Grooming to Win

ALSO BY SUSAN E. HARRIS

Horsemanship in Pictures

Grooming to Win

SECOND EDITION

How to Groom, Trim, Braid
and Prepare Your Horse for Show

Susan E. Harris

HOWELL
BOOK HOUSE

Wiley Publishing, Inc.

Howell Book House
Published by Wiley Publishing, Inc., New York, NY

For general information on our other products and services or to obtain technical support please contact our Customer Care Department within the U.S. at 800-762-2974, outside the U.S. at 317-572-3993 or fax 317-572-4002.

Wiley also publishes its books in a variety of electronic formats. Some content that appears in print may not be available in electronic books.

Library of Congress Cataloging-in-Publication Data:
Harris, Susan E. (Susan Elizabeth), 1949-
   Grooming to win: how to groom, trim, braid, and prepare your horse for show / Susan E. Harris.–2nd ed.
   p. cm.
   Includes index.
   ISBN 0-87605-892-6
   1. Horses–Grooming.   2. Horses–Showing.
SF285.7.H37   1991
636.1´0833–dc20   91-9217
                                                                          CIP

Manufactured in the United States of America.
20 19 18 17 16

Contents

Contents

Foreword

I first got to know Susan Harris when I was invited to give a hunter seat equitation clinic at the 5-H Acres School of Riding, the school she manages in upstate New York. Not only was I impressed by the basics she had taught her students about riding, but also by her standards of stable management and the knowledge of such that she imparted. Her stables were immaculately clean, her horses in beautiful condition, and I quickly got the impression that the residents of her school knew a good deal more than a smattering of how to take care of and present a show horse.

Many young authors, including myself, have contributed their share to horsemen's libraries with "how-to-ride" books, covering all breeds and divisions; very few have contributed anything in the way of "how-to-keep-a-horse" books. And, consequently, there are, sadly enough, many more good riders than there are good horsemen. Susan Harris's *Grooming to Win* will quickly and accurately help rectify that situation. Being a busy riding teacher with little time left over to teach the technology of caring for a horse, I am delighted to have Ms. Harris's book available to recommend to those sincere students of riding who want to make a comprehensive study of being a horseman.

Grooming to Win has been prepared and presented in a simple, clear, logical, step-by-step way, as only a teacher could do. The book is meant to explain and demonstrate in order for the reader to learn, and this it does. Ms. Harris's explanations are to the point and her pictorial efforts clear as a bell! The great beauty of this book is that it not only covers the essentials of caring for a horse at home but goes into great detail about every sophisticated nuance of preparing the show horse for the ring. Therefore, as a text, it should satisfy a wide spectrum of horsemen coming along in the future. We have all needed this book.

GEORGE H. MORRIS

Preface to the Second Edition

It has been more than twelve years since *Grooming to Win* was first published, and I've knocked a lot of dirt out of the old currycomb since then. The horse world, and especially the horse show world, never stands still—new people and new horses, new styles, trends and discoveries, new things to do with our horses and new ways of doing the old things keep emerging like new channels in an old river. Some changes are fads of the moment; others reflect a more basic change in the type of horse, the job he does in the show ring and the way in which we can best present him. In many ways, this book has needed updating, and I'm glad to have the chance to bring it in line with current show ring practices.

However, the more things change, the more they stay the same. I still find that the best horsemen still use the old, proven ways that are basic to good horsemanship and horse care—modern technology and show ring glitter have not supplanted the discipline, daily routine, attention to detail and plain hard work that go into the making of a champion. A true horseman still puts the horse's welfare first, ahead of his own convenience, the current fashion, and even his desire to win. The more demanding the specialty in which you compete, the more important real, thorough horsemanship is to the success of both horse and rider. Those people who can prepare their horses to meet the challenge of competition, weather the demands of the show circuit *and* do this while keeping their horses sound, healthy and happy in their work, are good horsemen and women indeed, and they deserve our respect along with their winnings. So too do people who keep their own horse fit, clean, healthy and happy, whether they compete or not!

One of the changes in the new edition of *Grooming to Win* is an increased emphasis on conditioning and the physiology which underlies the conditioning process. A real "show glow" comes from within, not from a brush or a bottle, and understanding how it happens helps keep us on the right track. Today the pendulum is swinging away from the slick, fat and overfed but underexercised show horse to the fit and well-conditioned animal that can perform and also look good—a healthier trend that will help horses stay sounder, perform better and last longer in their work.

As the level of competition, the costs and the pressures of showing increase, we have to be aware of the horse's mental health and attitude and his relationship with people along with his physique and his looks. While we have to meet show ring standards in the way we present horses, we can and must be aware of how we handle them and use good judgment about how far to follow a fashion. Some of the things frequently done to show horses in the name of beauty, fashion or winning are uncomfortable, unhealthy or down-right inhumane. We must remain sensitive to the individual horse's attitudes, needs and reactions whether we are grooming, conditioning, training or showing him, and do what we can to make his lot a happy one. It saddens me to see someone making a horse upset and miserable in order to make him clean or pretty, or keeping him unnaturally restricted for the convenience of the groom. Try to groom your horse with feeling; listen to what he tells you as you work with him, and as far as possible, let your horse have time to be a horse, even if it means you must brush off some mud later!

This book can never be the final word on grooming, as the subject is constantly evolving, yet I hope it will bring out some new and practical ideas while keeping the best of the old traditional methods. If you have a grooming tip or a different way of doing things, I'd love to know about it, and if your horses are shiny, healthy and happy, you must be doing it right.

SUSAN E. HARRIS

Cortland, New York

Grooming to Win

One

CONDITIONING

THE HORSE IN HIS NATURAL STATE

When horses live and develop as Nature intended, appearance is of little importance compared to survival, comfort and self-reliance under natural conditions. Horses living on the range or in large pastures are usually quite healthy and self-sufficient with little interference from man, as long as they have adequate range, forage and water and are not subject to disease or predators. The horse's systems, his habits and behavior, and the functions and physiology of his skin, hair coat, feet and mane and tail, as well as all his other parts, have developed over more than 50 million years. We should remember that free-living horses are designed to be comfortable, healthy and beautiful without human help or grooming, and it is only when we remove the horse from his natural environment and use him for our own purposes that he needs our care, attention and grooming. Practically speaking, most horses today are domesticated and are kept in pasture, paddock or stable, used for purposes ranging from breeding to pleasure riding, showing or racing, and hence need special care and grooming that their wild ancestors would neither need nor tolerate. Some horses, through generations of selective breeding, have become so refined and sensitive that they would suffer and deteriorate or even die if placed under range conditions or even under a lower standard of care. As those responsible for the condition and well-being of our horses, we must strike a sensible balance between the horse's natural ways, the demands of the show ring or our use of the horse, and the needs of each individual animal.

The horse's system is designed for a nomadic grazing life, eating small amounts of grass almost constantly and moving, usually at slow paces, over a wide territory. A horse "in the rough" is adapted to withstand rain, snow and cold remarkably well, and can fend off the attacks of flies in hot weather.

1

The natural oils and dandruff of the ungroomed coat help to waterproof the horse and prevent rain from soaking through to the skin. The long, heavy winter coat allows a horse to withstand quite bitter weather, as the thick coat traps air close to the skin and insulates his body, while the long "cat hairs" allow water to run off without penetrating the coat. A long, natural mane and tail provide an effective fly swatter and help to keep flies off the sensitive neck and head; in winter, the heavy mane and tail protect the horse against a loss of body heat at the top of the head and neck and protect sensitive areas beneath the tail and between the hind legs from cold. The bushy hair of the ears helps to filter out dust and repel flies and gnats, while the long hair under the jaw and on the lower legs and fetlocks allows water to run off and insulates areas which could otherwise become frostbitten. The long whiskers of the muzzle and above the eyes function as do a cat's whiskers—they allow the animal to feel when it is close to an object, even in the dark.

While range horses are usually quite physically fit, even if rough looking, horses kept in domestic pastures tend to lead a more sedentary life. They seldom have to range far for adequate feed and water, and may be overly fat. Inactive pastured horses may have grossly overgrown feet, which may crack off in chunks and which can lead to stumbling, sprains or gait abnormalities if the horse is put immediately into work. Some pastures, because of drought, overgrazing or poor location and terrain, may not offer sufficient nutrition to keep a horse in adequate weight. Certain thin-skinned individuals may be so harassed by biting flies that they cannot relax and eat; these horses may be thin and run-down. Other horses, particularly obese horses and ponies, may gorge themselves on rich grass, especially in the spring when the water content of the grass is high, resulting in the serious metabolic disorder known as grass founder. Perhaps the most pervasive problem of domestic horses pastured in confined areas is that of internal parasites, or "worms." While horses prefer to graze over clean areas where no manure has been dropped, in small pastures or overgrazed areas they cannot help but graze on grass that has been contaminated with manure and hence with the eggs and larvae of several types of internal parasites. The more horses and the smaller the pasture, the more severe the parasite infestation problem is likely to be.

In conditioning pleasure and show horses, we must realize to what extent we are asking a horse to adapt his natural lifestyle to an artificial system. We expect him to perform at demanding gaits and paces, rather than roam and graze at will. We confine him to a stall or a small paddock except during workouts, instead of allowing him the total freedom for which he was born. We feed him a concentrated diet high in energy, yet we don't want him to

FIGURE 1 *The confined horse being conditioned for show must adjust to stable life and restrictions on behavior and environment.*

develop a "hay belly," so he may not get the grazing or the constant "little and often" eating he prefers. We remove the need for a heavy winter coat by keeping him in a warm stall, sheeted and blanketed, and we may shorten his coat artificially, making him more vulnerable to chills and drafts. Finally we make demands on him for high action, athletic performance and stress on his mind and body that his natural life never would. A show horse is no longer self-sufficient. When we take away his ability to take care of himself as he would on the range, we have a heavy responsibility to take the best possible care of him. The success we have in producing and keeping a horse healthy, sound, happy and fit to show at his very best depends on how much time, attention and effort we are willing to put forth for him.

In order to bring a horse from soft, pasture condition into top show shape, we must prepare his system for the new demands to be made on it. His digestive system must slowly become accustomed to more concentrated energy-producing food. His muscles, tendons, ligaments and even bones must be conditioned for more strenuous work. His immune system must be prepared to meet the challenges of stress and exposure to disease. His feet will need proper trimming and shoeing to produce correct movement for the show ring, and his coat and skin will need to be conditioned for best appearance and to act efficiently to cool his body when he works hard and sweats. All these things take time to accomplish, so plan to begin preparing your horse well in advance of the show season. A horse that is only slightly out of condition might take a month to condition; a horse that is quite out of shape might need three months or more to reach peak condition.

TYPES OF MANAGEMENT

When beginning to condition your horse, you must take into account your goals for using him and your resources, including the facilities available to you. Are you a pleasure rider who wants to show at one or two local shows, or are you hauling your horse on the circuit for the season, in pursuit of breed or national awards? Do you have a pasture and shed, a stable or an indoor arena? Does your horse need to be fit for endurance-demanding events like competitive trail riding, foxhunting or eventing, or in "halter condition"? Most important, how much daily time and effort can you devote to his conditioning, grooming and other care?

The ultimate use of the horse may sometimes dictate the type of management. For instance, a gaited show horse with built-up feet and a set tail will have to be kept stabled, groomed and exercised meticulously and can seldom be turned out safely. At the other extreme, a competitive trail horse usually does best when kept in a pasture or paddock and seldom stabled. A pleasure horse used for occasional showing can usually be kept just about as he would be for ordinary pleasure riding, with a little extra attention to show details.

Your show schedule will be important both to your conditioning plans and your day-to-day management. Major competitions and "prep" shows should be marked on the calendar. This allows you to plan for the process of bringing the horse to peak condition at the right time and allowing some "let-down" time between major shows. No horse can maintain peak condition indefinitely, and the greater the stress and physical demands on your horse, the more important it is to allow some rest and recuperation time at home. Routine but essential procedures such as shoeing, deworming, innoculations and dental care should be scheduled when they will not interfere with the horse's preparation for a major effort, but they must not be put off until overdue.

Try to permit your horse the most natural life-style possible. Allow him access to a pasture or paddock as often as you can, or give him some time to graze on a lead line when turnout is impossible. Try to arrange your feeding schedule so that he has several small meals spaced out throughout the day, and

4

allow free access to water, salt and, if possible, hay or grass. Don't impose procedures on your horse that limit his lifestyle (such as blanketing or body clipping) unless they are necessary for your activities or for his comfort, and if you do, you must be conscientious about such details as changing blankets according to the weather. If possible, allow your horse to "be a horse" by rolling and playing (no matter how dirty he gets, you can always get him clean!) and let him have another horse as a "buddy" if you can. A horse should have exercise every day—nothing is worse for a horse than standing in confinement, particularly when he is fit.

Since most show horses are stabled much of the time, the stall will have to be cleaned and picked out more often and more carefully, and the horse needs plenty of bedding to cushion his legs and encourage him to lie down comfortably. A clean stall also helps to keep the horse from becoming dirty and staining his coat, mane and tail. Feed tubs and water buckets should be scrubbed out daily and kept fresh and clean. Fly control is especially important for show horses—they often have their manes and tails shortened, tied up or otherwise altered, and they may have fine coats and skin that are extremely sensitive to fly bites. Some fly-control measures are: the use of screens on stalls; scrim fly sheets, ear covers and face masks; meticulous stall cleaning and manure removal; use of fly repellents and (carefully!) insecticides; turning horses out at night instead of during the day.

HEALTH CARE

A horse must be healthy inside and outside to respond to a conditioning program. Good conditioning starts with a veterinary checkup. This should include a check of present condition and general soundness; it would be a shame to spend weeks preparing a horse only to have him break down under training. The horse's general condition should be evaluated with your veterinarian, who may have suggestions for meeting his special needs while conditioning. Many professionals have a blood count done as an initial evaluation; if a horse is slightly anemic, this will have to be corrected before he can be conditioned. If the blood test is normal, this provides a base line against which later blood tests can be compared. The normal resting pulse rate, temperature and respiration rates should be taken and recorded, as individual horses have slightly different normal vital signs. If you know what your horse's normal temperature is, you will be able to tell when he is running a degree of fever or is otherwise slightly off color.

Since a show horse is exposed to large numbers of strange horses while his resistance may be lowered by the stress of showing and shipping, he must be innoculated against tetanus and all common contagious diseases. Most horsemen today innoculate against tetanus, Eastern and Western encephalomyletis, influenza and rhinopneumonitis as a minimum. Many also vaccinate for Potomac horse fever, Venezuelan equine encephalomyletis, rabies and strangles. Your veterinarian can advise you on which vaccinations are important for your horse, given your show schedule and the diseases currently common in your area. While certain vaccines can be given as a multivalent shot (as many as four vaccines in one shot), you need to know how long the protection lasts for each type of vaccine and when booster shots are required. (For example, tetanus shots are good for a year, but influenza protection should be renewed every three months.) Booster shots should be scheduled on your calendar so that they will not be forgotten. Remember that innoculations may cause a mild reaction or at least a couple of "off" days for your horse; you should not give shots right before a show or a demanding training day. Also, it may require two to three weeks and two shots before the horse's immunity is high enough to protect him.

Along with innoculations, your veterinarian should draw blood for a Coggins test (for swamp fever or equine infectious anemia). Most states and many shows require a negative Coggins test within a certain time period in order to transport horses or enter a show. You may be required to forward a copy of a current Coggins test when entering, so extra copies are desirable. A record of Coggins test, all current innoculations and a veterinarian's health certificate should be kept in a folder to travel with your horse. If your horse shows in FEI (Fédération Equestre Internationale) competitions, your veterinarian must help you complete the identification information for the horse's FEI passport.

Your veterinarian can also perform a fecal parasite count to determine what kind and how many internal parasites (or "worms") your horse may be carrying, and can advise you on a deworming and parasite control program. No horse can respond to conditioning if he is carrying a load of internal parasites, and a large proportion of fatal colics have been linked to parasite damage. It is no exaggeration to say that your entire conditioning program rests on the effectiveness of your parasite control program. Show horses are usually dewormed at least every two months; some veterinarians prefer to deworm more often. Since a wide variety of dewormers are now available in oral paste form, many horsemen now see no need for the fuss and bother of deworming by stomach tube. Ivermectin is a broad-spectrum wormer that is very effective against all types of internal parasites; while some claim that it is not necessary to rotate products when using ivermectin, most prudent horse-men prefer to rotate dewormers at least twice a year to guard against develop-ing parasites with resistance to the product. Along with regular deworming, it is important to keep feed and hay from becoming contaminated by manure, and to mow, drag and pick up manure in paddocks regularly. Like innocula-tions, deworming may cause horses to feel under the weather for a day or two, and should not be scheduled immediately before a show or a heavy workout.

The horse's teeth should be checked by the veterinarian or an equine dental specialist, particularly if the horse shows signs of mouth trouble or is underweight. Spitting out wads of partially chewed hay (called "quidding") or eating sloppily, allowing food to fall out of the mouth while chewing, are both signs of a sore mouth or teeth that need attention. Tossing the head, difficulty in bridling and excessive "mouthing" or getting the tongue over the bit may point to a bad tooth or a sore mouth. Horses may have sharp edges or "hooks" worn into their molars by their natural chewing motion, or some may have failed to shed a baby tooth or "cap," which can cause abnormal chewing. Occasionally a horse may have a "wolf tooth"—a tiny extra premolar embed-ded in the gum in front of the premolars—which needs to be removed for comfort. Teeth should be checked by an expert twice a year.

You will need to evaluate your horse's overall condition and decide on your conditioning goals. Is your horse presently overweight, lacking in muscle tone or too thin? You cannot change his basic structure, but you can get him into the shape that shows him off best. Most show horses look best with a *little* fat—just enough to round their body contours a bit and produce a nice overall "bloom." Judges discriminate against horses that are too thin and look "poor," and this gives a poor impression of the exhibitor's management. Some horses are inclined to become obese, which presents functional problems even if the horse looks fat and shiny. Overweight horses are soft, lack endurance and are easily injured. They are especially prone to serious metabolic and digestive upsets like laminitis and colic. While fashion in the show world has unfortunately favored overfed, overweight and underexercised horses, particu-larly in halter classes, it is an unhealthy trend which has cost many horses their show careers and even their lives. A horse that is round and sleek but 150 pounds overweight is handicapped in performance and is no more healthy than an obese human athlete. Instead of overfattening your horse, why not condition him for correct muscle development and the health and stamina to do his job in the show ring and last out the season? This takes more work, skill and judgment than fattening a horse, but the results are lasting and worth the trouble. Happily, more and more judges are selecting well-conditioned

FIGURE 2 *Condition—obese, show condition, poor condition*

horses over the excessively fat "feed 'em and lead 'em" type.

If your horse has been out of work, he may be soft and out of condition. Many pastured horses and especially ponies put on so much weight that they are in danger of founder or laminitis (a serious metabolic disorder which causes painful inflammation of the feet and can cripple the horse.) These need to be kept on a "diet pasture"—an overgrazed or nearly bare lot, with their grass intake carefully controlled. A thin horse kept on a low-quality, weedy pasture or fed mostly on low-quality hay may have to ingest so much roughage to keep himself alive that he develops a "hay belly." This is due partly to enlargement of the cecum or "water gut"—the part of the intestine responsible for digesting the large amounts of cellulose found in weeds and stalks—and partly to saggy, unfit abdominal muscles. The hay belly will disappear with proper feeding and exercise, and can be prevented in the same way. A horse that is ridden less often than three times a week is likely to be soft and out of shape, and can be injured by doing too much too soon, just like a human "weekend athlete." A horse that has been ridden regularly even if lightly will be easier to condition and less prone to injury during the conditioning process.

PHYSIOLOGY OF CONDITIONING

Conditioning is the process by which the body becomes stronger and more efficient—in short, body-building. While most people think of conditioning as developing muscles, it involves the whole body and all its systems, and any part of the body that is placed under stress will respond. While we may think in terms of conditioning a show horse in order to make him look better (by slimming him down, developing his muscles, etc.), good conditioning makes him healthier and better able to perform, with less fatigue and less chance of breaking down. All horses should be in good, functional condition for the work they are asked to do; this has the secondary benefit of making them look their best, too.

Conditioning really takes place at the cellular level. The body has a wonderful ability to respond to stress. When a system or a part of the body (for instance, muscle fibers) is stressed by more work than it is used to, the body reacts by strengthening that part. Muscle fibers become larger and thicker; bone becomes more dense; the heart and lungs develop more capacity to pump blood and deliver oxygen, and the circulation develops more capillaries to deliver oxygen and nutrients and carry off waste products. We may see the result in bigger muscles, increased endurance, greater strength and a faster recovery rate after work. Some other benefits are a shiny coat, extra energy and a spirited, zestful attitude.

The stress that triggers this process must be just enough and not too much. Too little stress (or work) does not activate the conditioning process. Too much stress, especially without rest, depletes the cells' resources, allows waste products to pile up and eventually results in damage or injury. In order to condition without hurting the horse, the exercise must be just enough to tire him, but not enough to cause injury or to wear him down. Excessive stress that burns up a horse's resources is called overtraining; it leads to a thin, nervous horse that may be chronically fatigued, sour and difficult to train. Too much exercise all at once (for example, strenuous jumping or hill work on a soft horse) can cause sore muscles, tendonitis or sprained ligaments.

In order to condition cells, systems and the whole body, work or stress must be balanced against rest. Rest gives the body time to clear away wastes, deliver nutrients to the cells and build tissue. Rest doesn't mean standing idle—it can mean dropping back to a slower gait or a lower level of stress, or changing to an exercise that works different muscles. If you trot a horse for five minutes, then walk him for five minutes and then work at the canter, you are working and then resting different muscles. The entire workout should not be more than he can take at his stage of fitness, however. Injuries happen most easily and most often to tired horses at the end of a session, just as human athletes are most likely to injure themselves on the last ski run or late in a game.

FIGURE 3 *Taking pulse—artery under lower jaw*

The conditioning process is fueled by essential nutrients—carbohydrates, fats, protein, vitamins and minerals—and by oxygen, all of which are delivered to the cells by circulation of the blood. Good nutrition is essential; if the horse is not getting enough of an essential element such as protein or iron, he cannot become fit. The circulation improves with exercise, but remember that an unfit horse is unable to deliver as much oxygen to the cells as a fit horse—that's why he huffs and puffs when he works. The pulse recovery rate is used as a measure of a horse's fitness, and it can guide you in how much work your horse can take.

To determine the recovery rate, work the horse for a certain distance and length of time that is within his ability at this stage. (For instance, trot him for five minutes on level ground. (This must be done after the horse is well warmed up.) Then stop him and immediately take his pulse rate at the mandibular artery, which crosses the inside edge of his jawbone. Walk him quietly for ten minutes, then take his pulse rate again. The difference between the two pulse rates is the recovery rate. A fit horse's pulse drops back to nearly normal very quickly, even if it has gone very high during exercise. An unfit horse's pulse remains elevated for much longer. Some trainers in demanding specialties use high-tech equipment such as on-board heart-rate monitors to record the horse's pulse rates and recovery rates more accurately while training and during rest periods. Remember that heat and humidity will have a great effect on heart rate and respiration, so the recovery rate will be slower on hot, muggy days. A wise trainer will take it easy in such conditions, anyway.

To condition a horse, exercise must be regular and consistent, increasing gradually as the horse becomes fitter and able to handle more. All horses need some exercise every day, even if they simply walk around in a pasture or are led out in hand. When deprived of exercise, the muscles, circulation and other structures deteriorate, causing a horse to become first unfit and eventually unhealthy. A horse should be worked a minimum of three times per week (with turnout or maintenance exercise on the other days) in order to keep a basic level of fitness, and in order to condition a horse, he needs to work six days per week, with one rest day with turnout.

Tendons, ligaments, joints and feet condition more slowly than muscle. This can be a problem if the horse's muscles quickly strengthen and the trainer forgets that the other tissues are still soft; hard work for fit muscles can easily pull a tendon, sprain a ligament or overstress the structures of the foot. If the conditioning process starts with a sufficient "base" of long, slow distance work before beginning speed, sharp turns or jumping, the tendon and joint structures will have time to strengthen and are less apt to be injured. Ligaments in particular have less blood supply than muscles or tendons, so they condition more slowly and are slower to heal if injured.

The hoof can adapt to the demands placed on it by extra work and the ground it works on, but this takes time. Exercise pumps more blood through the soft inner structures of the foot, increasing circulation and growth and keeping the foot flexible to absorb shock. Lack of exercise can contribute to contracted heels and unhealthy feet. However, overwork on hard surfaces or rough ground can cause sole bruises or can damage the sensitive laminae, causing lameness. It is essential that the hoof be trimmed so that it is balanced naturally and the bones of the hoof and pastern are correctly alligned according to the horse's conformation. Some showmen try to camouflage conformation faults such as straight pasterns by having the feet trimmed with excessively low heels, or have too-large feet pared down to make them appear smaller. These practices can contribute to chronic lamenesses such as navicular disease and sheared heels, and make it impossible for the horse to move athletically.

One of the advantages of good conditioning is that you can change your horse's shape, way of going and his outline by proper work over a period of time. Horses that are weak in the top line tend to travel with a high head and a hollow back; they develop a bulging underneck and a saggy belly. By training your horse to move with long, swinging and rhythmic strides in a "round" frame, you can develop his neck, back, loin and hindquarter muscles and tighten up his abdominal muscles. This cannot be forced by tie-downs and head-setting devices. Good riding and an understanding of good movement develop muscles, while devices only teach a horse a habit of carrying his head in a certain way. Riding up and downhill with long, free-moving gaits, cavaletti work, frequent transitions and riding in well-balanced working gaits all

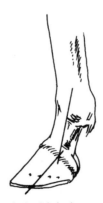

FIGURE 4 *Foot shod with broken angle—incorrect*

FIGURE 5 A. *Moving with hollow back—poor muscling*

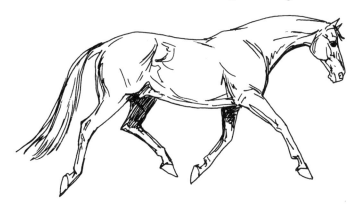

B. *Moving with round outline—better muscling*

help to develop the muscles that make a horse look more attractive as well as making him move better.

METHODS OF EXERCISE

Various exercise methods are employed with different types of horses. Many exercise methods incorporate some training of the horse in the skills he will be performing in the show ring. Others are strictly for conditioning purposes. It is a good idea to vary the exercise methods in order to condition the horse in different ways and exercise other muscles, and also to keep him interested and happy in his work.

Riding—the most common method of exercise, as it lets the rider train the horse, practice his own riding and enjoy himself at the same time. Trail riding is excellent for conditioning purposes, because the changes in terrain and footing condition the horse more than work in a level arena. The new sights and places also keep the horse (and the rider!) from becoming bored and sour. Working uphill at a walk and trot is an excellent muscle and wind exercise, but downhill grades should be taken slowly, as they increase the concussion on bones and joints. Deep sand or riding on a beach is also good for strengthening muscles, but it is easy to overdo with an unfit horse. An easy hack or trail ride is an excellent "let-down" after concentrated training, or when the horse needs an easy day's work.

Driving—is also good exercise and is frequently used by trainers of saddle horses for training young horses as well as conditioning. Driving can be used for young horses that are not yet ready to carry weight on their backs, and it is a good developer of the back and hindquarter muscles. Because the driver is not working as hard as the horse, he must stay alert for signs of fatigue and give the horse breaks when necessary.

Ponying—or leading one horse while riding another, can be used to condition two horses at once or to exercise a young horse that is not yet ready to be ridden. It requires a good horse handler with a reliable pony horse, and should be done in an enclosed area, especially with green horses. While a pony rider may pass the lead rope around the saddle horn for leverage, he should never tie one horse to the saddle of another. Ponying can be done at slow gaits for basic conditioning; polo ponies and some race horses are galloped while being ponied, but this takes a skilled pony rider and a safe field or track and is not a good idea for most riders.

Longeing—more strenuous than it looks. Working on a small circle at a trot or canter puts lateral stress on the horse's legs and body. Longeing should be done by an experienced person, using a line at least 30 feet long. The horse's legs should be protected with boots or bandages, and the trainer must be careful to warm up properly, to maintain rhythmic, well-balanced gaits and to make changes of direction in order to prevent one side from being over-stressed. Very young horses, especially foals and yearlings, should not be longed, as they are more vulnerable to injuries from too much speed on too small a circle. When used correctly as part of a training program, longeing can help to condition a horse while developing his muscles, flexion and carriage and acceptance of the bit.

Free-schooling—or working at liberty is an alternative to longeing. It is best done in a round pen 40 to 60 feet in diameter with good footing. Because there is no sideways pull on the longe line, there is less likelihood that a horse will interfere (strike one foot against the other leg), and it is a more acceptable training and conditioning method for weanlings, yearlings and young horses than excessive longeing. As in longeing, the trainer should work the horse at a rhythmic gait, giving breaks and making changes of direction often enough to prevent overstressing the muscles of one side. Indiscriminate chasing of horses makes them hot, nervous and hard to handle and can lead to injuries if they run wildly. If the schooling ring is surfaced with deep sand, free-schooling will develop the muscles through harder work, but it is important to build up slowly and not to overdo it, especially in the beginning of the conditioning program. As in longeing, horses should wear protective boots or polo bandages to prevent accidental interference injuries.

Cavaletti—refers to a grid of poles spaced at intervals, usually raised to about 6″ by blocks or trestles. The horse walks or trots through the grid and must adjust his stride to the even spacing. When ridden, the rider should assume a half-seat or 2-point position that frees the horse's back to round up, or if he is well balanced he may post to the trot. The object of cavaletti work is to encourage the horse to regulate his stride while reaching out and down with his neck and rounding his back. This develops the muscles of his neck, shoulders, back, loin and hindquarters, while the raised poles make him flex the joints of his legs at each step. It is essential that cavaletti grids be set at a comfortable distance for the individual horse. For an average (15.3 to 16.0 hand) horse, the cavaletti should be placed 3′3″ to 3′6″ apart for walking, and 4′3″ to 4′6″ apart for trotting. After trying these distances, the spacing should be lengthened or shortened until it is comfortable for the horse and he can place his feet in the middle of the space between the poles without tripping or reaching. Walking cavaletti can be useful in limbering up a horse's muscles during a warmup, but trotting cavaletti should be saved for later. Each pass through the cavalettis is hard work—don't overdo it!

Galloping, jumping, reining—and other strenuous activities will be re-quired in some horses' performance classes, so they will necessarily be practiced in training. These should not be practiced until the horse has reached a reasonable level of fitness, and they should be introduced gradually, a few minutes at a time. While activities like jumping do condition the parts that are used in jumping, it is all too easy to injure a horse by overdoing the fast, strenuous and, for many riders, the most enjoyable work. Horses should always be warmed up well before fast or strenuous work, and it should not be prolonged to the point of fatigue.

Some trainers, especially those preparing halter horses, use mechanized treadmills or automatic walkers to give horses long, slow exercise. Both machines require a thorough understanding of the working of the machine, its safety precautions and proper use, and skilled supervision whenever a horse is being worked. Automatic walkers work horses in a relatively small circle, which has the same disadvantages as too much longeing. They are a labor-saving device, because several horses can be exercised at once, but when used too mechanically without adapting the exercise to the needs of the individual horse, they can produce a sour, stiff or even lame horse. Automatic walkers are best used for what they were designed for—cooling horses out. Treadmills are more likely to be adapted to the individual horse's program, as only one horse can work on the treadmill at a time and he must be constantly supervised by a trainer. The treadmill can also be set on a slope to simulate hill work and develop the hindquarters. Treadmill work is primarily for muscle development.

A few high-tech training centers offer an equine swimming pool as a conditioning or therapeutic option. The horse is led down a ramp into the water and then guided around a dock or a round pool, swimming laps until he is led out again. Swimming allows the horse to work his heart and lungs and exercise his muscles without weight on his back or the effects of concussion. It was first used for conditioning racehorses suffering from foot and leg ailments, and is now used for other types of horses to improve cardiovascular fitness. It requires a trained attendant and, of course, special pool facilities. Most horses seem to enjoy swimming.

A SIMPLE CONDITIONING PROGRAM

If you are starting with a soft, unfit horse right out of pasture, a basic conditioning program is necessary to bring him to ordinary fitness—the level of a pleasure or show horse in training and showing. Here is a basic program for a mature horse, lasting two months. Horses that start in a more fit state can start in at a higher level of exercise and will take less time.

First ten days—Walk, starting with twenty minutes and increasing to thirty minutes. Make the horse move out in a working walk. Toward the end of the ten days, add one or two brief stretches of trotting (slowly).

Next ten days—Add walking up medium hills and gradually replace some walking with three-minute trots. Keep trotting slow and easy. Rides should last forty-five minutes.

Next ten days—Gradually increase riding time to one hour, adding three to five minute trots. One or two of the trots can be up a gentle hill. Always walk as much as you trot. At the end of ten days, add one or two brief canters on level ground.

Second month—Gradually increase the amount of trot and canter work, always keeping trotting in five-minute segments and walking for five minutes afterward. Gradually substitute three-minute canters for some trot segments. By the end of the month, workouts can last one hour and fifteen minutes, with fifteen minutes of walking to warm up and the same to cool down, twenty minutes of trot (in five-minute segments), fifteen minutes of canter (in three-minute segments), and the remaining walking time sandwiched in between trot and canter segments. By the end of the month, some trotting can be done up easy hills, and brief cavaletti work could be included once or twice a week.

Third month—By now your horse is up to ordinary walk-trot-canter fitness. He is ready to work in riding lessons on the flat, to begin light jumping (gradually!) and to start specialized work such as lead changes. Since he is used to being ridden about an hour and a quarter per day, his workload should not exceed this when he is entered in a show—remember how much you may have to ride him in the warmup ring and in the class itself, and limit the number of classes you enter accordingly. If you plan to enter many classes each show day, or if you are showing in a demanding event like barrel racing or jumping, you will need to condition him further.

While extending his conditioning schedule, remember to intersperse periods of trot or canter with walking, and to gradually lengthen the distance of trots and canters rather than going faster. Two-minute intervals of hand-gallop (450 meters per minute) can be interspersed in the work, but galloping should be done on good footing and no more than twice a week. Trotting up hills (five minute trots) will develop wind fitness with less risk of injury than galloping. Total riding time will now be one and a half hours. If you feel that the horse needs more work, try to ride him twice a day for shorter sessions. This can also be a training advantage.

Always, *always* walk the first fifteen minutes and the last fifteen minutes of every ride! Proper warmup and cool-down will do more to prevent injuries than anything else you can do. Keep track of your horse's fitness by being aware of his breathing; if he starts to huff and puff, he is feeling the strain and needs to walk soon. If his breathing and recovery rate show that he is handling the work well, you can safely move on to the next phase of your conditioning program. If he's breathing hard, tiring rapidly or taking a long time to recover, or if his attitude is cranky or listless, go slower and give him time to gain condition before making any new demands. Keep weather and footing conditions in mind—hot, humid weather takes a lot out of a horse, and hard footing can pound his legs into unsoundness if you ignore it.

TURNOUT

Horses are freedom-loving creatures by nature. Their most natural setting is a pasture, and some freedom to graze, play, roll, run and just to "be a horse" is essential to their mental health. Show horses are often deprived of turnout time because they are too valuable to risk injury in a herd environment, there may be no safe area for turnout while on the circuit, or they may have built-up shoes and pads that could lead to injury if they ran and played freely. The fact that a horse will get dirty when he rolls is *not* a valid excuse for limiting turnout, however—any dirt he picks up can be brushed or shampooed away, or if he gets really filthy he can be turned out in a turnout rug or sheet.

The first requisite is a safe turnout paddock or pasture, fenced so that the horse cannot get out and is safe from injuring himself. Barbed wire is dangerous and can certainly cause a blemish that can ruin a horse's show career, and square wire or hog fence is not much better. A high, visible and smooth fence, possibly protected by an electric wire, is best. Ideally the paddock will offer some grass, shade, water and a sandy place to roll.

Since a show horse may be spirited and full of himself, it makes sense to protect his legs with boots if he is apt to run and play when turned out. Splint boots or polo wraps on the legs and bell boots on the front feet are standard precautions used by many stables when valuable horses are turned out. If he is left out with a halter on, it should be a leather halter or a halter with a leather crownpiece that would break if he should get caught up in it. When leading a horse to turnout, it is safest to use a chain end lead shank, run over the nose if necessary for control. In cold weather, clipped or blanketed horses should be turned out wearing a turnout rug or turnout sheet with leg straps, which will keep the blanket in place if he rolls or bucks. An ordinary blanket can slip underneath the horse and become caught around his legs, scaring and possibly injuring him.

Some horses are unhappy if turned out alone; instead of relaxing and enjoying their freedom, they may pace, run or simply hang mournfully over the gate. If a quiet and compatible turnout buddy can be found for them, they will often settle down. The hind shoes should be removed, in case of kicking, and for valuable horses, no more than two should go out together. Turn the dominant horse of the pair out after his mate is already out, and bring the dominant horse in first. If you plan to put a new horse with another, let them get acquainted through adjoining stalls or over adjoining paddocks before turning them out together, and stay within sight until you are sure they are getting along well when they first go out together.

Show horses usually have fine coats and are often supersensitive to fly bites. Try to avoid turning them out during the "buggiest" times of day, or be sure that they have a shady spot or a shelter to get into away from the flies. Use a fly repellent and be sure that any horses with their tails tied up have an artificial fly swatter (such as the Farnam fly strips) attached to their tail ties. Sometimes it works better to turn horses out at night—the flies may be less troublesome and their coats will not be bleached by the sun. If you must turn horses out during the day, try to avoid the midday hours of strongest sunlight, and use a sunscreen ointment on any horses that have extensive white face markings—they sunburn! There are fly sprays on the market that have sunscreen, and are said to help prevent the coat from fading in the sun.

If you cannot turn a horse out, try taking him out for a walk and to graze on a lead line as often as possible. This is a good way to let him relax and get used to the sights at a horse show, and the grazing is good for his digestion and his peace of mind.

FEEDING

As your horse adapts from pasture condition to show condition, you will need to change his diet. A show horse will usually require more concentrated feed, usually in the form of more grain, richer hay and sometimes special supplements, in order to provide energy for work and weight gain; protein for growth, maintenance and repair of tissues, and vitamins and minerals necessary to meet his needs under the demands of shipping, training and competition. While most show horses get a more concentrated diet (more grain and less hay than other diets), it is important to remember that all horses need enough roughage to keep their digestive system healthy. Feeding large quantities of grain and not enough roughage can cause real problems in the horse's health, condition and behavior, especially if the change is made too quickly. As a rule, at least 50 percent of the horse's total daily diet should be made up of roughage. Roughage does not have to be in the form of hay or grass; there are other sources of fiber such as beet pulp, range cubes and certain types of pelleted or extruded feed.

A horse should be changed over gradually to any new ration, especially if it is a major change such as switching from pasture grass to hay and grain. The horse's digestion depends in part on the action of certain beneficial bacteria in his gut. It takes ten days to two weeks for these bacteria to adapt to a different kind of feed, so any change in feeding should be made gradually over this period or colic may result.

If your horse is used to being on pasture all the time, one way to begin is to bring him into the stable during the day and turn him out at night for a couple of weeks or more. While inside, he can have a small feed of grain twice a day and can be groomed, trimmed, shod and have his veterinary needs taken care of; he can also start on his exercise program. Eventually he may be kept in a night also, with turnout time in a paddock according to his schedule, and hay will replace the grass in his diet.

The kind of feed you give your show horse will depend on many factors—the horse's age, temperament and nutritional and conditioning needs; the level of work; and also what feeds are available and practical to feed while on the show circuit. Oats are preferred by many horsemen because they contain adequate protein, energy and fiber, are palatable and are usually available even on the road. Others prefer a "complete feed," which contains both grain and hay in pelleted form. Bags of pellets are easier to store and transport than hay and grain, and the horse's intake can be carefully controlled. However, some horses miss the constant browsing that hay provides and may chew wood or eat their bedding in boredom. Horses with allergies or respiratory problems may need special feeds that contain beet pulp as a hay substitute. If you feed hay, you will have to decide whether to feed a grass hay (such as timothy, orchard grass or bermuda) or a legume hay (alfalfa or clover), or a mixture of the two types. It is an excellent idea to have your hay analyzed, and your grain too if you grow your own feed. (For commercial feeds, you can consult the feed label for an analysis.) Feed testing and analysis is available inexpensively through your county agent or land grant college. Such an analysis can determine the levels of protein, energy, vitamins and minerals actually present in your horse's ration, and whether any need to be supplemented. Once you have taken the trouble to balance your horse's ration, you can make small adjustments in the amount as needed. Balancing a ration takes a little math and some charts and tables (and possibly some help from your county agent or a feed man), but it can save you money and make sure that your horse's feed meets his nutritional needs.

Many show horse owners overfeed and oversupplement in their zeal to achieve a high show bloom. This can be wasteful and sometimes even dangerous. Excess energy (calories) turns to fat; too much protein either creates fat or is excreted through the kidneys, and overloading most vitamins is simply a waste of money. Some minerals can build up to toxic levels, however, and an imbalance of certain minerals may block the horse's ability to absorb other minerals and lead to serious deficiency disorders. This is particularly true of phosphorous and calcium, which must be kept in proper balance, especially in broodmares and young, growing horses. Feeding a single supplement according to directions may be beneficial; feeding several supplements and extra doses is more likely to waste money and may harm the horse instead of hastening the conditioning process.

Whatever kind of feed you use, it must be of good quality. Grain should be clean and fresh, not moldy or musty. Corn should be checked for mold under ultraviolet light at the feed mill to prevent moldy corn disease, which can cause brain damage and death. Sweet feed, or grain containing molasses, may spoil in hot or humid weather—sniff it before you feed it and don't let large quantities of grain sit around for a long time before you use it. Hay should be clean, soft, leafy and sweet-smelling and must be free from dust and mold. Mold spores can damage a horse's lungs and give him an allergy and a chronic cough. Alfalfa hay grown in the South and Southwest must be checked for blister beetles, which can be fatal to horses when eaten with the hay.

Stabled horses must have their grain intake carefully balanced against their work and condition. Although feed changes should be made slowly, grain can be cut back or even withheld completely without harm, and it is safer to err on the side of too little than too much. For a horse starting to exercise, begin with a small amount of grain per day (a pound or two) and increase it gradually as you increase the work. As you increase the feed, it is better to spread it over several small feeds given throughout the day than to give a large feed once or twice a day. You can also follow the same plan with hay, giving a flake or two at a time several times a day instead of a large amount all at once. This is closer to the horse's natural "little and often" eating habits and allows him to use the feed most efficiently, besides preventing waste and staving off boredom.

Whenever a horse must be kept in without exercise (for instance, if he is rested because of an injury), his grain should be cut to half or less of his usual ration. This is especially important as the horse nears peak condition, when he may be receiving a great deal of grain and a ration high in calories and protein. Fit horses receiving a high-carbohydrate diet are subject to a metabolic disorder called azoturia or tying up syndrome, especially if they are kept in without exercise for a day or two without sufficiently cutting the grain ration. When the horse starts work, it suddenly suffers muscle cramps and then partial paralysis of the muscles of the hindquarters; the muscle tissue may break down and be excreted in the urine, which is as dark as coffee. Signs of tying up are: cold sweat, especially over the hindquarters; trembling, corded hindquarter muscles; short, crampy steps leading to inability to move, and hindquarter muscles that tighten until the horse appears to stand on tiptoe or knuckle over. There are several degrees of tying up, which is a syndrome rather than a disease. If you suspect that a horse may be tying up, stop him from work (he will soon become immobile anyway) and blanket his hindquarters; call the veterinarian and apply heat and massage to the affected muscles until he arrives. Gently rubbing and pulling on the ears from base to tip may help give him some relief (this is an acupressure treatment for shock), but the veterinarian will probably inject muscle relaxants and vitamin E. Azoturia or tying up is more common in fit, heavily muscled horses; some veterinarians believe it is associated with selenium deficiency and possibly a deficiency of vitamin E. A horse that has had one attack is more prone to have another, so prevention by careful attention to grain and exercise balance is very important.

The most important thing in feeding is close attention to the needs and eating patterns of each horse. The same person should feed each day, as he will be able to note minor changes that may be significant, such as a horse failing to eat as much as usual. Feeding should be done on a regular schedule, as horses become accustomed to regular feeding times and get upset if they are late. Notice the horse's feeding behavior—if he gets agitated or impatient, feed him first instead of making him wait until he has worked himself into a frenzy. If he is a shy, picky eater, notice which feeds he likes and under what

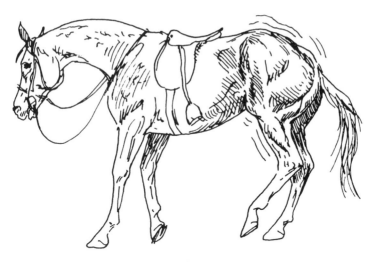

FIGURE 6 *Azoturia*

conditions he eats best. If you feed hay first, horses will be less ravenous and are less apt to bolt their grain down (which can cause colic); however, some greedy eaters may have to have their feed spread out in a thin layer or have large rocks placed in the feed tub to slow them down. Be sure that feeding times are taken into account when planning the work and exercise schedule—a horse should not be worked for an hour after a grain feed, and he should not be given grain until he is completely cooled out after work or he may colic. Finally, all feed tubs and water buckets should be kept clean and fresh and scrubbed out daily, with any uneaten feed removed before it becomes stale and musty and puts the horse off his feed.

Horses should always have access to clean water, except when they are overheated after work. Some, especially large horses or nursing mares, may need two buckets. Buckets are more work than automatic waterers, but they allow you to keep track of how much the horse drinks, which may be important if he is a fussy type who refuses to drink unfamiliar water away from home. An old trick is to flavor the water at home with peppermint, molasses or some other flavor; once the horse is used to the taste, the same flavor can be added to water at a show to make it more likely that the horse will drink as much as he needs to. A horse that does not drink enough can become dehydrated, especially in hot, humid weather.

Horses need free access to salt, especially in hot weather and whenever

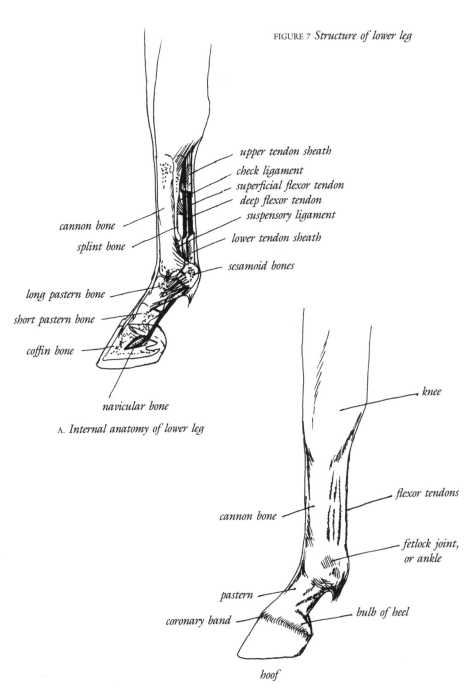

FIGURE 7 *Structure of lower leg*

upper tendon sheath
check ligament
superficial flexor tendon
deep flexor tendon
suspensory ligament
cannon bone
lower tendon sheath
splint bone
sesamoid bones
long pastern bone
short pastern bone
coffin bone
navicular bone

A. *Internal anatomy of lower leg*

knee

flexor tendons

cannon bone

fetlock joint,
or ankle

pastern

coronary band

bulb of heel

hoof

B. *External anatomy of lower leg*

they work hard and sweat. They lose salt and essential minerals in their sweat and cannot replace it sufficiently unless they have a salt block or salt is added to their feed. Electrolytes (a mixture of salts and potassium) may be necessary when horses are worked extremely hard in hot weather, in order to replace those lost during heavy sweating and to prevent dehydration. Electrolytes can be given in the water, in the feed or by oral paste. The last method is best, as some horses do not like the taste of the electrolyte mixture and may refuse to drink or may leave their feed. Electrolytes serve the same purpose for horses as Gatorade does for human athletes. They should be given only when the weather conditions and the demands of the horse's work warrant it—under ordinary conditions, salt is all that is necessary.

A simple test for dehydration is the "pinch test." If you pinch the skin at the point of the horse's shoulder into a tiny "tent" and then release it, the skin should fall back into place almost immediately. If the little tent of skin remains raised for a second or so or subsides slowly over several seconds, the horse is noticeably dehydrated and should have water and probably electrolytes immediately.

FOOT AND LEG CARE

In order to show and win, a horse must first get to the show ring on four good legs! Considering the strain of carrying a rider and the hazards of work, showing and just being a horse, this isn't always as simple as it sounds. The feet and legs are among the parts of the horse most vulnerable to injury, and like the rest of the horse, they must be properly conditioned to carry him through training and into the show ring.

Before starting conditioning, the horse's feet and legs should be evaluated by the trainer along with the veterinarian and the horseshoer. If the horse has been out of work, the tendons, ligaments and joints will be weak and soft and vulnerable to injury, so they will need to be conditioned slowly. The horse's conformation should be assessed. Does he have conformation faults that are functional defects that can affect his way of moving or predispose him to injury? Are there any old injuries that may point to a weakness, or that will need special consideration during training? Is the structure of his feet and legs basically strong and correct, or are there structural weaknesses that will need to be watched closely for signs of strain? Are his feet too hard or too soft, brittle, cracked or contracted?

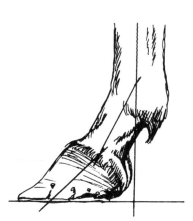

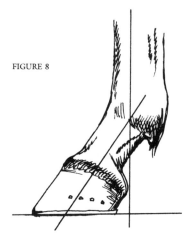

FIGURE 8

A. *Overgrown foot, needs resetting; broken angle*

B. *Foot correctly shod with hoof and pastern in alignment*

Horses that have not been kept trimmed or regularly worked tend to grow long toes and low heels. This must be trimmed to give the bones of the foot a proper angle before the horse can begin serious work. Riding with too-long toes and low heels can cause tripping and stumbling; it also puts strain on the flexor tendons and can lead to tendonitis. Some horses' feet crack and break off until the horse is tender-footed. Such horses will need shoes, and if their soles are thin or bruised, they may need pads to protect their feet. If the horse will have to undergo drastic changes to the angle and shape of the foot or the weight of the shoes, this should be accomplished gradually so as not to strain joints and ligaments with too great a change at once.

At one time, it was common practice for horseshoers to perform "corrective" shoeing or trimming in an effort to force horses with crooked legs to travel straight and stand as if their legs were correct and square. While this had some cosmetic effects, it often caused strain and lameness by forcing the bones and joints out of their natural, although crooked, alignment. Most horseshoers today feel that corrective shoeing or trimming to straighten crooked legs must be done while the leg bones are still growing, preferably during the horse's first year. For mature horses, whether straight or crooked, the emphasis is on trimming or shoeing the foot to allow it to travel and land in its best natural balance. Much can be done to help a horse with less than perfectly formed legs, but overcorrection can cause more trouble than the original problem.

Most horses will need to be trimmed or have their shoes reset every six to eight weeks. Horses that need to have their shoeing "fine-tuned" may require reshoeing every four weeks or so. If your horse wears special shoes, it is prudent to have your regular horseshoer make and fit an extra set, which can be taken along to shows. Should he lose a shoe, you can have a local horseshoer replace a shoe that has already been custom fitted, with only minor alterations on the spot.

Daily foot care should include picking out the feet and brushing the sole clean so that the ground surface of the foot can be inspected closely. Some grooms wash the feet, which makes it easier to check it. If the feet are dry, the sole may be packed with prepared mud or clay such as White Rock, which is left in the foot overnight. If the outer surface of the foot seems dry or peels, it can be painted with an oil-based hoof dressing, or a lanolin dressing can be rubbed into the coronary band. The foot absorbs moisture through the sole and ground surface of the foot; the circulation of the blood through the soft inner structures of the foot also moisturizes it. Hoof dressings applied to the outer wall of the foot have a cosmetic effect and can soften the coronary band, but the wall of the foot does not absorb moisture. The wall of the foot should never be rasped or sanded to make it look cleaner, as this removes the periople (the shiny outer coating of the hoof). Removing the periople is like sandpapering the surface of your fingernails—it can cause the hoof to dry out and crack. If you want to keep the feet looking clean, scrub them with a nail brush and then apply a clear hoof polish. Sticky dressings build up on the outside of the foot and collect dirt; they should be applied only sparingly to the coronary band and should be rubbed in, with the excess wiped off.

The legs require daily attention, too. The horse owner or groom should make a habit of examining each leg closely each day when he first takes the horse out, during grooming and later, after exercise. If you look closely at each leg and run your hand over it, feeling for heat, filling or swelling, you will come to know your horse's legs and feet so well that you will notice any little bump, swelling or heat before the problem has a chance to escalate. A normal leg is clean, tight and hard, without puffiness, swellings or hot places. The tendons and other structures should stand out clearly under the skin, and the horse should not show tenderness at any particular spot when the leg is palpated. Some horses have an old injury such as an old "set" bowed tendon that is long healed; this area should be watched for any signs of flaring up with inflammation.

Stocking up is a common problem in older horses and horses that stand up in the stable when they need to exercise. It is a generalized, cool swelling of both hind legs or all four legs, caused by poor circulation. It does not cause

FIGURE 9

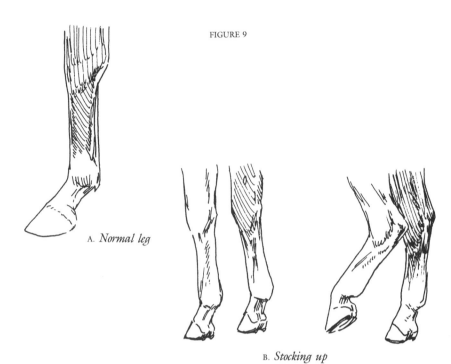

A. *Normal leg*

B. *Stocking up*

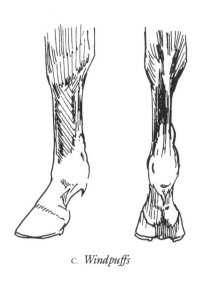

C. *Windpuffs*

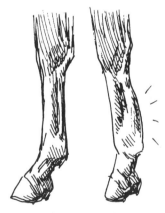

D. *Filled leg—injury*

lameness, but horses that stock up may be stiff when they are first brought out in the morning. Horses that do not lie down to rest are more likely to stock up, and standing on hard surfaces with insufficient bedding aggravates the problem. If the horse can be turned out in a pasture or paddock with a shed or stall to run into, stocking up rarely occurs. If he must be kept in, the use of standing bandages and leg braces will help to alleviate the swelling; massaging the legs is also helpful, but at least ten minutes per leg is necessary to do much good. Horses that stock up should have a long, easy walking warmup and benefit from being hand walked to loosen them up before being worked.

Windpuffs are soft, bunchy swellings on or near the fetlock joints of the front or hind legs. They are caused by an excess secretion of synovial fluid in the joint area and especially in the tendon sheaths near the joint. The excess fluid is secreted when the joint is stressed; eventually the joint capsule stretches and the swelling is permanent. Windpuffs are unsightly but usually are not a functional problem. They do point to stress, however, so if a horse develops puffy ankles the day after a hard workout, it is a sign that he has done more than he was fit for and serious injury may follow if he is stressed further. Old windpuffs are cool; a hot, puffy swelling probably points to a fresh sprain or strain, which should be taken seriously, instead of an old blemish. Stable bandages, leg sweats and leg braces will temporarily reduce old windpuffs so that they are not as noticeable for a Halter class, but they will soon reappear. Windpuffs are best prevented by avoiding overstressing tendons and fetlock joints and bracing and bandaging the legs after severe work to prevent swelling.

Windpuffs and stocking up should not be confused with heat and "filling" in a leg, which points to active inflammation and injury. When checking legs, compare one leg with the other. If one leg is puffy, warmer or thicker than the other, or if the horse flinches when one leg is palpated, the leg should be carefully examined. When an injury takes place, the inflammation results in "cellulitis"—the area becomes engorged with fluid, which makes it hot, tender and swollen. Although cellulitis is part of the body's healing process, the sooner it is reduced the better for the injury. Cold-hosing, or running a stream of cool water over the swollen area for ten to fifteen minutes, is good first aid. The area should be hosed for ten to fifteen minutes, then dried and left alone for an hour, and the hosing repeated several times a day. Applying a support bandage (stable or treatment bandage) also helps to reduce the swelling and minimize the damage. Whenever a "hot" leg is discovered, it should be treated immediately—don't wait a day to see if it will get worse! The horse should be rested (hand walking, no work) until the injury is obviously better.

Unfit horses tire more quickly and are more likely to injure themselves by interfering (striking one leg with the opposite hoof) or overreaching (grabbing the back of the heel or sometimes higher on the front leg with the toe of the hind foot.) They should be protected with boots or polo wraps when they are doing work that might result in such injuries—especially longeing, lateral movements and fast turns or jumping. Some trainers routinely brace and bandage the legs after the horse's workout, but horses do become dependent upon the support of the bandages if they are used constantly. Any bandages must be applied evenly, securely and correctly or they may cause injury to the tendons or come loose, tripping the horse. Boots must be kept clean so that dirt and sweat do not rub sores on the legs, and some horses are allergic to certain types of rubber or plastic liners—these horses may need a thin sheet of cotton next to their skin if boots are to be worn. (For directions for applying bandages, see page 92.)

CONDITIONING THE SKIN AND HAIR COAT

The skin is the largest organ of the horse's body; besides enclosing the body, it protects against injury and harmful organisms and serves as a sense organ. Besides providing beauty, the hair coat protects and insulates the skin.

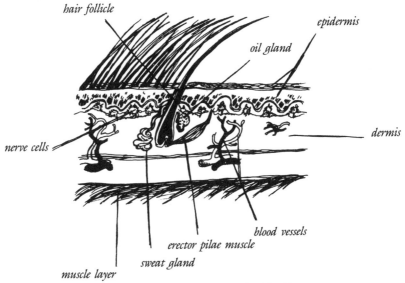

FIGURE 10 *Skin structures—healthy skin*

The skin consists of an outer layer, the smooth, pliable dermis, from which the hairs grow, and a thicker inner layer, the dermis, which contains the support system for the skin and hair: hair follicles, sweat glands, sebaceous glands and blood vessels. The skin's health depends on good nutrition and exercise, which produce good circulation and deliver the necessary proteins, oils, vitamins and other nutrients to grow a healthy, functioning skin and a shiny hair coat.

The skin oil called sebum is secreted by the sebaceous glands. Sebum is a source of moisture for the skin and hair and helps to keep the skin and hair follicles smooth and pliable. When it is distributed over the hair shafts evenly, it waterproofs the coat and makes it shine. Stimulating the skin to produce enough sebum and distributing it evenly over the hairs are two of the main essentials in producing a beautiful, shiny coat. Exercise and sweat help in this process—exercise and skin movement stimulate the sebaceous glands, and sweat rinses the coat and helps to distribute the skin oil over the hairs. Vigorous grooming also helps this process.

The sweating mechanism plays a vital role in regulating the horse's temperature. When the blood and inner body temperature rise, the part of the brain called the hypothalamus triggers sweating. The sweat glands release a watery sweat, which wets the skin and hair. As the watery sweat evaporates, it cools the skin and the network of blood vessels within it; the cooled blood is pumped back into the body, cooling it in much the same way that a car's radiator cools the engine. The difference is that the horse's "radiator" is all over his body.

A fit, well-groomed horse sweats a thin, watery sweat that evaporates easily. The sweat contains salt and other minerals, but it is mostly water. An unfit horse's sweat is less watery, containing more salts and waste products, and it mixes with sebum, dandruff and dirt to form a thick, scummy lather that evaporates slowly. This makes the skin less efficient at cooling the body, and the unfit horse gets hotter and cools more slowly, with a greater risk of heat exhaustion. In cold weather, the lathery sweat soaks the hair coat and removes its insulating qualities—the coat becomes wet right through but dries slowly and the horse is susceptible to chills. One of the most important reasons for grooming horses that work hard is to clear away the excess sebum, dirt and dandruff (called scurf—the whitish grease that you notice on brushes, tack and your hands when grooming dirty horses) so that the skin may function effectively in sweating and drying to cool the horse.

When the horse is cold, the skin can warm him up by shivering, and by increasing the loft of the coat. Each hair follicle is attached to a tiny muscle

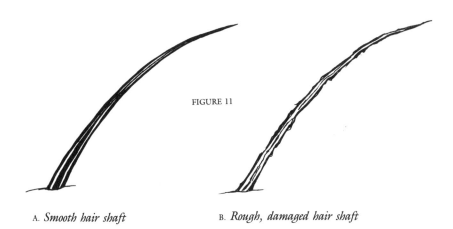

FIGURE 11

A. *Smooth hair shaft*   B. *Rough, damaged hair shaft*

that can make the hair stand up straight. This traps air within the coat, insulating the horse and protecting him from a loss of body heat. On a very cold day, the horse's coat will look extra fluffy, as the hairs stand out. Horses that are sick and having chills and fever may have a "staring" coat, as the hairs stand up in an effort to conserve body heat. This makes the coat appear dull and rumpled.

The hairs themselves are made up of an outer shaft, the cuticle, and an inner core, the cortex. A healthy, shiny hair coat has many smooth, uniform, straight hairs that taper toward their tips. The hairs lie flat except in cold weather. Thin, broken and irregular hairs, fewer in number, with many uneven, bent hairs and a rough surface on the hair shafts produce a dull, uneven and unhealthy coat. Crusty, scaling skin, excessive dandruff, poor circulation and inactive sweat glands and sebaceous glands all result in poor coat condition. Itching, rubbing, sunburn and the effects of harsh chemicals can also damage the hair and skin.

To condition the skin and hair coat, the extra scurf and dirt must first be removed from the skin. This is best done by regular good grooming, using a rubber currycomb to loosen the scurf and massage the skin and the dandy and body brushes to sweep the skin clean. In stubborn cases it may help to use a vacuum cleaner and/or bathe the horse to get the coat reasonably clean. Bathing, especially with detergents, temporarily removes some of the skin's natural oils and so may decrease the shine of the coat for a short while. This is one reason why bathing cannot be substituted for good daily grooming.

However, rinsing the horse's coat with clean water and a small amount of body wash after exercise does not harm the hair and makes it easier to keep the skin clean and working efficiently. Leaving the coat full of dried sweat and salt will make the horse itch and want to rub himself; if the horse is left out in strong sunlight, the coat may bleach and change color where the saddle marks are.

Once the worst of the scurf is removed, vigorous daily grooming will keep the skin and hair clean and condition the skin. Grooming stimulates the production of sebum or skin oil and distributes it evenly over the surface of the hairs. It also removes debris and loose hairs. Grooming is most effective when done right after exercise, when the skin is warm and the pores are open, but horses must be cleaned before being ridden in order to prevent friction sores.

The coat can be protected by using a scrim fly sheet during the day and a light sheet at night; this encourages the hair to lie flat, which makes the coat smoother and shiny. A silicone coat dressing can be applied to the clean hair—the silicone coats the cuticle or outer surface of the hairs, making them smooth and slippery and helping them to reflect light. Silicone or polymer dressings help to repel stains for several days at a time. They are cosmetic, not therapeutic, however—they make the coat look better and protect it against staining, but they do not improve the quality of the hair.

If your horse's hair quality needs improvement, you can help him through nutrition as well as therapeutic coat products. If a horse lacks vitamin A, or if he has an excess of vitamin A, zinc or sulfur in his diet, he may have dull or dry, scaly skin. Feeding unsaturated fats (corn oil, soybean oil or canola oil), biotin or lysine may help coat quality and hair growth. Some feed supplements are especially formulated to develop a shiny coat—these usually contain some oil or oil meal and a vitamin supplement.

Topical products are those applied directly on the coat for therapeutic purposes. These smooth and coat the hair shafts, bonding with the keratin of the cuticle and making the hair smoother and more flexible and restoring moisture. Some excellent ingredients are aloe vera, lanolin and protein. If the horse's skin is dry, flaky, itchy or produces too much dandruff, he can be bathed with a medicated shampoo. If shampooing does not help the problem, the veterinarian should be consulted, as the trouble may be an allergy, dermatitis or a condition that requires prescription medication.

Horses normally shed their winter coats beginning in midwinter and being completely shed out by the middle of May. The winter coat begins growing during the late summer and becomes longer and thicker during the fall. The rate at which the winter coat grows in is influenced by fall temperatures—a few nippy nights will cause horses to grow their winter hair faster. In the spring, the shedding-out process is triggered by the lengthening daylight as well as warmer temperatures.

The long winter coat may be altered for winter showing by body clipping or by blanketing (for more on body clipping, see Chapter 5). An unclipped coat is usually softer and richer in color than if it is clipped. To induce the horse to grow very little coat, he wears a sheet whenever the temperature dips below 60 degrees. As the weather becomes cooler, the sheet is replaced by a light blanket, a heavier blanket and eventually as many as two blankets, a blanket liner and a full hood. In addition, as daylight shortens, the stall lights (at least 200 watts) are left on from 6 A.M. to 9 P.M. to simulate long summer light. The stable temperature is regulated to between 45° and 50° Farenheit by paying close attention to opening or closing doors and windows according to the outside temperature. This process acts on the horse's hypothalamus (the part of the brain which reacts to changing seasons) and stimulates the horse to grow a summer coat or, if it is begun in January, to shed his winter coat early. It will also bring mares into their spring reproductive cycle early.

If you choose to keep the coat short by blanketing and/or body clipping, remember that the horse needs more care. He is very vulnerable to drafts, yet he needs fresh air and good ventilation. His blankets must be clean, must fit properly and must be added or taken off when the temperature changes. When riding, he should be kept moving and should be covered if he must stand still when it is cool. Since blanketing requires more care, attention and knowledge, it makes sense to leave a horse natural unless you really need him to keep an artificially short coat.

One important aspect of conditioning is toughening portions of the skin that must tolerate sweat, friction and saddle pressure. A soft horse has soft skin and is apt to develop girth and saddle sores when he first starts to work. Hot weather and long hair increase the problems of heat, sweating and friction and the likelihood of sores. It is much easier to prevent sores and galls than to treat them; treatment usually requires the horse to be laid up while he heals.

The skin should be inspected after every ride and washed with clean water, or a little body wash may be added. When the saddle is removed, notice the wet saddle mark—if there are small dry patches in the wet spot, these indicate pressure points. The pressure that creates dry spots will eventually lead to tissue damage and a serious sore. Pain in the skin tissues or underlying muscles can cause the horse to move stiffly, throw his head, limp or even buck or rear. If you notice a rubbed spot, it can be treated with strong tea—the tannic acid in the tea toughens the skin. If the skin is already raw, it must be treated as

FIGURE 12 *Saddle mark with dry pressure point*

an open wound and protected from any further contact until it is healed. The penalty for inflicting a girth sore on your horse is to ride bareback until it has healed! Padding up a sore to keep working is risky, as it may slip as the horse moves and grind dirt and sweat into the sore, making it many times worse. There is no padding that will make pressure on a raw sore tolerable, and to work a horse in this condition is a cruelty.

FITTING OF TACK AND EQUIPMENT

Equipment must fit the horse without excessive pressure concentrated at pressure points, pinching, friction or rocking. A saddle must rest on the "saddle muscles" along the top of the ribs—*it cannot touch the withers or spine at any point.* It must also permit the top of the shoulder blade to move freely back at each stride without pinching, and it must not throw the rider into a backward balance that could hurt the horse's back as well as hinder his riding. This is not always easy to achieve, especially if the horse is fatter or thinner than he should be when you start to condition him.

Check the fit of a saddle by running your hand under the gullet and down the front edge of the saddle on each side. You should be able to fit two fingers between the withers and the saddle, and the saddle should allow your hand to slide confortably over the back of the shoulder blade. If the tree is too wide, it will sit down on the withers. This can be helped temporarily by using a full back protector pad. If the tree is too narrow, the saddle will ride high in front

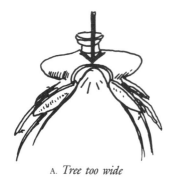

A. *Tree too wide*   B. *Tree too narrow*

FIGURE 13 *Saddle Problems*

A. *Correctly fitted saddle*

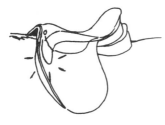

B. *Too high in back (too much padding);* C. *Too high in front (tree too narrow);*
jabs shoulder blades and throws rider *jabs shoulder blades and throws rider*
forward   *back on loins*

FIGURE 14 *Saddle Fitting*

and will jab the horse in the shoulder blades; it will also throw the rider backward. Simply raising the cantle with a lift-back pad may level the seat, but it makes the pinching worse. The only real solution is to use a wider saddle.

The rider should be able to sit in a good position in the deepest part of the saddle. If the saddle is low in back, he will be thrown into a backward balance. If the saddle tilts too far forward, he will be overbalanced forward. A correctly sized saddle is essential in order to ride in good balance. The advice of an instructor is helpful when choosing a saddle.

The saddle pad cushions and protects the horse's back and protects the bottom of the saddle. It should be clean, neat and complement the show outfit. English pads should be white only, of sheepskin or washable fleece, and should fit the saddle with a neat two-inch border. Pads should be secured to the saddle by billet tabs, Velcro strips or a girth slot. Square English pads are used only in dressage, eventing and jumper classes—never for any other English class. Western riders may use a show pad or a folded Navajo-style blanket. Since the show pad may not be washable, it is sensible to use a smaller cotton pad underneath it. Some horses may require extra padding in the form of a back protector pad, a cut-back pad or a lift-back pad to balance the saddle and protect the back.

Protective equipment can sometimes help to prevent sores. Cut-back saddle pads keep the saddle from touching the withers, and a specially formed back protector pad may temporarily fill in an area that is lacking in muscle

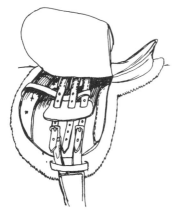 

A. *Pad secured with loop to last billet above buckle guard; girth loop at bottom of pad*   B. *Correctly fitted hunter saddle pad*

FIGURE 15 *Saddle pads*

alongside the withers while it dissipates shock and protects the back. Girths, breastcollars, harness backpads and saddle pads are available in a range of washable materials ranging from sheepskin to artificial fleece, cotton, hospital felt and other materials. Girth tubes and fleece "cinch safes" can be slipped over a girth or cinch ring to prevent sores. A shaped, molded girth keeps the elbow area free from friction, and string girths grip with less friction and allow air to penetrate, keeping the skin cooler. With some ingenuity, it is possible to pad or alter almost any piece of equipment that tends to pinch or rub by padding it, covering it with fleece or wrapping it with padded rubber tape.

Bits and bridles must fit so that they are secure, comfortable and effective. No part of the bridle or headstall should rub or pinch—check the browband to be sure that the headstall does not pinch the ears. The throatlash should admit four fingers at the side of the cheek; if too tight, it binds when the horse flexes correctly at the poll. Nosebands and cavessons should be high on the face (within a half inch of the cheekbone) and snug but comfortable. Over-tightening the noseband for control purposes can cause the horse to throw his head, grind his teeth or move stiffly in discomfort. The buckles of the cheekpiece, cavesson headstall and throatlash should lie in line with the horse's eye. When a double or Weymouth bridle is used, the bradoon carrier buckles on the right side. The reins should be of plain leather and the snaffle rein is slightly wider than the curb rein.

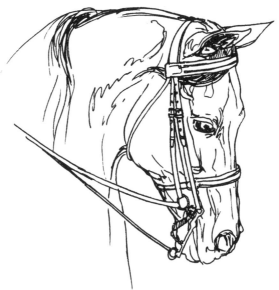

FIGURE 16 *Correctly fitted double show bridle*

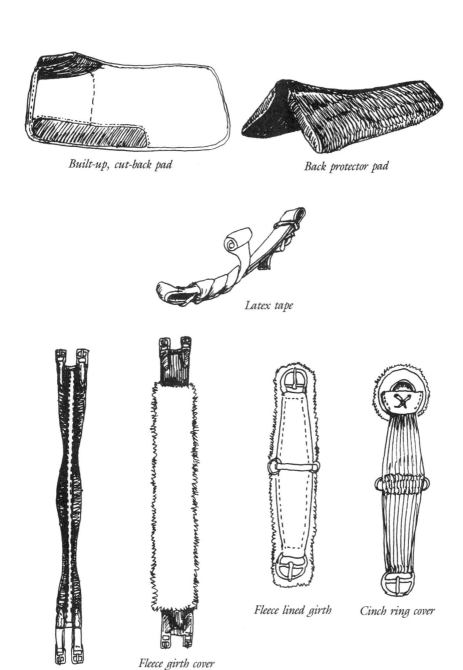

Built-up, cut-back pad

Back protector pad

Latex tape

Fleece lined girth

Cinch ring cover

Fleece girth cover

Shaped girth

FIGURE 17 *Protective equipment*

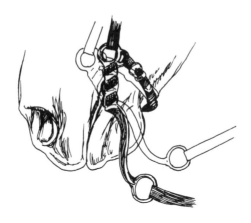

FIGURE 18 *Fitting curb bit and curb strap or chain*
Bit shank should rotate 45° to tighten curb chain.

The bit must be wide enough to fit without pinching but not so wide as to rock sideways. Snaffle bits should be adjusted to form one or two gentle wrinkles in the lips; the horse may get his tongue over the bit if it is placed too low. Curbs, pelhams and kimberwickes are placed lower—just touching the corner or the lips without a wrinkle. The curb chain must be twisted clockwise until it lies flat and should be adjusted so that the bit shank rotates exactly 45 degrees to tighten the chain or strap against the jaw. Some bits can be equipped with a lip strap which prevents the horse from lipping the shank of the bit.

MENTAL ATTITUDE

The horse's mental attitude should be taken into consideration along with his physical conditioning. Horses are not machines that can be worked when it is convenient and then turned off when the trainer goes home for the day. Concentrated work and confinement are not natural to a horse, and horses may develop unpleasant dispositions or neurotic habits if they are treated without sympathy and understanding for their nature. A happy horse is healthier, more resistant to stress and disease and shows better, too.

Horses feel more secure when a steady routine is followed, so try to keep to a regular daily schedule for feeding, grooming, exercise and turnout, etc. Try to break up long periods of idleness by spacing out feedings, breaking exercise into two shorter periods instead of one long one and allowing the horse as much access to a paddock as possible. If he must be kept stabled a great deal of the time, he should have a roomy box stall with a large window or Dutch door that permits him to see other horses and activities going on around him. Feed several small meals throughout the day instead of one or two big feedings; not only is this better for his digestion, but it gives him something to do. If you feed an all-pellet ration, the horse may eat up his pellets and then chew wood or begin eating his bedding if he has nothing else to do. Providing a few flakes of hay to nibble on may help. Without something to do, a stalled horse may find himself a "hobby" such as chewing wood, digging holes or perhaps stall-walking, weaving or cribbing. The last three can be nervous habits, though they are more often caused by boredom, and may be an indication that a horse is being handled unsympathetically or trained too hard for his mental and physical good. (It is important to note that cribbing especially is an addiction, so a horse that cribs may continue his habit even under the best of management. In this case, the only solution is to keep a cribbing strap on him to prevent the habit.) Some horses are happier if they are stabled or turned out with a favorite stablemate or if they have the companionship of a "pet" such as a dog, cat or goat; and there are some exuberant clowns who delight in bouncing a rubber ball, a plastic bottle or an old tire around their stall or paddock.

A good trainer will try to keep his horse in a pleasant and confident state of mind. He should be aware of the horse's interest in his work—or lack of it—and be alert to a change in attitude that might signify fatigue, sourness, illness or fear. The treatment a horse receives in his daily care is just as important to his performance in the show ring as his formal ring training—a horse that is confused, hurt, frightened and frustrated in the barn will carry these attitudes over into training under saddle. If a horse is gradually introduced to such things as noises, strangers, trailer loading and strange places with a quiet, confident handler and a minimum of fuss, he will handle the new experiences of showing better and will settle down faster to show his best.

As horses reach peak condition they will be—and should be—full of high spirits and playfulness. A show horse that feels full of himself is consequently more difficult to handle than the placid pleasure horse in the pasture. It takes a firm but sympathetic handler with his mind on his job to keep such a bundle of equine energy under control without resorting to abuse. Show grooms are always busy and often harried; don't let yourself get distracted and inattentive or a horse's high spirits can cause an accident, and don't let your temper get the better of you. Anticipate the keen horse's playfulness and energy, insist on ordinary good manners and obedience, but don't punish him for feeling good; this is what you have been working so hard to achieve all along!

Two

GROOMING AND DAILY CARE

BASIC GROOMING

All show conditioning and good horse care includes a thorough daily grooming. Any horse that is kept stabled and in work should be groomed every day whether he is ridden or not. Grooming is important for health and comfort as well as appearance; it massages the skin and promotes good circulation, and picking out the feet helps to prevent thrush. One of the most important aspects of grooming is that the groom performs a daily close examination of the horse; in this way, small problems such as a scrape, rash or swelling are treated before they become major problems. Horses living in pasture need less grooming than stabled horses, as they use rolling and dust baths to keep themselves comfortable. They should be cleaned before they are ridden, however, and need their feet picked out daily and a check for injuries, ticks and skin problems such as rainrot.

Grooming can be excellent training for simple obedience and stable manners and is a good way to establish trust and respect between horse and handler. Horses use mutual grooming (scratching, nibbling and brushing flies off each other) as a gesture of trust and friendship. When you groom your horse and make him feel good, he learns to relax and enjoy your handling. However, don't let him return the favor by nibbling on you; he must treat you with more respect than one of his herd buddies or he could hurt you accidentally.

SAFETY IN TYING AND HANDLING DURING GROOMING

You should groom your horse in a safe, convenient area where your tools and grooming items are handy but not underfoot, and where the horse is safely restrained. A horse may be tied in a stable yard, tied up in his stall, cross-tied or perhaps even ground-tied in a barn aisle while you work. The ideal place to work is a grooming stall with good lighting, safe footing and cross-ties, hot and cold water available and shelves or cupboards to hold your grooming items. Trying to groom a horse while loose in a stall without even a halter on his head is foolish and unsafe; if the horse nips, kicks or turns around suddenly, you are helpless to control him.

While any kind of halter will do for grooming, it is convenient to have the type in which the throatlash unsnaps to permit grooming of the head, or perhaps a simple grooming slip, which has no throatlash. The halter should have rings on each side of the noseband to permit cross-tying. When grooming an aggressive horse or one that fidgets and does not pay attention to you, pass a thirty-inch chain end lead shank through the side halter ring, over the noseband of the halter, out through the off-side halter ring and snap it to the

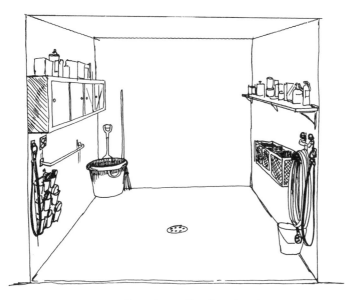

FIGURE 1 *Grooming stall and wash rack*

43

FIGURE 2 *How to put a chain over the nose*
   A. *Run snap from outside to inside.*
   B. *Pass chain across halter noseband and through offside ring from inside to outside.*

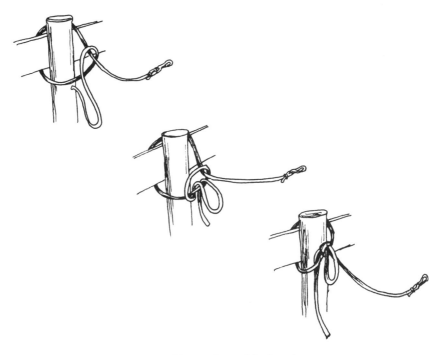

FIGURE 3 *How to tie a quick-release knot*

upper ring on the far side of the halter. Never jerk on a chain over the nose—a light tug is sufficient to get a horse's attention and to remind him of his manners. *Never* tie a horse with a chain shank over the nose or under the chin—should he pull back, he can severely injure or even fracture his nose or chin. This also applies to letting the end of the shank hang on the ground where the horse could step on it.

Anytime a horse is tied for grooming, he should be tied with a halter and tie rope, using a quick-release knot. Beware of tying with leather straps or light, flat nylon leads, as these may jam or break even if a quick release knot is used. Tie only to a solid object that the horse cannot move or break off (never a fence board or a door, for instance), and be sure that there is nothing nearby that the horse could injure himself on or catch a foot in, such as a wire fence or a bucket with a loose handle. The tie rope should be tied at the height of the horse's back or slightly higher; if tied too low, a horse can injure his neck if he should pull back. The length should just allow him to turn his head but not quite touch the ground; if tied with too much slack, he could get a leg over the rope and get rope-burned or catch the rope over his poll and scare or injure himself. Never tie by the bridle reins or snap cross-ties to the bit rings; a pulling horse may panic and severely injure his mouth.

Cross-ties restrain a horse best for most grooming, but they are not without their own hazards. Horses are often cross-tied in a busy barn aisle, with people, wheelbarrows and other horses passing by them. Cross-ties pre-

FIGURE 4 *Safe cross-ties with breakaway links*

vent a horse from turning his head to see what is going on, and if a horse pulls back he can lose his footing and hang from the cross-ties or even flip over backwards.

Some Sensible Cross-tie Precautions Are:

1. Equip cross-ties with a breakaway link (easily made by fastening the cross-tie to the wall ring with a piece of baling twine.) A breakaway link can also be placed on the rings of the halter.
2. Place cross-ties at wither height, not up high. Be sure the footing is not slippery.
3. If possible, cross-tie a horse with a solid wall several feet behind his hind-quarters. Should he pull back, the wall will stop him before he gets into trouble on the cross-ties. Cross-ties inside a box stall are safer than in the aisle.
4. If someone wants to pass by, unsnap one cross-tie and move the horse over. Don't duck under cross-ties, especially when leading another horse! Unsnap one cross-tie when bridling or for any procedure that might cause a horse to pull back.
5. Be aware of activities going on in the barn that could spook your horse, and never leave a horse unattended on the cross-ties.

If you must deal with a nipper, a fidgety horse or a horse that pulls back when cross-tied, a hand-held cross-tie can make your job safer and easier. First run the chain end lead shank over the nose from the left side, as previously described. Next, snap or tie a piece of clothesline to the right halter ring, pass it through a cross-tie ring or around a post, then run it back through the chin ring of the halter and hold the end along with the lead shank in your hand. You can let the hand-held cross-tie slip so that the horse is not held too tightly and scared, or use the clothesline to keep his head turned slightly away from you if he is nippy. Do not jerk on the chain shank or try to hold the horse in place forcibly with this cross-tie—instead, use it to teach the horse gently that he can stand where he is asked without getting excited or swinging around. This method works well for introducing green horses to being cross-tied. To handle the horse on the other side, reverse the shank and hand-held cross-tie.

When grooming a horse that nips or bites, the hand-held cross-tie can help. You can also take hold of the cheekpiece of the halter while you groom the head, neck and forequarters, keeping your arm firm enough to prevent him from turning and nipping. If a horse nips at you when you are not holding

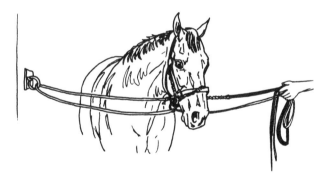

FIGURE 5 *Hand-held cross-tie*

the halter, let his cheek bump into your ready elbow while you keep a casual attitude and continue to groom. Slapping, jerking or making a fuss tends to make a nipper into a sneaky biter who takes his bite and then jerks away, rather than curing him. Letting him punish himself while continuing to groom quietly works much better.

When grooming the belly, flanks or legs, keep your free hand on the horse's loin or back. You can feel him tense up if he is planning to kick and can head off a kick by a warning word, or move to a safe position. If you must pass behind a horse, stay close to him and keep a hand on his tail or rump. Your hand pressure lets him know where you are and a firm pull downward may discourage a kick. If the horse should kick out and you are close to his legs, you will not get the full force of the blow as you might if you were several feet away. Of course, with a kicky horse it is safest to walk around the front or safely out of range instead.

If your horse is tied to a fence, wall or horse trailer, never duck under his neck and tie rope to get to the other side. By doing so, you pass into his blind spot beneath his head and can startle him into pulling back. If anything makes him jump forward, you are in trouble!

Be aware of your body position whenever you work around a horse— especially a young, green or nervous horse. Horses do not look where they put their feet, especially if they are excited and dancing around, and they can step on you without even knowing it. If a horse does step on your foot, push against him—this will get him off faster and with less injury to you than if you try to pull away from him. Keep your head out of the danger zone around the horse's head—his skull can weigh as much as fifty pounds and can really hurt if he throws his head up suddenly and your face is in the way. Pay attention also to the forelegs—horses instinctively strike at a fly or bee that buzzes under their chin, and they can hurt you quite by accident in fly time if you are in the way. Never sit down or kneel when working around a horse; bend your knees to get lower, but be able to move away in case the horse should move or kick.

When leading a horse, even for a short distance, always use a lead rope or shank—never lead with only your hand on the halter. If anything should make the horse act up or bolt, you would either be dragged or have to let go, which is a good way to teach him a bad habit. Wear shoes or boots that offer some protection in case a horse should step on your foot, but never metal-toed work boots—these could bend under the weight of a horse and injure your toes more than the horse himself.

Lastly, a neat barn is a safer barn, for horses and people alike. Pick up trash and put away unused tools; clear the aisles or grooming areas when you plan to handle horses there, and notice hazards such as protruding nails or open gate latches that could cause injury if a horse bumps into them. Keep wire fencing, lead ropes and longe lines, etc., neatly coiled and away from horses' legs, and be sure that a tied dog cannot wrap his rope or chain around a passing horse's legs.

BASIC GROOMING PROCEDURE

To begin grooming a horse, first remove the sheet or blanket and standing bandages if these are used. Sheets and blankets should always be unfastened at the rear surcingles or leg straps first, the chest fastenings last. (Unfastening the chest strap first can cause the blanket to slip back and "flank" the horse in front of the hind legs, just like a bucking strap on a rodeo bronc. A real "rodeo" may follow!) Bandages are removed quickly, not by rerolling them off the leg. Never kneel or sit when removing bandages or working around a horse's legs; this is unsafe. The clothing should be brushed clean and hung up; bandages may be rerolled for reuse or put aside to wash. Use a rub rag or towel to quickly wipe surface dust off the horse's head, neck, body and legs.

Groom systematically, starting at the same place with each tool and working over the body in the same order. Besides being more efficient, the horse will get to learn the routine and feel secure; he may even cooperate by holding up the next foot for you when he knows that you are ready for it. Currying, brushing and rubbing are forms of massage and should be done vigorously, one right after the other for the best effect. If you find you get tired before finishing one operation, switch to picking out the feet or do the mane or tail; this will give you a rest so you can go back to grooming with energy. Of course, you will have to moderate your grooming efforts according to the sensitivity of the horse. Pay attention to his ticklish spots and the kind of grooming he likes best; don't groom so hard you make him upset or sore. Grooming is supposed to make the horse feel good!

The first tool to use is the currycomb, which loosens dirt, scurf and dandruff and massages the skin and muscle beneath the coat. Use a soft, bendable rubber or plastic currycomb (hint: rubber works best for removing loose hairs, as it is slightly "tacky") that can flex with your hand so you can bear down and massage the skin well. Too many people buy a stiff currycomb and then cannot use it hard enough to do any good or else they drive the horse to rebellion at the intense discomfort. Scrub in a circular or side-to-side motion, bearing down on the heavily muscled, less sensitive areas and lightly rubbing the sensitive spots. Knock the loose scurf out of the currycomb from time to time. The currycomb is primarily a massage tool intended for use on the neck and body, but if you are gentle you can use it to loosen caked dirt on the cheek, legs and belly. Never run it harshly over bony or sensitive places, and do not use a metal currycomb for grooming, as it is far too sharp.

A metal currycomb can be used very gently to break up heavily caked mud on the less sensitive parts of the body when the horse has a long winter coat, and it can help to shed out thick winter hair. Remember that the metal teeth can scratch the skin, and most fine-coated horses are far too sensitive to tolerate a metal currycomb at all.

Next, take up the dandy or stiff brush. With the brush at arm's length, use short, hard, snapping strokes to get between the hairs and down to the skin. This brush sweeps the skin free of larger particles of dirt. Since the bristles are quite coarse and stiff, be careful when brushing sensitive areas like the face. The dandy brush should be used all over the body in the direction of the growth of hair. It should be used lightly but thoroughly on the legs, head and belly. When brushing the legs, hold the brush vertically (pointing up and down); it will clean the hair more efficiently. Do not "pet" the hair with a dandy brush; hard, short strokes are necessary to penetrate the hair to the skin and to lift the dirt out. You should see a little cloud of dirt fly out of the skin at every stroke. Clean the brush frequently by brushing the bristles against a currycomb, stall screen or any hard object.

When you have finished with the dandy brush (not neglecting the elbows, the roots of the mane and the pasterns), if you part the hair and look closely at the skin, you will find it clean, but the hair will be filled with fine dust and the whitish, greasy dust called scurf. The body brush is used to remove the fine dust and scurf from the skin and hairs and to distribute the sebum or skin oil over the hairs by friction. Its rubbing action is also good for the skin.

Use the body brush to rub the horse firmly in the direction of the hair growth all over the head, neck, body and legs. The short, close-set bristles penetrate the coat when enough pressure is applied at each stroke, and the dust and scurf cling to the bristles of the brush instead of the hair coat. The heat and friction generated by vigorous body brushing helps to distribute the sebum over each hair and brings up the shine of the coat. The body brush will pick up a considerable amount of dust and scurf as you work; once it becomes full of scurf, the brush is less effective at gathering it. You can clean the brush every few strokes by scraping it across the teeth of a metal currycomb; the dust goes into the brush and then out into the air, not back onto the horse. (This is the *only* correct use of a metal currycomb on fine horses!)

The body brush is a good tool for removing dust from hard-to-clean areas like the head and the top of the croup, especially when you cannot give the horse a bath. It will also help remove dandruff from the roots of the mane.

Next, using a large body sponge or turkish towel dampened with warm water, go over the face, ears and lower legs. Clean out the lips, nostrils and corners of the eyes very gently (this can be done with disposable cotton balls, which are more sanitary). Use a separate sponge to wipe the underside of the dock and the area beneath the tail, along with the sheath or udder. When cleaning under the tail, notice if there is a grayish or dry yellow discharge from the anus; this is a sign of pinworms, and the irritation they cause will often lead to tail rubbing. Most deworming preparations will remove pinworms along with other internal parasites.

If your horse is light colored or has white markings, he may have manure, mud or grass stains that do not come out with normal grooming. Most stains will come out with vigorous rubbing with a damp rub rag, turkish towel or cactus cloth. Dampen the towel slightly with hot, soapy water and rub the stain until the part of the towel around your hand becomes darkened; then shift to a clean portion of the towel. Another method is to make a paste with Bon Ami cleanser and water and work the paste into the stained area. After it dries, the powder can be brushed out of the coat, taking the stain along with it. There are various commercial preparations for loosening and removing stains, but large or stubborn stains may have to be shampooed out. Once the hair is clean, a little silicone coat dressing sprayed on the spot will help to repel future stains.

To do the mane and tail, pick all snarls out gently by hand. If you must use a comb, a smooth plastic comb or a dog brush is less likely to break off hairs than a metal comb, but any tool will pull out and break off at least a few hairs every time it is used. Many show stables forbid the use of anything but the hand alone on the precious mane and tail hair. If the hair is tangled and full of bedding or other debris, spray it lightly with a silicone coat dressing. As the silicone drys, the hair will become slippery and the tangles and debris will slip out more easily. A human hairbrush or a pet brush (the type with wire bristles set into a rubber backing) is a good compromise when you do not have time to pick the hairs out properly. But don't brush long hair rapidly with it or the hairs will fly out and wrap around the brush and pull out. When working with long mane or tail hair, first brush the tips of the hairs until they are free. Then separate a small section of hair and gently work it free from the bottom to the top, carefully loosening snarled hairs. Never rip through a mane or tail with a comb or a currycomb unless you like short, bushy and broken-off hairs!

The roots and skin of the mane and tail need to be kept clean, with healthy skin. Brush across the crest of the neck or the dock of the tail, parting the hairs to get right down to the skin in small sections. Check the tail and mane for ticks—ticks like to crawl up the long tail hairs and fasten themselves to the end of the dock. Crusts of amber fluid or scabs show where a tick has been, or you may find one still attached. To remove a tick, use tweezers or wear plastic gloves and be sure to get the entire tick, not just the body—if you pull the body off and leave the head embedded, it can cause an infection later. The tick should be dropped into a can of alcohol and the spot where it was attached disinfected with alcohol. Since ticks can carry a variety of serious diseases, including Lyme disease, you should wash your hands after checking for ticks or removing them. Horses really suffer from tick infestation—if neglected, ticks can cause a nasty infection or infect a horse with Lyme disease.

As a final touch, you can "lay" the mane over to the proper side by brushing it with a wet brush. The top hairs of the tail may be treated similarly, and for formal occasions, hunters and sport horses often have a tail bandage applied to the dock for an hour or two to shape the dampened hair and make it appear neat and trim later when the tail bandage is removed.

CLEANING THE FEET AND DAILY FOOT CARE

The feet should be picked out carefully every day and the foot checked for condition, small injuries or cracks and foreign objects like stones. The shoes should be checked, as a loose nail or a sprung shoe can cause the loss of a shoe or injure the horse. If the feet are too dry, brittle, contracted or soft and chalky, the problem must be addressed before the foot becomes too damaged to hold a shoe or causes lameness. Even a horse that is not being worked should have his feet checked regularly.

To ask a horse to lift a front foot, stand facing backward and press against his shoulder or elbow until he shifts his weight to the opposite leg. Then, slide your hand down to the flexor tendons below the knee and squeeze briefly, giving a voice command to pick up the foot. If he ignores the request, you can tap gently on the coronary band or gently squeeze the skin around the chestnut, which will usually make him lift his leg. As the leg comes up, cradle the hoof with the hand closest to the horse. Hold the hoof, not the pastern—it is more secure.

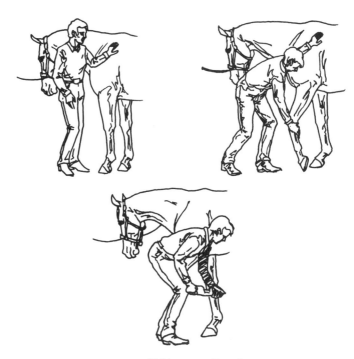

FIGURE 6 *Picking up a front leg*

52

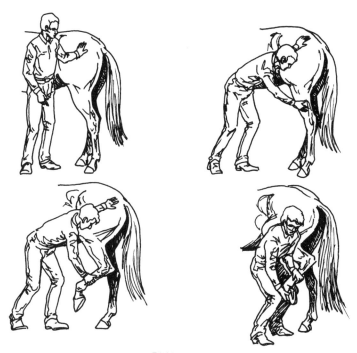

FIGURE 7 *Picking up a hind leg*

To lift a horse's hind leg, stand next to his hip facing backward and press against the hip with the hand closest to the horse, asking him to shift his weight over. Slide your other hand down the outside of the leg to the flexor tendons, below the hock, and squeeze briefly; pull forward against the tendon. If you keep your hand on the outside of the hind leg, you can deflect a kick if a horse should try one. Do not run your hand and arm around the inside of the hind leg, especially on a strange horse—if he should snatch up the leg suddenly or should kick, he could trap your arm as he flexes his hock. Remember that the hind leg will come up and forward, as though the horse was going to take a step forward; as it comes up, your other hand can take the cannon bone and help to bring the leg backward, a bit behind the horse's hindquarter. Bend your knees and assume a half-squatting position, with your thigh behind and supporting the hind leg. If the horse should want to kick or take his leg away, he cannot kick you but can only stretch it out behind him. Never pull the leg too high or too far out to the side—this causes the horse pain in the hip and stifle and hindquarter muscles and can make him struggle to kick or to get his leg away.

When you are holding up a foot, insist on good manners from your horse. He should be given time to balance on three legs; he is not allowed to lean on you! If he leans or tries to take his leg away, take a toe hold: place the palm of the hand nearest the horse over the sole of the foot, with your spread fingers holding the toe. In this position, a resisting horse will simply flex his own ankle more, and you can move with him if necessary. If you should have to let go, you can easily get out of the way.

Never snatch up a foot without warning, pull or twist it uncomfortably high or out to the side, or drop it down suddenly. If the horse sets his foot down before you are finished, make him pick it right up again. If you are patient, persistent and consistent in your handling, most horses will learn to pick up their feet easily on command and stand politely without leaning. Be sure to reward with praise and perhaps a food reward when teaching a green or difficult horse, and don't get into a fight—a tense or angry horse is more apt to freeze in place, snatch his foot up violently or kick.

When cleaning the foot, use the hoof pick from back to front in order to avoid accidentally digging it into the frog. Pick quickly, so that the horse doesn't have to hold his foot up for too long. If you can dig the point of the pick under a packed-in mass of dirt and lever it out, it cleans the foot faster and more efficiently than picking or scraping a little at a time. Be sure to get the commissures (the depressions on each side of the frog) clean all the way to the bottom, and pick out the cleft (the crease in the center of the frog) carefully but thoroughly. Use a stiff brush to brush the ground surface of the foot clean so you can inspect it.

Thrush

Thrush is a fungus infection that can attack the soft parts of the foot. It usually starts in the cleft of the frog but can spread to the commissures or to holes and depressions in the surface of the frog. Thrush needs a moist, dirty and airless environment; it is often found in horses that stand in wet, dirty conditions, but can occur in any horse if the cleft is deep or there are holes and pockets in the surface of the frog. The characteristic signs of thrush are a watery discharge and a particularly foul odor. The surfaces of the frog within the cleft or pockets of thrush will be raw and tender, and the area will be filled with blackish debris or dead cells and foreign material such as rotting manure and bedding. To treat thrush, wrap the end of your hoof pick in cotton and gently pick out the area, discarding each piece of cotton and replacing it until the discharge and debris are cleaned away. The farrier or veterinarian may need to pare away the diseased parts of the frog to open the area to light and air—you should not try to cut out the cleft, as you could cut too deeply and damage it further. Stand the horse with his foot in a rubber bucket filled with hot water to which a little iodine and a handful of Epsom salts have been added; the foot should be soaked for 15 to 20 minutes and then carefully dried with cotton. Cotton balls can then be packed into the cleft and into any deep holes and saturated with a liquid thrush remedy or with diluted Clorox. The cotton should be removed and the medication renewed daily. Antibiotics may be needed to clean the thrush up quickly, or in an extensive case. In the meantime, the horse should be kept out of mud, urine and wet conditions and his feet should be picked out clean twice a day.

Hoof Dressing and Packing

Hoof dressings are used to improve the texture and condition of the feet and for their cosmetic effect. The foot is moisturized primarily by its internal blood supply, which is stimulated by exercise and inhibited when he stands without working for long periods. The hoof wall is made up of tiny tubules, which run down from the coronary band to the ground surface. These tubules are hollow, so they can absorb moisture from the ground. The coronary band is also soft and can absorb moisture, like the cuticle of your fingernails. The hoof wall is covered with a shiny, varnishlike outer layer called the periople, which prevents moisture from escaping or from being absorbed through the outer hoof wall. Hoof dressing applied to the coronary band can help to keep it soft and flexible, especially if it is rubbed in. When applied to the outer wall, it does not do much to moisturize the foot but can make it look better, especially when the horse works in sandy conditions that make the periople appear scratchy, peeled or uneven. Thick, sticky hoof dressings can build up on the outside of the feet, picking up dirt; they do not do much for the actual condition of the feet. The best place to apply hoof dressing is in a ring around the coronary band and across the heels, rubbing off any excess.

The outer wall of the foot may be scrubbed clean, especially on horses with light-colored feet, but the natural coating of the periople should never be removed. Scrubbing the wall of the hoof with steel wool, a wire brush or an electric sander is no better for the feet than sanding the outside of your fingernails would be for your nails. Without the periople, the hoof may become excessively dry and cracking may follow; it will have to be treated with a sealant. This is never as good as the natural coating Nature provides. To clean the hoof safely, scrub with a nail brush or a vegetable brush. An old method of polishing white feet is to scrub them with a cut onion. Avoid using dark, sticky hoof dressings on white feet and you will not have stained walls with a buildup of dirt and dressing to clean. Lanolin, animal fats and pine tar are common ingredients in hoof dressings. Do not use old motor oil to darken the feet—it contains chemicals and additives that are detrimental to the feet.

Packing or Stopping the Feet

After the foot is clean, it may be packed or stopped with a prepared clay such as White Rock. This exposes the sole of the foot to moisture for twenty-four hours and will soften feet that are excessively hard and dry, so that they are less apt to sting on impact with the hard ground. Hoof packing can be overdone—packing too often or in feet that do not need it can make the sole too soft, and the horse may not hold his shoes. It is not a good idea on horses that are prone to thrush, as it creates a moist and airless environment that would make it easier for thrush to thrive. It can help to pack the feet if a horse suffers a stone bruise—the moist clay seems to act like a poultice and draws out the soreness.

To pack the feet, the mud must be prepared—it will have to soak overnight. It should be the consistency of stiff clay, not runny or Jell-O-like. Using a wooden spoon or a spatula, place a large ball of clay in the sole of the newly cleaned foot. Use the spatula to press the clay down into the commissures and fill the bottom of the foot so the packing sticks up slightly above the level of the shoe. Place a piece of brown paper over the packing and let the horse set his foot down. His weight will compress the packing into the foot, and the paper will fall off as the surface dries. When you pick out the feet the next morning, the mud should come out in a single mass molded to the shape of the foot, and the foot should be damp, cool and flexible.

FINAL DETAILS

If you discover any scrapes, wounds or irritations as you groom, they should be taken care of immediately. An open cut or scrape should be cleaned with plain water and dusted lightly with nitrafurazone powder or a dab of salve, or it may do best if left clean but unmedicated. Never put Vaseline or a harsh antiseptic on an open cut—this can cause proud flesh (overgrowth of granulation tissue). A scab can be softened with Vaseline, but Epicoat Coat Restorer will cause the hair to grow back faster and is less likely to result in the hair growing back white.

Any botfly eggs you notice should be removed. The botfly looks like a large bee but it does not sting—it lays small yellow eggs that are attached to individual hairs of the legs, the shoulder and sometimes the mane. When the horse rubs his mouth against these areas, the friction opens the eggs and the larvae inside find their way into the horse's mouth and eventually his stomach. There they mature into "bots," internal parasites that fasten themselves to the lining of the stomach. Every botfly egg you see is a parasite just waiting to invade your horse; they should be removed for his health as well as for neatness' sake. You can scrape the eggs off with a hard styrofoam block (for example, Bot Block or Slick 'n Easy Block). It helps to lubricate the hair with a dab of shampoo or baby oil first. You can also use a special serrated edge "bot knife" to scrape them off the hairs, or a piece of fine sandpaper.

In fly season, the horse should be protected with fly repellent. This can be sprayed on or wiped on. Be careful of the ingredients—some horses have a skin reaction to certain brands of fly repellent, especially if they are applied heavily. A small amount should be tested on a small patch of hair when trying a new product before applying fly spray all over. For the ears, eyes and muzzle, Avon Skin-So-Soft bath oil seems to work well—flies hate it and it is gentle to the skin.

Finally, to remove the last of the dust, spread the sebum or skin oil over the hair and bring up the shine of the coat, rub the horse thoroughly all over with a soft rub rag or with your bare hand. The longer and harder you rub, the more you stimulate the skin to produce skin oil and distribute it over the hairs. The rub rag is folded and rubbed firmly back and forth across the hair coat, finishing by rubbing in the direction of the hair to straighten the coat. The coat should be rubbed for thirty minutes or more each day in order to achieve the high "bloom" so desirable on a show horse. The horse may also be massaged or "wisped" to improve muscle tone and skin and hair condition, but grooming should finish with soft wisping, rubbing or hand rubbing for best results. (See page 85 for more on massage, wisping and rubbing.)

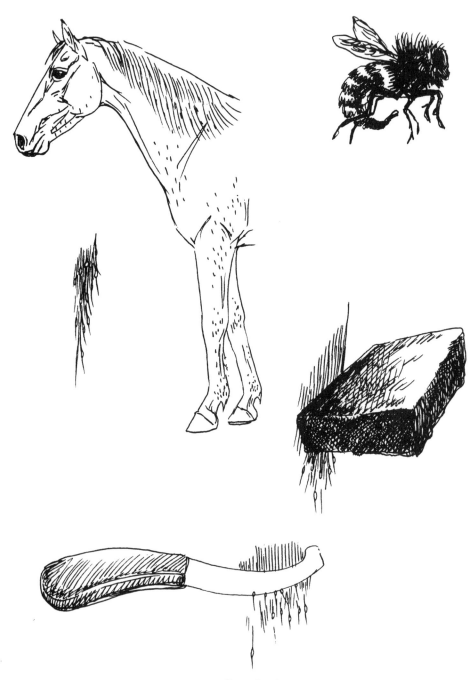

FIGURE 8 *Removing bot eggs*

GROOMING THE SENSITIVE OR DIFFICULT HORSE

Grooming should be pleasant for the horse and should develop confidence, cooperation and trust between horse and groom, but too often it is anything but a pleasure. Some horses dislike being groomed with certain tools or on certain parts of their bodies, or special procedures like bathing, clipping or applying fly spray. Their behavior can range from expressions of discomfort and protest such as making faces, head tossing, grinding the teeth or pawing to defensive measures like head-shyness, prancing or making snapping or kicking gestures. Some horses act aggressively, biting, kicking or striking with purpose. It is not fun for horse or groom to have to follow a dancing, squirming horse, dodge teeth or feet or avoid getting stepped on or hurt by an agitated horse. When a horse hates grooming, he may eventually come to hate the person who grooms him, and the dislike may become mutual.

The underlying factor in all such behavior is pain and the anticipation of pain. If grooming makes a horse feel good, he will cooperate and enjoy it instead of fighting it. Many horses are so sensitive that ordinary grooming tools and techniques irritate them beyond their tolerance level; some have been abused in connection with grooming. A horse with a painful condition or chronic tension and muscle soreness may feel as touchy as a person with a tension headache or a bad backache—even gentle grooming may be really painful to him. While you must protect yourself from getting hurt, threats or punishments only momentarily suppress the behavior and will make the problem worse. To provoke a horse to defensive behavior by grooming him painfully and then punish him for saying "Ouch!" is abusive, but it is all too common. Remember, the horse is not "being a jerk" just to thwart you, and he does not plan or plot his actions. Allowing yourself to get angry with him makes it harder to change his attitude and behavior and can lead to losing your temper, punishing him inappropriately and perhaps causing an incident you will regret. It takes a thinking handler with patience, self-control and sympathy for the horse to make a difficult horse easy to groom, especially if he is very sensitive or has been mishandled.

When a horse is difficult to groom, the first thing to check is your grooming tools and technique. While some horses love to be curried hard, others find it unbearable and tell you so by becoming agitated or defensive when you curry or brush them. If your horse paws, dances, makes faces, grinds his teeth or snaps, give up the currycomb and stiff brush and try softer implements such as a rubber grooming mitt or a soft body brush. Some horses can only tolerate a sheepskin mit and the softest of brushes, or gentle wiping with a soft rag. Don't scrub severely or brush vigorously; slow down your motions and use long, slow and very gentle strokes until you find a level he can tolerate without protesting. You can still get him clean by using a hot, damp towel, which will also feel good if he has sore muscles (see page 79 for hot towel directions), and stains can be removed with a damp sponge and dry towel. Supersensitive horses often have very fine coats that do not need hard currying or rough brushing to get them clean.

Horses that have associated long-term discomfort or severe punishment with grooming or tacking up often have strong habit patterns that are triggered by the usual grooming or tacking procedures, even before the horse is actually hurt. For instance, a head-shy horse will throw his head up out of reach before you even touch it, or a "girthy" horse may snap at you before the girth comes in contact with his belly. (Perhaps you have similar ingrained responses to injections or while in the dentist's chair!) Changing to a non-habitual way of doing things (such as girthing up from the right side instead of the left) may avoid triggering the ingrained "automatic" response. Threats or punishments sometimes temporarily suppress the behavior, but usually make the problem worse over time and can lead to a real explosion—they certainly do nothing to teach the horse that the procedure will not hurt him.

If you are slow, smooth and gentle in your grooming and your grooming tools would feel comfortable on your own skin, the problem may be chronic muscle soreness or mental and physical tension. Race horses, some show horses and stallions that are "wound up tight" in high condition and young horses that are kept stalled without enough turnout time seem to have more energy than they know what to do with. They often "fire off" excess energy by dancing, pawing or kicking backward, apparently at nothing. Sometimes the best thing to do is to place them in a situation where they cannot hurt themselves or you, such as a grooming stall, and groom as gently, efficiently and quietly as possible, ignoring the occasional kicks and fussing. Punishment makes such horses more agitated and can provoke an explosion, but the groom will have to stay alert and careful to protect himself from accidental injury. Such horses should not be picked at or fussed over—if possible, they should be groomed after they have been turned out or worked and then left alone to relax.

Chronic muscle soreness may occur in any horse, but is especially common in tense, high-strung horses and horses in demanding athletic specialities. Often the soreness is specific to a certain muscle group that is worked hard or held in tension when the horse is trained or performs. The back, loins, neck and shoulder muscles are all common sites of painful tension. This may not show up as actual lameness, but the horse may cringe or make defensive gestures when that area is gently touched or groomed. Hot towels, massage therapy or T.E.A.M. body work can help to relieve muscle tension and soreness, which is important for the horse's ability to perform even more than for his grooming behavior.

One of the most effective methods for retraining sensitive and difficult horses is T.E.A.M., or the Tellington-Jones Equine Awareness Method. Developed by Linda Tellington-Jones, T.E.A.M. uses special hand touches (not the same as massage), bodywork and work in hand that can later be incorporated with riding to bring relaxation, awareness and cooperation to the horse without force or pain. T.E.A.M. has been used successfully for all kinds of problem horses, for young horses and also on other species; it is used by many Olympic teams to keep their horses at their physical and mental best. T.E.A.M. training is available through clinics, training centers and videotapes, or through the book *The Tellington-Jones Equine Awareness Method* by Linda Tellington-Jones (published by Breakthrough Publications, Millwood, NY).

When grooming a difficult horse, you must protect yourself from injury. Keep one hand resting gently on the horse while you groom with the other—this will allow you to feel him tensing to kick or move and may help you deflect a kick. If you must work low down, bend your knees but never kneel or sit near him. Keep your head away from the "line of fire" should he toss his head or paw with a foreleg, and hold the cheekpiece of the halter while grooming near the forequarters, to prevent nipping or biting. Tying a nervous horse too tightly can scare him or lead to pulling back—he may be quieter if he can turn his head to see what you are doing. A hand-held cross-tie (See page 47) can be useful in keeping him where you want him without using too severe a restraint; you can let the off-side rope slip a little so he is not held solidly enough to panic him. A hand-held cross-tie works well when teaching a green horse to accept cross-ties, too. Some horses are content to stand if ground-tied in a quiet aisle (but *never* leave the horse alone!) or if they are allowed to munch from a hay net during grooming.

Try to be aware of your horse's comfort range, and especially of any places he likes to be groomed or particularly dislikes. You can use grooming he likes (such as scratching his favorite "itchy spot") as a reward for tolerating a little grooming on a spot he would rather you did not touch. Start your grooming stroke on a place he doesn't mind (perhaps the back or shoulder) and slide it down across the ticklish place (such as the flank or belly), returning quickly and smoothly to "neutral territory" before he can get upset. If your horse is difficult about being touched on the hind legs, try stroking him gently with a long, fairly stiff stick or dressage whip down the legs and around the hind-quarters until he relaxes and accepts it. Hitting him with the whip, even if he kicks, is counterproductive—simply use the stick to reach the hind legs while you stay safely out of kicking range and be quietly persistent. Once he accepts the stroking of the stick, you can move closer and work with a brush or soft rub rag.

This is not to say that the horse is always right and that you should tolerate any and all behavior. There are times when a horse must be repri-manded for actions that are clearly beyond the limits. You need to distinguish between behavior that is provoked by fear, discomfort or tension, or that is triggered by past abuse, and behavior that is deliberately and clearly aggressive. When a horse tries to bully you, he is usually quite calm and purposeful and he may bite or kick and then watch you to see what you will do about it. When a horse deliberately and aggressively bites, kicks or strikes, correct him immedi-ately with a deep-voiced growl of "NO!" or "Quit!" and hit him hard but *only once* on the offending neck, shoulder or hindquarter. One firm, well-timed and unemotional correction can work wonders; irritable or fearful nagging, jerks or little slaps can drive many horses, particularly stallions, to the point of violence. If you must deliver a correction, do it effectively *once* without anger and let that be the end of the incident—don't carry a grudge. Be sure that neither you nor anyone else who handles the horse acts in a provocative, annoying way that can be taken by the horse as teasing, and switch instantly to a pleasant and rewarding attitude after you have made your point. For corrective purposes, a hard swat with the open hand or a flat bat is better than a crop or a whip, as this makes noise rather than cutting pain. Avoid using a chain over the nose or under the jaw for punishment—"shanking a horse down" severely can cause the horse to rear, run backwards or flip over back-ward and can cause severe and permanent damage to the nose or chin. Use a light tug on a chain shank to get a horse's attention or to warn him, but do not rely on the chain shank for correction, and *never* tie a horse with a chain over the nose or under the chin!

GROOMING TOOLS AND PRODUCTS

The saying, "A workman is only as good as his tools" is never more true than in show grooming. While it is possible to do an adequate job with only fair equipment, it is easier and more efficient to have the right tools for the job and to keep them in good working order.

The basic grooming tools are currycombs, stiff brushes or dandy brushes, soft brushes or body brushes, scrapers, sponges, hoof picks, combs and rub rags. There are many other specialty items that make specific chores easier. You will need a convenient grooming kit or carryall to keep your tools together, and it helps to paint them in a distinctive color so it is obvious whose tools they are. If you are managing a stable, it is best for each horse to have his own set of brushes and basic grooming tools and not to use the same brushes on other horses. This can help prevent the spread of fungus or other skin infections. The grooming tools should be cleaned and disinfected periodically.

Currycombs come in several shapes and types. Rubber currycombs are apt to be softer and their slightly tacky surface makes them good for removing loose hair. Two useful models are the groom mitt, which is shaped like a

A. *Rubber currycomb*

B. *Grooma*

C. *Plastic currycomb with hose connection*

D. *Rubber curry mitt*

E. *Metal currycomb*

FIGURE 9 *Currycombs*

rubber mitten and covered with small raised dots, and the "Grooma," a massage tool with flexible rubber "fingers." Grooming mitts work especially well on clipped horses or those with sensitive skin, and the massage tool does a good job on shedding out winter hair as well as thoroughly massaging the skin and underlying muscle. Plastic currycombs are usually stiffer; many horses find them uncomfortable if they are used for massage, but they do shed out long hair well. They should not be used to brush tails, as they break off and pull out the tail hair and the currycomb teeth break off to short, hard "nubs" that are uncomfortable to the horse's skin when currying. Metal currycombs are too sharp and harsh to be used on the horse's skin; they should be used to clean the body brush while working, or they can be used with care to break up heavily caked mud and to shed out horses with thick coats.

When buying brushes, especially body brushes, it often is most economical to buy a good-quality tool and then take good care of it than to make do with less well made brushes that do not work as well or last as long. This doesn't apply to all tools, of course—a fifty-cent hoof pick will do just as good a job as a two-dollar one!

The best brushes are wire drawn—the bristles are drawn through one half of the back and fastened with wire, and the top half is then attached. On a wooden-backed brush, you will see four screws holding the two halves of the brush together; leather-backed brushes are glued or stitched together. Cheaper brushes are machine drilled—the bristles are stuck into the holes by machine and held in place by glue. Under hard use and wetting and drying, the glue loosens and the bristles come out.

The body brush is the most important tool in hand grooming the coat and producing a deep bloom, so you will probably find that a quality body brush is worth the fairly high initial cost. A good leather-backed brush with short, close-set natural bristles and a flexible back will remove dust and spread skin oil over the hairs more thoroughly and can get a horse really clean. You may also want a second body brush with stiffer, synthetic bristles for working on thicker coats. A good body brush will last for years if it is not abused.

Dandy brushes have longer bristles and also come in machine-drilled or wire-drawn types. Remember that the bristles will not remove particles much smaller than the size of the bristle. Stiff, heavy bassine-fiber brushes are used for breaking up mud and brushing thick winter hair; medium natural or plastic fibers are used for initial cleaning of the body and legs, and finer fibers work best on short, fine hair such as the head and legs. Some dandy brushes have a mix of coarse and finer fibers; these make a good general-purpose brush. A brush with long, soft bristles is called a finishing brush; these are used to

A. *Dandy brush or stiff brush*

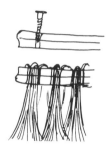

B. *Wire drawn dandy brush*

C. *Machine drilled brush*

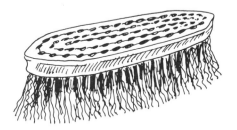

D. *Open backed rice-root brush*

FIGURE 10 *Dandy brushes*

A. *Leather-backed body brush*

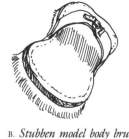

B. *Stubben model body brush*

C. *Wooden backed soft brush*

D. *English water brush*

FIGURE 11 *Body brushes*

A. *Squeegee sweat scraper*

C. *Shedding blade and sweat scraper*

B. *Sweat stick*

D. *Sponge*

E. *Styrofoam block (Slick 'n Easy block)*

F. *Cactus cloth and fleece mitt*

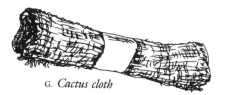

G. *Cactus cloth*

H. *Hoof pick with brush*

I. *Hoof pick*

FIGURE 12 *Grooming tools: assorted grooming aids*

remove dust from the face and surface of the coat but will not penetrate the hair and spread skin oil to produce a shine as will the body brush with its short, close-set bristles. A small finishing brush is useful for the head and ears.

Water brushes are used to lay the mane and tail over and when making quarter marks. An open-backed brush allows the water to drain through; the English water brush has close-set natural bristles like a body brush and is tapered to a point at each end. It is used for quarter marks and fine work. An inexpensive plastic scrub brush or a large nail brush is useful for washing feet; there are also small brushes made especially for scrubbing feet. Rice-root bristles or synthetic bristles that are crimped retain water better and are useful for bathing or scrubbing out stains.

Hoof picks come in all colors and in plastic or metal. A useful type is a pick with a small brush attached, which can be used to brush the sole of the foot after it is cleaned. Some grooms like to snap a hoof pick to their belt so that it is always handy.

The cactus cloth is a loosely woven grooming cloth made from the fibers of the maguey plant. It contains a little natural oil and helps to shine the coat. The rough surface makes it easy to scrub away sweat marks and dried mud; it can also be rubbed briskly over a stain to remove it. Cactus cloths are available as a large grooming cloth or in the form of a mitt backed with fleece.

You can buy a special rub rag, but turkish towels work just as well. Get them in a light color so you will notice when they are dirty and launder them. It is better to have several medium-sized towels than just one large one.

Sponges may be natural sea sponges or synthetic. You will need a large body sponge for washing your horse and a couple of smaller sponges for the face and dock. Sponges should be stored so they can dry out—hang them in a bag or an open-mesh basket. Another useful item is the Moisture Magnet, a soft cloth like an artificial chamois. It can be used to dry the face, head and belly or for getting stains out of the coat. A sweat scraper will also be needed for washing and cooling out; you can use the simple "sweat stick" or the Squeegee type that comes with a handle and a strip of rubber to squeeze more water out of the hair.

A shedding blade is used to shed out the long winter hair in the spring. It has a flexible blade with a serrated edge for shedding; the smooth edge can be used as a sweat scraper. Don't bend it backward or the blade will break. You can make a homemade shedding blade by taping each end of an old hacksaw blade to form handles.

For the mane and tail, you may want a hairbrush or a comb. A plastic hairbrush from the drugstore works well on manes and tails and pulls out less hair than a metal comb or currycomb. Another good brush is the pet slicker brush, which has a rubber backing with metal pins set into it. Metal mane and tail combs are not recommended for ordinary grooming of the mane and tail hair, as they break off and pull out too many hairs and can leave the mane and tail short and bushy. If you must use a comb, it should be plastic and the teeth should be very smooth. Small metal pulling combs are used to thin and shorten the mane or to pull the tail. A trimmer with a serrated edge can be used for shortening without thinning, but this can leave the hair thick and stubbly looking unless used with skill.

Wash mitts or scrubbing mitts are useful for bathing, as is the plastic currycomb with a hose attachment, which allows you to massage the horse as you rinse him.

A Styrofoam block can be useful to remove bot eggs and also for scrubbing away stained places, caked-on dirt and loose hair. The edge of the block works well when shedding out hard-to-reach places around the head. These blocks are sold as Slick 'n Easy Blocks or Bot Blocks. You can also use the type of gray Styrofoam blocks that are sold for cleaning barbecue grills.

A fleece applicator mitt is useful for applying fly repellent, particularly to the head, where most horses will not tolerate fly spray. You can also use a fleece mitt for rubbing the coat. For real luxury, you can use a real sheepskin mitt; the lanolin in the natural fleece will help to shine the coat, and sensitive horses enjoy the softness of the fleece.

For hard wisping or "banging," you will have to make a hay wisp. Wisping

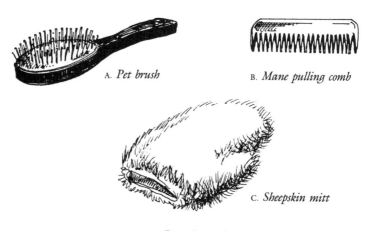

A. *Pet brush*

B. *Mane pulling comb*

C. *Sheepskin mitt*

FIGURE 13 *Grooming tools*

is a traditional English form of grooming and massage; while special massage pads are sold in England and Europe, they have not yet made their way into American tack stores, probably because this type of massage is not widely known here. A hay wisp is made from old, soft grass hay (not from alfalfa!), twisted into a rope and then plaited into a hand-sized block.

To Make a Hay Wisp, You Must First Twist a Long, Thin Hay Rope:

1. Make a long pile of hay on the floor, about 10 feet long and a foot wide and about 6 inches to a foot deep—similar to a windrow in a hayfield that has been cut for baling. Wet it down with a bucket of warm water.
2. Begin to twist a hay rope, keeping one end of the rope down under the pile so that it turns around and around, forming a bulky rope as you twist the ends. As you work down the rope, give the end to an assistant, who will keep twisting against you so that the rope does not unravel.
3. As you work, pluck pieces of hay from the twisting rope to keep it from becoming too thick. Keep the rope twisted very tightly, and don't let it get too thick. It should be no more than 3/4 inch to 1 inch in diameter.
4. When the rope is about 10 to 12 feet long, two people must keep it tightly stretched while another helper snips off pieces of hay and trims it down. Be careful not to trim so much that the rope is weakened.

Next, you must plait the wisp. This takes two people: one to hold the end of the rope and one to do the plaiting.

To Plait the Wisp:

1. Form two loops 10 to 12 inches long, as shown in the diagram. The long end of the rope goes behind and between the loops to the assistant who holds the rope and keeps it taut.
2. Lower the right-hand loop so that the rope is passed back through the center and across the back of the loop.
3. Lower the left-hand loop and bring the rope back through the center and across behind the left loop.
4. Continue weaving the rope alternately around each loop and back through the center by lowering and rotating each loop to pass the rope around it. Keep the rope taut.
5. This weaving is continued until the loops are almost completely covered by plaiting except for two small loops at the top, about 1 to 2 inches in diameter.
6. Pass the end of the rope through the left-hand loop, into the center and

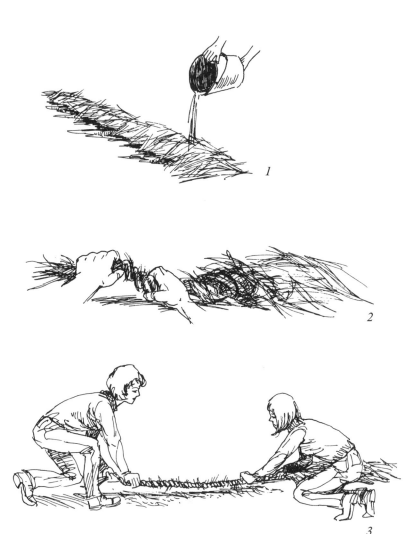

FIGURE 14 *Steps in making a wisp*

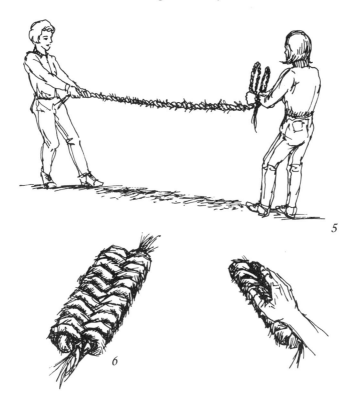

5

6

around the right-hand loop, then finish by pulling it through the right-hand loop. The loops should be very tight.

7. Cut or pluck out any extra hay rope at the top and bottom of the wisp. Firm and shape the finished wisp by striking it several times against a wall or board.

Your finished wisp should be about 10 to 12 inches long and 4 to 6 inches wide and should be easily held in one hand. It should be dampened before use. Keep it out of your horse's reach or he may eat it!

Whatever grooming tools you have deserve proper use and good care. A dirty brush will not make a horse clean; it will waste your time. Clean your brushes frequently as you work by scraping the bristles against the teeth of a currycomb or across a stall screen; this way, the dust goes into the brush and out into the air, not back onto the horse. Tools should be put away clean of

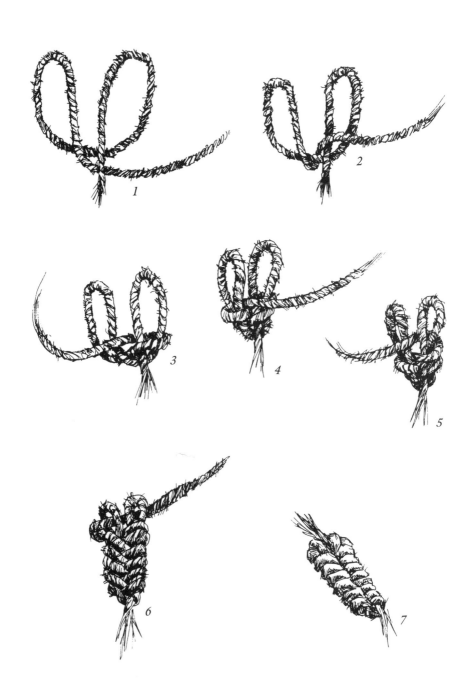

FIGURE 15 *Plaiting the wisp*

hair and dirt. Try not to get your good brushes wet—save a water brush or scrub brush for removing stains or washing feet. Never rub wet, dirty surfaces with an expensive body brush—it should be saved for rubbing and polishing the coat.

Currycombs, plastic brushes and other waterproof items can be washed with pine oil soap or a similar disinfectant. Leather-backed body brushes or those with natural bristles should not be immersed in water but can be cleaned by working through the bristles with a damp soapy towel and then a dry one. When a brush is wet, stand it on the bristles to dry so that water will not run down into the back and loosen the glue or damage the bristles. Towels and rub rags should be laundered frequently, and sponges should be rinsed out and wrung out clean before putting them away.

Vacuum Cleaners and Grooming Machines

A vacuum cleaner can be a great help in getting horses clean, especially when horses are turned out and get muddy but need to be gotten "show ring clean." A full-power livestock vacuum does the best job, particularly for a large stable, but a shop vacuum or a smaller cannister model will work well for most horse owners.

The vacuum gets dirt, dust and dandruff out of the coat, but it does not rub the coat or distribute the skin oils as currying and hand grooming does. A good compromise is to vacuum every other day, grooming by hand on alternate days. For grooms who are allergic to horse dander, the vacuum can cut down on the amount of dust, hair and scurf one is exposed to.

You may curry the horse first, or use the vacuum currycomb attachment to break up and vacuum away caked-on mud and dirt. Press the tool well down against the skin so the suction gets all the loose dirt, and work it back and forth across and against the lay of the hair. You can use the vacuum on the neck and body, and carefully on the larger muscles of the legs, but do not use it on the head, mane, tail or any areas where the horse is especially ticklish.

Some vacuum cleaners have a rotating brush that stimulates the skin while the vacuum cleans it. There is also a rotating brush that can be attached to a hand-held electric drill. Electric brushes can cause havoc if they are run into the long hair of the mane; they will wrap up the mane and pull the hairs out in a flash! In general, hand brushing is more work but safer and more easily adapted to the various areas and sensitivity of the horse.

Most horses get used to a vacuum cleaner quite easily, as they find the suction pleasant even if they dislike the noise. Have someone hold the horse when you introduce him to the vacuum cleaner, and start on a less sensitive area of the body. Rub him with the hose and the brush or curry attachment before turning the motor on, and try feeding him some grain or tidbits during his first experience with the vacuum. All vacuum cleaners, blow driers and grooming machines should be used on a dry surface and should have a grounded plug. Don't leave them plugged in within reach of a horse while you do something else; an experimental nibble on the cord can give him a jolt of electricity.

Grooming Products

While there are so many grooming products that they could fill a catalog and more are being developed all the time, there are some standard products that are found in most show stables. It is helpful to try out different brands and new products to decide which works best for your purposes. Some of the most commonly used grooming products include:

Shampoos—for bathing and removing stains. Iodine-based and antifungal shampoos are used to treat dermatitis and fungus infections of the skin. Some shampoos have coat conditioners or a whitening agent that helps to remove stains from white markings and to prevent yellowing of white hair.

Body wash—mild astringent and cleanser added to rinse water when washing horses down after exercise. They help to remove salt and sweat and keep the skin from itching. Some liniments can be diluted to use as a body wash.

Stain removers—used to remove stains while grooming and as a last-minute touch-up at shows. Commercial stain removers are available, or you can make your own by combining a capful of blue or purple shampoo, 10 ounces of rubbing alcohol and 10 ounces of water in a spray bottle. Spray on the stain and rub out with a towel. Bon Ami cleanser may also be used—make a paste of Bon Ami and water and rub into the stain; when it is dry, brush the powder out of the hair.

Ivory or other mild soap—for cleaning the sheath and other chores.

Creme rinse or mane and tail conditioner—is applied after shampooing the mane and tail to condition the hair. Special de-tangling conditioners are available.

Silicone coat spray—can be used to prevent the mane and tail from tangling, to repel stains and dirt and to make the coat slick and shiny.

Coat polish—high-gloss spray used to enhance the coat at shows.

Highlighter—gel applied to the fine skin of the face to enhance highlights and draw attention to the eyes, ears and contours of the face.

Liniment or rubbing alcohol—for rubbing, bracing and wrapping legs. Alcohol can also serve as a quick stain remover.

Hoof dressing—to condition the feet, especially the coronary band and heels. Dark oil hoof dressing is used to darken and shine the hoofs for some types of show horses.

Hoof packing—a prepared clay (sometimes called White Rock) that is packed into the sole of the foot to moisturize it and keep it free from bedding, manure or foreign objects.

Hoof polish—used to enhance the shine of the hoof for showing; comes in clear, black or brown. Use *hoof polish remover* to take it off after showing.

Poultice—a prepared medicated clay used under bandages to draw heat and soreness out of the legs.

Fly repellent—in spray or wipe-on form, may contain natural pyrethrins or synthetic repellents. Some are oil-based, others water-based; may contain sunscreen to prevent sunburning of the coat. When you first use a new fly repellent, try a small amount on a small patch of hair for twenty-four hours before spraying or wiping it on more liberally. Some horses can have a skin reaction to certain ingredients. Roll-on repellents, gels and creams are available to keep flies off the face and away from the eyes. Avon Skin-So-Soft bath oil works well to keep flies off the face and ears and is gentle to the skin. You can make your own fly repellent by combining 3 ounces of Skin-So-Soft, 1 ounce of oil of citronella, 12 ounces of white vinegar and 12 ounces of water in a spray bottle.

Hot oil treatment—used to condition the coat after clipping and to condition the mane and tail if they become dry and brittle.

Setting gel—used to lay down the mane hairs or to make quarter marks.

Epicoat Coat Restorer—applied to scrapes or scabs to bring back hair growth as quickly as possible and minimize scarring.

Neck sweat or glycerine—used under a plastic sweat wrap to reduce a heavy neck temporarily.

Three

SPECIAL PROCEDURES

BATHING

When your horse has to be extra clean for a show, or when he has gotten stained or especially dirty, you may want to give him a bath. Bathing is no substitute for good and regular grooming, however; too frequent use of detergents removes too much sebum from the skin and hair and causes dry skin and a dull coat. If you groom your horse thoroughly every day, you will not need to bathe him very often. However, horses do get stains, and the lighter colored the horse, the more he seems to enjoy rolling in the mud, so washing is sometimes the best way to get him clean. When you are first starting to condition a horse whose coat is very dirty and full of scurf and grease, a bath is the first step in getting the coat into more manageable condition. If you must bathe a horse thoroughly before a show, it is better to do this a day or two beforehand so that his coat has time to regain its maximum shine by show time. Any stains or small dirty spots can be touched up on show day, particularly if you keep a light sheet on him at night to keep him clean.

A horse should not be bathed when the weather is cold, any more than you would go swimming when it is chilly. If you have access to a heated wash stall and a draft-free area where he can dry, you can bathe him even in the winter, but if it is too cold, try a thorough grooming, vacuum him and give him a hot towel bath instead. (Hot toweling is described on page 79.) If the weather is at all cool, you will need a clean cooler or walking cover to protect him while he dries.

To bathe a horse, you will need several buckets of warm water, a large body sponge, a rubber currycomb, a sweat scraper, towels and a cooler or walking cover. Use a halter that will not be hurt by being wet and that will not run and stain him (beware of red or yellow latigo leather!). There are many good shampoos made especially for horses, including some that will whiten grey coats and some with aloe vera, lanolin or other coat conditioners. You may want to apply a silicone coat dressing like Showsheen to the hair coat after bathing, or use a creme rinse on the mane and tail. A wash stall is the ideal place to work, with safe-footing, cross-ties, a hose and grooming supplies at hand, but you can tie the horse in any safe place outdoors. If you can get warm water from a hose, this will make washing and rinsing much easier. Most horses can be taught to accept the use of a hose if you keep the water a comfortable temperature, use a slow stream and do not spray their head or ears.

First, wet the horse all over down to the skin, using the hose or a body sponge. Horses will accept this better if you start with a trickle of water and work up from the hoofs, wetting the legs and then the body gradually. (How would you like to have someone splash you or spray you with a hose without warning?) Wet the mane and tail down, too.

Make up a bucket of soapy water by squirting shampoo into a bucket of water, and sponge this liberally over the horse, working from the neck back and down. As each section is soaped, use the currycomb to massage the skin and work up a lather. You can also use your fingers as when shampooing your own hair. Keep the soapy parts wet, and rinse as you work by running the hose or squeezing out a large spongeful of clean water above the part where you are scrubbing until the water runs clean. The hair and skin should feel "squeaky clean" and free of soap before you move on. Any soap that dries on the coat will leave a sticky scum and a dull coat. A hose attachment that resembles a perforated currycomb lets you massage as you rinse and makes the job easier.

The face and head should be washed with as much water as the horse will tolerate and as little soap as you can use and get them clean. Often hot toweling works better, especially on horses that throw their heads up and resist. If you use a lot of soap, you will have to rinse many times and the horse may not cooperate. Don't let water run into the ears or soap get into the eyes. Be careful and gentle when working on the head; most horses hate water on their heads, and a bad experience can make your horse difficult the next time.

The mane and tail should also be washed and thoroughly rinsed, with special attention given to the skin and roots of the hair. The skirt of the tail can be doubled up and dunked into a bucket to rinse it. If you want the mane and tail to be especially full and flowing, you can apply a creme rinse after the shampoo is rinsed out. Never use a creme rinse on a mane or tail you intend to braid—it will make the hairs too slippery to hold onto and your braids will be inclined to come loose.

If your horse is a grey or has white markings, these can be whitened by applying a whitening shampoo such as Quick Silver full strength and leaving it on the hair for ten to fifteen minutes. It should be kept wet, and occasionally scrubbed into a lather to prevent it from drying into the coat. When rinsed out, it removes stains and yellowing and gives the coat a silvery cast. Some grooms add a capful of laundry bluing to a large bucket of rinse water to give a grey horse a whiter coat, but don't overdo it—too much can turn your horse green!

The wet coat should be scraped, starting high on the neck and working down and backward, in the direction the hair grows. Use a body sponge that has been wrung out nearly dry to pick up water from the head, legs, flank and other areas that are hard to scrape. The tail is gently wrung out and and the skirt can be given a snap to the side to remove excess water.

A silicone coat dressing such as Showsheen can now be sprayed over the damp coat. Silicone dressings coat the hairs with a slick, shiny surface that repels stains and reflects light, making the coat glossy. It will repel stains for several days, and makes them easier to remove. Because it makes the surface of the hair slippery, it should not be used on the area beneath the saddle, or on the horse's back if you plan to ride in Bareback Equitation!

After bathing the horse should be covered with a cooler, walking cover or light sheet according to the weather and kept out of drafts until he is dry. Don't leave him where he can lie down—newly bathed horses love to roll in the mud!

HOT TOWELING

Hot toweling is used to clean the coat when it is impractical to give the horse a bath. It is a good way to remove stubborn dust and excess scurf from places like the head, the croup and the roots of the mane. Since the horse is not wet down, hot toweling can be done when the weather is too cold to wash a horse or expose him to chills. It can help on days when the air and the horse's coat seem electrically charged and dust sticks to the hairs as if magnetized.

To hot-towel a horse, you will need a large, light-colored turkish towel or two, a pail of very hot water, rubber gloves to protect your hands and a small amount of detergent or shampoo. The small amount of soap (less than a capful in a large bucket) changes the pH of the water so that the dirt and dust are attracted to the towel. Wearing the rubber gloves, dunk the towel in the bucket and wring it out until it is almost dry—it should be too hot to handle comfortably without rubber gloves, as it will lose heat quickly. Place one hand behind the towel and rub it quickly through the roots of the coat. The hair should not be wet, but dirt and scurf will quickly blacken the towel. Shift your hand to a clean place and continue. When the towel begins to lose its heat, dunk it and wring it out again. Continue until the area is clean. If the hair coat is becoming more damp than you would like, rub with a second, dry towel immediately behind the hot towel.

This procedure feels good to most horses and produces a clean coat very quickly. It is a good procedure to use before body clipping or when the horse needs to be extra clean for showing. Coat dressing can be applied to the clean hair coat after hot toweling.

COOLING OUT A HOT HORSE

A horse is never so much in need of good, skillful care as when he is hot and very tired. After hard work, his muscles, cardiovascular system, skin and entire system must "wind down" from the state required for hard effort. In the meantime, the horse is very vulnerable to chills, aches and muscle cramps. A horse that has raced, run a cross-country course or finished a maximum effort may still be feeling the effects of adrenalin. He may have sustained bumps, cuts or sprains and may not feel them yet, and he may be very excited. The groom's job is to get him back to a normal state gradually and safely, so that he can recover as quickly and efficiently as possible.

A horse that is turned over to you hot and blowing immediately after hard work should be protected from a quick loss of body heat. Quickly cover him with a cooler, light walking cover or net anti-sweat sheet according to the weather, loosen his girth and noseband, and get him walking without delay. He should keep on walking until his breathing comes back to normal and his nostrils are no longer distended and showing the red lining. You can quickly substitute a halter for the bridle and wash out his mouth with lukewarm water if he is slobbering, and lift the saddle to allow air to reach his back, but leave the saddle in place for five to ten minutes while he walks. This allows the circulation to return to normal slowly in the areas compressed by the saddle.

Once the horse's breathing has returned to normal, his tack can be removed and he may be quickly scraped off. He should then go back to walking without delay. Only when he has walked for fifteen minutes or more and is beginning to look nearly normal should you stop him long enough to wash him down. You will need several buckets of tepid or lukewarm water, or if your horse will tolerate it, a hose that can supply warm water, a large body sponge and a scraper. Never use cold water on a hot horse; it can cause the large muscles of the back, loins and hindquarters to go into cramps. Use lots of water to float away the salt and sweat, and rub out any caked-on mud and sweat with the body sponge. The horse should not be left wet any longer than necessary, so scrape each part as you go and get him finished as quickly as possible. A little body wash added to the rinse water acts as an astringent and helps clean the coat. Use the big sponge, wrung out as dry as you can, to pick up any excess water from the head, legs, belly and parts that are hard to scrape dry. Cover him again with a dry cover and resume walking until he dries.

If you set out a bucket of tepid water in your walking area, you can allow the horse a swallow or two each time you pass by. By the time he has had as much as he wants to drink in small increments, he should be walked dry and be safely cooled out. This way he is less likely to gorge himself on water when he returns to his stall.

In very hot or humid weather, cooling out may become more critical and require unusual measures. Cold water can be applied by sponge or wet towel along the jugular groove, on the head, between the hind legs and to the large blood vessels close to the surface on the legs. This helps the body to cool down faster when it is overheated. However, never apply cold water to large muscles or they may go into spasm. Keep the horse in the shade and take advantage of any breeze, which will hasten evaporation and cooling. An electric fan can be used to create a breeze, but don't turn it directly on the horse or it may chill him. Electrolyte solution may be administered, preferably by oral paste, and small sips of tepid water should be given frequently as he walks.

Ordinary cooling out is usually less extreme but just as important. A horse should be allowed to walk for a minimum of fifteen minutes following work, whether this is done under saddle or after the rider dismounts. This allows his heart and breathing to return to normal, waste products to be removed from muscle cells and other tissue, and the circulation in his feet and legs to return to normal. Skipping walking time or neglecting cooling out can lead to colic, laminitis (founder) or muscle cramps. The horse should be cool and dry to the touch on his chest before he is put away, and he should be completely cooled out for an hour before being fed grain or shipped in a trailer.

Coolers, walking covers and anti-sweat sheets can be an aid in cooling out. In cool, windy or downright cold weather, the horse must be protected from chilling when he is hot and sweaty. He should be covered promptly with a warm woolen cooler, which will allow the sweat to evaporate slowly and conserve his body heat. If the day is windy, a cooler clamp is snapped onto the underside of the cooler beneath his belly, creating a warm "envelope" and preventing the cooler from blowing off and spooking him. A lighter walking cover can be used on a moderately cool day.

Thermal anti-sweat sheets have a loose weave that traps air next to the horse, stabilizing his temperature and allowing him to cool and dry slowly. In warm weather an anti-sweat sheet can be used alone; when it is cold or windy, it should be used under a cooler or sheet. The Irish-knit type has a slightly closer weave than the open mesh type and can be used in cooler weather. Anti-sweat sheets are useful for safely drying horses with long hair, which may remain damp long after the horse's body temperature has returned to normal. The anti-sweat sheet can be used after the horse has returned to his stall, or as a precaution against sweating up while shipping. It should not be left on a horse that is free to roll, as the sheet can be torn easily.

Some horses appear to cool out normally and then break out in a sweat later. This may be due to nerves and fatigue, incomplete cooling out at first, or hot, humid weather. Check on your horse later if he has been very hot, and if you find he has "broken out" and is sweaty again, he should be scraped, covered with an anti-sweat sheet and walked until he is back to normal. If humidity is the problem, getting him out of the close confines of the stall will often help.

An old method of drying a wet coat in cool weather is "thatching." The horse's blanket is put on inside out (to keep the lining from becoming damp) and straw is stuffed up under the blanket next to the horse. This creates an air space and allows the coat to dry, and the straw absorbs some moisture. When the horse is dry, the straw is brushed away and the blanket can be put on right side out.

CLEANING THE SHEATH OR UDDER

Cleaning the sheath is a distasteful chore to many people, but it is necessary for the comfort of a gelding or stallion. The skin of the sheath secretes a waxy substance called smegma; this combines with dirt, bedding and skin debris to form an accumulation of hard lumps and dead skin that collects inside the sheath and on the surface of the penis. A small lump of smegma, called a bean, may form in the opening of the urethra. If this accumulation is not removed, urination can become painful and some horses will refuse to "let down" to urinate; the area can become inflamed and even infected. The sheath should be cleaned every two to three months, depending on the

FIGURE 1 *The sheath*

individual horse. Streaks of smegma found on the inside of the hind legs, refusal to "let down" for urination or a strong odor are signs that the horse needs attention.

Mares sometimes form a similar accumulation of smegma and dirt between the folds of the udder. This should be checked occasionally when grooming, but use caution, as mares are often touchy about being handled near the udder and some may kick.

To clean the sheath, you will need a mild soap such as Ivory, a small sponge and two buckets of warm water or a warm water hose if your horse is gentle enough to permit this. You will appreciate rubber gloves for your own hygiene; disposable latex or vinyl gloves are available. Most horses will behave while you clean the sheath as long as you are gentle and do not hurt them, but some horses may not have been handled well and you may need an assistant to restrain an uneasy horse by holding up a front foot or by applying a twitch at first. If you come across a horse that is really difficult to handle, have your veterinarian tranquilize him; the effect of the drug will cause him to let down his penis as well as calming him down, so cleaning is much easier.

Wet down the area gently with warm water, then lather your sponge well and gently enter the sheath. Use plenty of lather as a lubricant, and rinse frequently, using the warm water hose if possible. When you have removed all you can with gentle scrubbing, rinse thoroughly. If a horse is very dirty, it is better to wash him gently and then apply a little Vaseline to the area, and clean the sheath again in a few days. The Vaseline will soften the lumps and make it easier to remove them without irritating the skin. Be sure to check the blind pouch at the opening of the urethra for the bean, and remove it.

SWEATING THE NECK

Neck sweating is a form of "spot reduction" that is often practiced by trainers of Arabians, Quarter Horses, Morgans and other breeds that are sometimes thicker in the neck and jowl area than is desirable. The thickness is partly due to the individual horse's body type and conformation, and partly because these horses are usually overweight. The extra fat they carry gives them a fashionably rounded outline and a showy "bloom," but it also shows up in the form of fat deposits in the neck, crest, jowl area and forequarters. While neck sweating, jowl wraps and spot reducing has a cosmetic effect, this is temporary because it achieves its effects by pressure and by sweating water out of the areas. (Overweight humans have found that plastic exercise suits, body wraps and the like have a similarly short-lived effect!) Unfortunately, for horse or human, fat cells are not eliminated by heat, sweating or pressure, only temporarily reduced.

The area most often targeted is the throatlash and jowl area. Thick, fat-throated horses have difficulty in flexing at the poll and do not present a refined, clean-cut throttle in conformation classes. Some trainers may wish to sweat the whole neck or the throat, neck and shoulder area. Sweating of larger areas, such as the body, is less advisable and can result in dehydration if overdone. A better plan for the grossly overweight horse would be to put him on a reducing diet and condition him with sensible exercise instead of severe sweating.

To sweat the neck or throat, you will need a sweat wrap. Some trainers augment the sweat wrap with plastic food wrap applied next to the skin; then

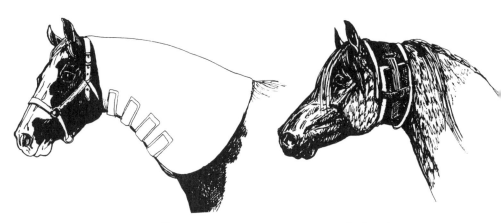

FIGURE 2 A. *Sweat wrap*   B. *Jowl strap*

the rubber or vinyl sweat wrap is applied over it. For increased sweating, you can apply glycerine, Listerine antiseptic or a commercial neck sweat preparation to the skin under the wrap. After applying the wrap, the horse is tied and left to stand for an hour before being exercised with the wrap in place. After exercise, the horse is cooled out completely before the wrap is removed and the neck is washed clean of sweat and any remaining preparation.

Some horses' skin may be irritated by certain sweating preparations; these are better off with only glycerine or nothing applied under the sweat wrap. In cool weather, plastic or even a second sweat wrap may be needed to achieve enough sweat to be effective. Keep a close eye on a horse that is being sweated—it is easy to cause too great a loss of moisture and allow the horse to become severely dehydrated, especially in hot weather. Test the horse by pinching up a fold of skin at the point of the shoulder—if the skin remains tented for 3 seconds or more instead of snapping back into place when you release it, the horse is becoming dehydrated and needs water, electrolytes and relief from exercise and sweating.

Stallions and thick-necked horses may need to be sweated every day to maintain a clean-looking neck. If much sweating is required, two shorter sessions per day are often more effective than one long one, and they are less stressful for the horse.

A jowl strap or jowl hood may be worn in the stable to keep the throttle slimmed down by heat and pressure. This is a fleece- or felt-lined strap or a hood which incorporates a jowl strap, not a rubber- or vinyl-lined sweat hood. The jowl strap is worn snugly but not so tightly that the horse cannot eat, drink and move comfortably. It supports the muscles of the throttle, which sometimes appear loose and flabby in certain horses, and helps to maintain the slim appearance achieved by sweating. Sweat lotions should not be applied under a jowl strap, as the lining may absorb the active ingredient and cause the skin to blister or hair to come out.

MASSAGE, BANGING AND WISPING

Massage can be very beneficial in relieving aches and pains, alleviating stiffness and helping a horse to recover after an injury or hard work. Some forms of massage help to develop or tone up certain muscles, much as isometric exercises or certain forms of massage do for human athletes. Therapeutic deep massage (using "trigger points") can be very helpful for some horses, but this requires expert application and is beyond the scope of this book. Rubbing, banging, soft wisping and simple massage also help to stimulate the skin and distribute the sebum or skin oil over the hair coat, improving the shine of the coat.

Hand rubbing may be used as a therapy for legs, sore muscles or to bring up the shine of the coat. When rubbing legs or joints, the area may be rubbed while dry but it is usually more comfortable for both horse and groom if the area is lubricated with rubbing alcohol, glycerine or, if heat is desired, a mild liniment such as Absorbine. (Some horses may have skin reactions to alcohol or to certain liniments, especially if they are rubbed in and then bandaged.) The fingers and palm are moved over the area with smooth, rhythmic pressure and a firm but flexible touch. Rubbing must be carried out for five to ten minutes to have any benefit; it is the rubbing, not the liniment, that gets results. (See pages 87–88 in the leg care section for directions for rubbing legs.)

Banging or hard wisping is a form of massage traditionally practiced by English grooms. It tones up and develops muscles in specific locations by causing a rhythmic contraction and relaxation, and can be carried out to work on the muscles even when the horse cannot be taken out and ridden. Banging is used to build up muscle in areas where muscle development is deficient or when the muscles are flabby. It is done with a hay wisp or a massage pad. (For directions for making a hay wisp, see pages 70–71).

To practice banging or wisping, first dampen the hay wisp. It should be firm and a size that can easily be held in one hand, like a body brush. Start by swinging your arm slowly and gently striking the wisp against a muscled area you wish to work on, such as the large muscle of the neck. Strike the muscle slowly and gently at first, sliding the wisp down and off the body with a long, firm sweep. As the horse gets used to the steady bang-and-sweep, he will learn to contract his muscles and then relax them with each bang. As he gets used to it, you can build up to harder strokes—about ten on each muscle area to begin with. As you progress, add a few strokes each day until you are banging each muscle area thirty times or more, putting all your weight into each "bang" and stroke.

Banging should be practiced only over large muscle masses, never over bony or thinly muscled areas and never over the sensitive loin area or any place that is tender or sore. Some horses obviously enjoy it and lean into the bangs; others may be too sensitive or nervous to tolerate it. Try starting slowly and gently and your horse may learn to like it; if not, it is better to omit banging or hard wisping than to risk hurting a sensitive horse or spoiling his trust in you. Banging is of value only if carried out faithfully and vigorously every day. It will certainly develop muscles in the groom!

FIGURE 3 *Banging or hard wisping*

Soft wisping is a milder form of rubbing, used to rub the skin and coat. A hay wisp, rub rag or folded towel can be used. The wisp or massage pad is rubbed firmly back and forth across the hair coat to stimulate circulation and work the skin oils throughout the coat. The coat should be rubbed for thirty minutes or more in order to shine up the coat and warm the skin. Some grooms finish off the job by rubbing the horse with the bare palms of the hands. This form of rubbing is so effective that it must be used with moderation on fine-coated horses—you can literally rub the hair off in places!

Massaging or hand rubbing the legs is a good thing to do for your horse, especially when he is tired, stiff or sore or when he is recovering from an injury. Good massage stimulates the circulation and helps the lymph system carry away cellular debris. Massage is good for stiff, arthritic horses to warm up their joints before work; it also helps when a horse is stiff or tired from a hard workout the day before. You should rub the legs after strenuous work such as galloping or jumping, and when removing bandages. Don't massage a bruise or any area that is swollen because of infection, however.

When hand rubbing legs, it helps to lubricate the area with rubbing alcohol or a mild astringent leg brace. (Some horses are allergic to alcohol, however.) Be careful about rubbing in liniments and leg preparations—some can blister the skin if rubbed in too hard or too long. It is the rubbing that does the most good, not the liniment, so don't just dab on a little liniment and give it a lick and a promise. It is necessary to rub each leg for at least five minutes to do any good.

FIGURE 4 *Hand rubbing a leg*

How to Hand-rub a Foreleg:

1. Lubricate your hand and the leg with alcohol or leg brace.
2. Facing toward the rear, bend down and take hold of the tendon with the hand nearest the horse. Your fingers should point down, with your thumb on the outside of the leg and your fingers on the inside, running along the tendon groove. By gently grasping the tendon, you can apply pressure with your fingers as you move your hand up and down.
3. Rub the leg by moving your arm up and down while your fingers and palm slide over the flexor tendons, the check ligament and suspensory ligament, the fetlock joint and the pastern. Apply most pressure upward, toward the heart.

To rub the shin or knee, you would face toward the front. The hind leg can be rubbed in the same way as the front. When working on a horse's legs, bend over but never sit or kneel—you might have to get out of his way if he should jump or kick.

BRACING AND BANDAGING THE LEGS

The feet and legs should be examined carefully each day when the horse is first brought out and later after his workout. Run your hand slowly over the surface of each leg from knee or hock to the hoof to check for heat, swelling, tenderness or scrapes, and treat any minor injuries before they have a chance to escalate. Many trainers of race and performance horses have the legs rubbed with a leg brace and wrapped with stable bandages after each workout as a precautionary measure; this also protects the horse from accidental injuries in the stall. Horses that are not routinely bandaged may benefit from support bandages when they have worked especially hard, when they have an injury or show signs of filling or stocking up, or when, at a show, they are stabled in temporary stalls that present more danger of the horse getting cast or getting his leg stuck through the slats than at home. If the legs are bandaged routinely, the horse will come to depend on the support of the bandages and the legs may develop temporary filling if bandaging is discontinued.

Bandaging materials include leg wraps or bandages and pads or "cottons." Leg wraps are usually of a knitted or semielastic material and are about 4 to 6 inches wide and 6 to 7 feet long. All leg wraps, except fleece polo wraps and special padded elastic wraps, must be used over a leg quilt, sheet cotton or other type of pad. It is quite dangerous to run a bandage directly on the leg without padding or to use uneven or insufficient padding, as the pressure can impair circulation and cause inflammation and injury to the tendons and soft structures. Leg wraps may fasten with Velcro closures, ties or safety pins; the closure is sometimes reinforced with masking tape or elastic adhesive tape.

There are various kinds of bandage materials with different purposes. Some common types are:

Knitted stockinette "track" bandages—the most common general-purpose bandage, used for leg wraps (always over a pad) and sometimes for tail bandages. They have some elasticity and are best for standing bandages, shipping bandages or tail wraps.

Flannel bandages—most often used by professionals for standing and shipping wraps, over thick cottons. They are not elastic but give good support. They are fastened with safety pins.

Elastic support bandages such as Ace bandages—very stretchy; can be used for support and working bandages over leg pads, but need skilled application because they can easily be pulled too tightly and damage the leg. Sometimes used for tail wraps over braided tails, but must be put on with care.

Vetrap—elastic crepe bandage that sticks only to itself and conforms to the leg or the padding beneath; may be reused once or twice but is disposable. Useful for wrapping injuries, wrapping tails for breeding or veterinary purposes or for exercise bandages when applied over padding. Not as strong as Ace bandage, but the same precautions regarding support bandages apply.

Elastic adhesive tape—useful for bandaging wounds or for reinforcing bandage closures.

Polo wraps—elastic bandages of a fleecy material, which incorporates its own padding into the bandage. Used to protect and support the legs during training and exercise, they are easily washable and easier to apply than other types of exercise bandages. They are used without leg pads underneath.

Types of padding used under bandages include:

Sheet cottons—six doubled sheets are used beneath standing or shipping bandages. They may be covered with cheesecloth to make them last longer. Sheet cotton is disposable; it cannot be washed.

Leg quilts or pads—made of quilting similar to bed pads, these should be sized to fit the horse's legs. They may be of cotton, washable felt or similar materials. They may be machine washed.

"Pillow" wraps—leg pads of cotton or acrylic batting covered with a cloth outer shell. They provide thick, soft and washable padding.

Other materials are available, and new wrapping materials are constantly being developed. Any padding should be soft, should compress into the contours of the leg without binding or creating lumps or wrinkles, and should be "breathable."

The legs may be "braced" before bandaging, especially after a workout and before stable bandages are applied. A mild liniment or leg brace or rubbing alcohol is massaged into the tendon, suspensory ligament and ankle areas until it is absorbed under the friction of the rubbing and the leg feels warm. Be careful to use a leg brace or liniment that is intended for use under bandages and that is not so strong as to cause skin irritation or blistering. The massage, along with the astringent and heating effect of the liniment, stimulates local circulation and encourages the absorption of excess fluid. The leg should be rubbed for at least five minutes and then bandaged immediately so as not to lose the effect of the liniment and massage. Do not use brace, liniment or heat over a bruise or a hot, swollen area—these conditions require cooling and support instead of heat, which can make the problem worse. (See pages 87–88 for directions for massaging legs.)

Stable or standing bandages are used to provide support and pressure for relief of tired legs, to treat strains and sprains and to take down swelling. They are also used as a precaution against accidental injury in the stall or while being walked in hand, especially when a horse is in a strange stall where he is more likely to get hurt than at home. A standing bandage should have plenty of padding; the wrap is pulled tightly enough to compress the padding into the contours of the leg and provide even pressure against the structures. It must be applied evenly from just below the knee to the pastern, and some padding should extend above and below the edge of the wraps to prevent them from binding against the knee or pastern.

To Apply a Standing Bandage, as Shown in Figure 5:

1. Place the padding evenly around the leg, starting with the edge in the groove of the tendon. On the left legs, the padding should be run counter-clockwise; on the right, clockwise. Do not start the padding on the shin or the tendon, and be sure it lies evenly without lumps or creases.
2. Start the bandage at the top of the ankle by slipping the end of the bandage inside the edge of the padding for 4 inches or so. Wrap one and a half times firmly over the tucked-in end, then begin to bandage downward, overlapping about one third the width of the bandage each time.
3. Wrap over the ankle and down to the pastern, keeping the wraps quite firm and even. The ankle is not as easily harmed by firm pressure as the tendons, and this gives a secure base from which to wrap the rest of the leg.
4. Pull the bandage up firmly beneath the pastern, for support.
5. Wrap back up the leg, keeping the wraps even, firm and parallel to the ground. Pull firmly against the shin, and feel the tension around the back of the tendon to keep it even with each wrap.
6. At the top, bring the last wrap well up to the bottom of the knee or hock. At least 1/2 inch of padding should extend upward beyond the bandage to prevent binding the back of the knee with the edge of the bandage.
7. Wrap back down to the middle of the leg. Fasten the bandage on the outside of the leg, never on the tendon, shin or inside. If the bandage is too long, it can be folded inward to adjust the length to come out right.
8. Fasten with Velcro closure, or with two safety pins in a horizontal position, pinning through several layers of bandage and into the padding beneath. The pins or Velcro can be covered with elastic adhesive tape for extra protection. If you use bandages with ties, they should be flat and must not

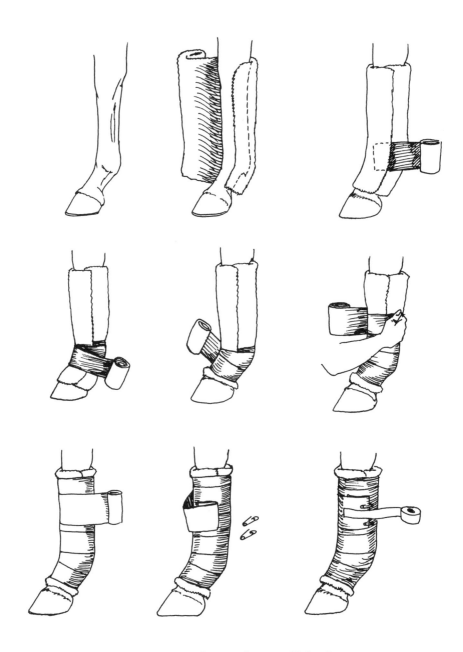

FIGURE 5 *How to apply a standing or stable bandage*

be pulled tight enough to indent the bandage. They must tie on the outside.

Now check the bandage—it should feel firm and even but not so tight that you cannot insert a finger under the wrap at the top and bottom.

Shipping bandages are used to protect and support the legs while traveling; they are applied like standing bandages but are extended down to cover the coronary band, in case the horse scrambles and steps on his own feet or is stepped on by another horse. The cottons and leg wraps will have to be extra long to cover the coronary band and also protect the tendons all the way to the knee or hock. Don't put on shipping bandages as "galoshes"—big lumpy bandages around the coronary band and ankle that end halfway up the tendon. These are clumsy and give no protection to the tendons and may cause uneven pressure on the leg. If you cannot run a neat, firm bandage from below the coronary band to the knee or hock, it is better to use rubber bell boots to protect the coronary band and apply a regular stable bandage over them, or to use shipping boots instead.

To Apply a Shipping Bandage, as Shown in Figure 6:

1. Place cotton or pad smoothly over the leg from below the heels to the knee or hock. On the left legs, wind the padding counterclockwise; on the right, clockwise. The edge of the padding should start at the side in the groove of the tendon.
2. Anchor the edge of the bandage under the cotton, starting at the top of the ankle.
3. Wrap one and a half times around the anchored end of the bandage, then wrap downward, using firm, even pressure. Overlap each wrap one third the width of the bandage, but do not waste bandage or you may run out of bandage at the end.
4. If the bandage gaps at the front of the pastern, give it a half twist.
5. Drop the bottom edge of the bandage at least 1 inch underneath the heel. Use a half twist if necessary to keep it tight. The padding should extend below the bandage, and both padding and bandage should be below the heels and the coronary band.
6. Wrap back up the leg, keeping the pressure firm and even for support. Check the tension over the tendon with each wrap, and pull most firmly against the shin, not against the tendon.
7. Wrap up the bottom of the knee or hock, leaving at least 1/2 inch of padding extended above the edge of the bandage to protect the back of the knee. Wrap back down over the leg to mid-cannon.

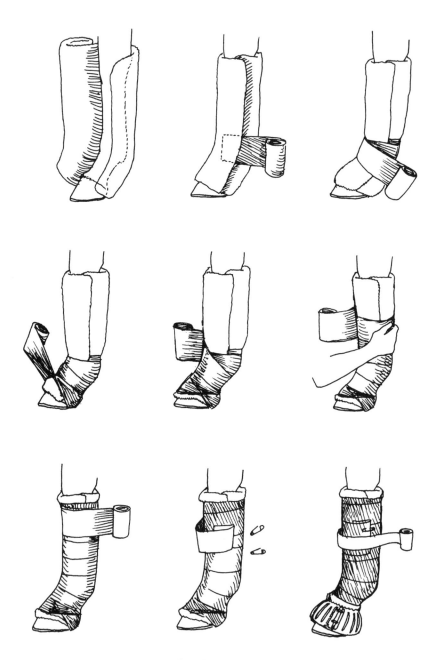

FIGURE 6 *How to apply a shipping bandage*
Shipping bandage applied over bell boot

8. Fasten the bandage on the outside of the leg. If necessary, fold the end back underneath to make the end finish in the right place.
9. Fasten with Velcro closure or with two safety pins in a horizontal position. Reinforce with a strip of elastic adhesive tape over the closure. Do not pull the tape tightly enough to indent the bandage.

Exercise bandages are used to protect the lower legs during work, longeing or turnout. They can also support tendons, ligaments and the fetlock joint when a horse is being returned to work after an injury. There are several types of exercise bandages for different purposes: tendon bandages, run-down bandages, ankle supports and others. Because exercise bandages are used when a horse is working, they must be secure or they can come loose, be stepped on and perhaps trip the horse. A bandage with too much or uneven pressure can damage the tendons under the strain of exercise. When learning to apply exercise bandages, you should have an experienced groom or trainer check your work, so that you learn exactly how much pressure to use and how to keep it even. Exercise bandages should not be used indiscriminately; if they are not necessary and especially if you do not know how to apply them correctly, leave them off!

The safest kind of exercise bandage for the average groom to apply is the fleece polo bandage. This wrap incorporates its own padding into the bandage and can safely be applied over the bare leg, without additional cottons or pads. They are easily washable, and are quick to put on when it is desirable to protect the legs during work, longeing or turnout. Polo wraps should not be used for cross-country work, as they become saturated with water and will slip and stretch when wet. They are not permitted in the show ring except on jumpers.

To Apply an Exercise Bandage Using Fleece Polo Wraps, as Shown in Figure 7:
1. Start the bandage at the edge of the tendon on the outside of the leg, wrapping counterclockwise on the left legs and clockwise on the right.
2. Wrap the bandage one and a half times around to anchor it, then begin wrapping downward, using even and fairly firm pressure. Do not pull as tightly as when wrapping a standing bandage because there is no padding to compress.
3. Most of the pressure should be applied backward against the shin instead of pulling forward against the tendons. Overlap each wrap about half the width of the bandage.

4. At the ankle, keep the front edge of the bandage high, above the bottom of the fetlock joint. Drop the bandage down and under the back of the fetlock joint and then back up in front. This will form an inverted **V** at the front of the ankle, giving room for the fetlock joint and pastern to flex.
5. Continue wrapping back up the leg, keeping the wraps parallel to the ground and the tension even and moderately firm. Wrap up to the bottom of the knee or hock.
6. Wrap back down, with a little less tension, over the previous wraps. Fasten the Velcro closure on the outside of the leg, never over the tendon or on the inside.
7. For extra security, the closure can be reinforced with a strip of elastic adhesive tape. Do not use a nonelastic tape, and do not pull the tape tightly enough to indent the bandage.

Exercise bandages are time-consuming and require some skill to apply, and they need frequent laundering, so many trainers prefer to use protective boots instead. Boots are quicker to apply and often offer more protection against a blow from a shod foot or a jump rail. They come in many styles to protect various parts of the leg, and usually have wide elastic closures that distribute pressure evenly, making them less likely to bind on a tendon or injure a leg than poorly applied exercise bandages. The boot lining must be clean when put on and cleaned after each use; mud, sand, sweat or grit against the skin can rub sores on the horse's legs. Some horses need a thin sheet of cotton worn beneath the boot.

Tendon boots, galloping boots and ankle boots should be applied high on the leg and then pulled down into position before adjusting the fastenings. The straps should be checked for adjustment after the horse has warmed up, as some horses' legs may go down in size as they warm up and the boots may need tightening.

Some common types of boots, shown in figure 8, are:

Tendon boots or galloping boots—protect the tendons and fetlock joint from interference injuries or high overreaches into the tendon area. They also protect the splint bones and the shins, and are frequently used on jumpers and event horses.

Open front boots—are used on jumpers to protect the tendons and sides of the leg, but let a horse feel a rap if he jumps carelessly.

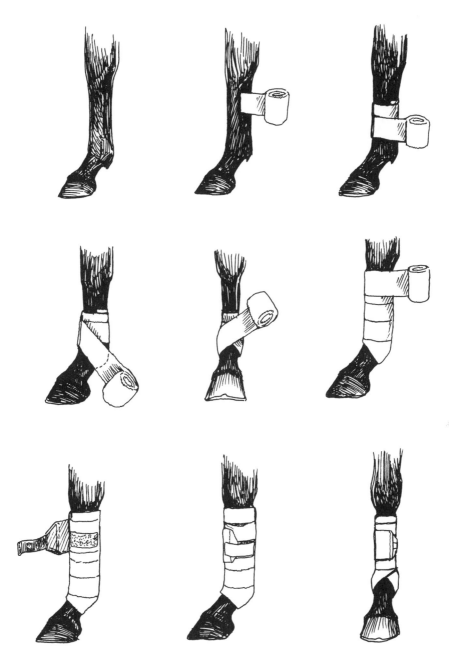

FIGURE 7 *How to apply fleece polo bandages*

Tendon boots or galloping boots   *Open front boot*   *Splint boots*

  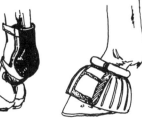 

Ankle boots and ankle cuffs   *Skid boots*   *Bell boots*   *Quarter boots*

Easyboot

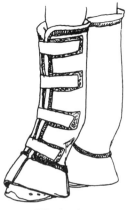

Shipping boots

FIGURE 8 *Types of protective boots*

Splint boots—protect the splint bones and inside of the leg from blows from the opposite foot when the horse is cutting, reining, longeing or doing lateral work, or on horses that interfere because of crooked leg conformation.

Ankle boots—protect against striking the inside of the ankle; they are usually used on hind legs. *Ankle cuffs* are folded felt ankle boots.

Skid boots—are used to protect the bottom of the ankles from abrasion on western horses that make sliding stops.

Bell boots—protect the heels and coronary band from "grabs" or overreach injuries. They are used on jumpers, during shipping and on any horse that is likely to injure his heels with the toe of the hind foot. Valuable horses often wear them during turnout.

Quarter boots—are used on saddle and harness horses that work with high action at speed. They protect against injury to the heels and quarters of the foot.

Easyboots—are fitted over the hoof like a slipper, taking the place of a shoe. They may be used for treatment or to protect the hoof until a lost shoe can be replaced, but they are not suitable for continuous use.

Shipping boots—take the place of shipping bandages, protecting the leg from coronary band to hock and knees during shipping. They should be made of a sturdy material that will not sweat the legs during hot weather.

Four

MANE AND TAIL GROOMING

The mane and tail are one of the horse's chief beauties. In nature, they also serve a practical purpose. The tail is an effective fly swatter (be careful around the tail in fly season, as the coarse hairs sting like a whip if they are lashed across your face!). The mane and forelock help to shade the horse's eyes and keep flies off his face and neck. In cold climates, the thick mane helps prevent the horse from losing body heat at the top of the head and neck, and the heavy tail protects the thin-skinned groin area as the horse habitually turns his rump to the wind and snow. Horses also use their tails for expression and communication. A frightened horse tucks its tail tightly against its rump; an irritated horse angrily switches the tail as it prepares to kick, and an animated, excited horse may "flag" its tail, carrying it in a high arch. The dock or tailbone is an extension of the spine; hence a rhythmically swinging tail denotes a relaxed, efficiently working back, while a crooked, stiff or wringing tail points to mental or physical distress.

Basic routine care of the mane and tail include careful untangling, keeping the skin clean and free from parasites, occasional washing and protection from damage and breakage of the hairs. Almost all show horses today are shown with the tail as long and full as it will grow; manes may be full, pulled or clipped short, depending on the type of horse. The only way to induce more growth of the hair is through proper nutrition and skin care; hair growth is stimulated from within, not by lotions or potions. However, good care of the mane and tail hair and the skin it grows from will reduce the problems of damage and breakage of the hair, and the texture of the hair itself can be helped with certain treatments, just as can human hair.

UNTANGLING THE MANE AND TAIL

Routine care starts with careful untangling of the mane and tail. While some long, thick manes and tails can take daily brushing, it is not a good idea to brush long hair too often, as each brushing pulls out and breaks off some hair. Neglecting untangling can cause long hair to become twisted into "ropes," which are then hard to untangle without breaking off and pulling out more hair.

If your horse's tail or long mane hair is tangled and full of debris, burrs or bedding, spray it with a silicone coat spray before untangling it. This makes the hairs slippery and allows the burrs and bedding to slide out easily with less chance of breaking off hairs. The best method is to hand-pick the mane or tail, taking a few hairs at a time and carefully separating them from any snarls. This is the only method that is permitted in many show stables, as the use of any brush or comb will break off a few hairs. If your horse has a long, thick and healthy mane or tail and you are not concerned about pulling out or breaking some hairs, you can brush it carefully with a hairbrush or a wire pet brush (the type with wire bristles set in a rubber backing), starting at the tips of the hairs and working carefully up to the roots, a small section at a time. Combs are more apt to damage the hair unless used with great care; plastic combs are smoother and less likely to cause damage than metal combs, which should only be used for pulling and shortening manes. The worst way to treat long hair is to drag a plastic or metal-toothed currycomb through it; this breaks off and pulls out the most hair and soon results in a short, bushy and bristling appearance.

How to Hand-pick a Mane or Tail:

1. Start at the edge of the mane or tail, holding the hair loosely in one hand. (If working on the tail, stand to one side.)
2. With the other hand, separate a few hairs (usually no more than three or four) and carefully work them free from the rest of the hair for their full length. Let these hairs fall to one side as you work.
3. Continue through the mane or tail until all the hairs have been separated and hang free from tangles from the roots down.
4. Part the roots of the hair and clean the skin, either with a soft, short-bristled body brush or with a damp sponge and towel. Brush only with short strokes to clean the skin, not brush the long hairs. Continue to part the hair along the mane or dock until all the skin is clean.

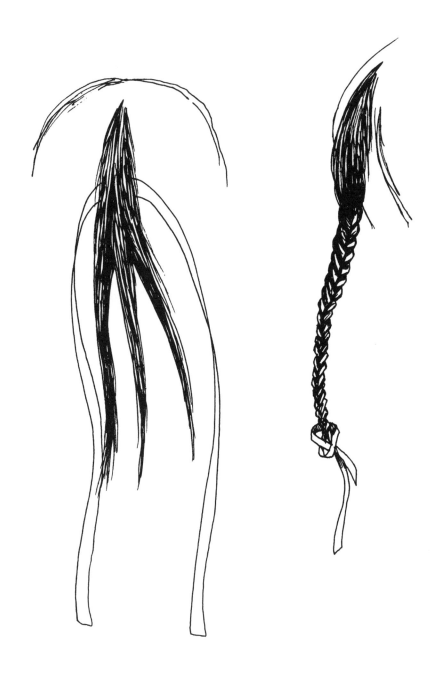

FIGURE 1 *How to braid the skirt of the tail*

FIGURE 2 *Tying up the skirt braid*

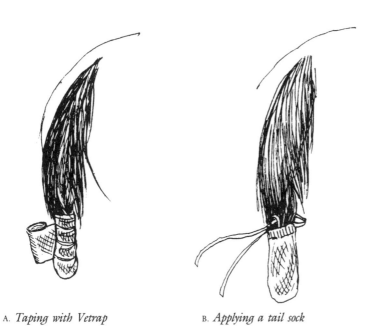

A. *Taping with Vetrap*   B. *Applying a tail sock*

FIGURE 3 *Protecting the braided skirt*

Some grooms moisten their fingers with baby oil or brilliantine, which gives a gloss to the hair as it is picked. However, both of these products will eventually have to be shampooed out, as they can build up on the hair and will pick up dirt and dust.

PROTECTING THE TAIL SKIRT

Horses that are shown with long, full tails usually have the skirt of the tail protected by braiding, bandaging or being kept in a tail bag. The longest hairs of the skirt can take several years to grow, so it is important to keep them from being pulled out or broken off by being caught on burrs, splinters, and various other "tail catchers" in the horse's environment. While you cannot make the tail hair grow faster, keeping the skirt protected leaves it much fuller and longer than it would normally be. Left to nature, the tail tends to become thin, stringy and straggly at the bottom and short, thick and bushy at the top. While this is practical in nature, it is just the opposite of the desired look for the show ring, where we would prefer to have the top of the tail slim and the skirt full, long and flowing.

The simplest way to protect the tail skirt is to keep it in a long braid. This prevents individual hairs from getting caught on splinters, etc., and broken off, yet the horse can use the long, soft braid as a fly swatter. It is most suitable for horses that are kept stabled most of the time and that do not have to contend with burrs and thistles or severe fly problems. The tail can be left braided even when the horse is worked, and it is only taken down once every week or two or when showing. For more protection, the braid can be covered with a long tube sock or a commercial tail sack. When the skirt hair is very long, the braid will have to be doubled and tied up to fit into the tube sock or tail sack. Some grooms cover the doubled-up braid with Vetrap, an elastic bandage that protects the hair without sticking to it. There are also special tail bags that fasten to a blanket or sheet and enclose the dock and entire tail in a protective nylon cover. These keep the tail clean and protected, and do not require that the skirt be braided.

How to Braid the Skirt for Protection:
1. You will need: a piece of cotton sheet, about 3 inches wide and 4 to 5 feet long (a piece torn off an old bedsheet works well), a large tube sock or a tail sack (sold in tack shops), electrical tape or Vetrap tape.
2. The tail should be clean and picked out. Starting at the end of the dock, divide the tail into three sections and begin to braid, not too tightly.

3. Partway down the braid, lay the center of the cotton strip behind the braid. Add one end to one of the hair sections and one end to the other. Continue braiding to the end of the hairs. The cotton sheeting will enclose the hairs, protecting them in the braid.
4. When you reach the ends of the hairs, the cotton ends should be 8 to 12 inches longer. Take one strip and pass it around the braid and pull it through, forming a slip knot around the end of the braid.
5. Double up the tail and pass the braid through the loosely braided upper section. Wrap it around and tie the cotton ends to keep it in place.
6. Pull the tail sack or tube sock over the doubled braid. Reinforce by wrapping tape around the top of the braid, 3 or 4 inches below the top of the tube sock. The tape must be applied at the top of the doubled braid but below the end of the dock.
7. Finally, pull the top of the sock down over the tape to protect the finished tail.

If the horse is to be turned out, Farnam fly strips or several strips of heavy cloth can be fastened to the bottom of the tail sack as a fly swatter. However, horses with tails tied up should not be turned out in bad fly conditions, as they will hit themselves with the tail bags and become irritated. For many owners, it is only practical to keep the tail tied up during the winter months when flies are not a problem. If you must keep tails tied up during fly season, the horse must be protected with scrim fly sheets, fly repellent, good barn cleaning and other fly-control measures.

SHAMPOOING

While horses do not need their hair shampooed as often as people do, there are times when washing the mane or tail is necessary. The tail may be soiled or stained, and sometimes the roots of the hair and the skin become excessively greasy or full of dandruff. Tails kept tied up or those exposed to sun and dust may become dry and need conditioning, and sometimes a horse may get his tail soaked with mud from working in a muddy ring.

For washing the tail, any mild shampoo will do, horse or human. A creme rinse may be used to make the tail hairs smoother, so that they will stand out and float. The tail may be sprayed with Showsheen or another silicone coat dressing, which makes the hairs shiny and slippery; this repels dirt and stains and makes it easier to pick or brush out the tail when it dries. No More Tangles shampoo or conditioner is sometimes used for the same purpose. If the roots of the hair and the skin are flaky and full of dandruff, Head and Shoulders or another human dandruff shampoo will help, and horses with dry skin or hair that is dry, brittle or sun-bleached can benefit from a hot oil treatment or a hair conditioner containing lanolin, aloe or protein. For gray or white tails, Quick Silver shampoo contains a whitening agent that removes stains and prevents yellowing of the tail, much as a similar rinse is used by gray-haired ladies. Too frequent tail washing can remove the natural skin oils and result in dry skin and hair, so it should not be done more often than necessary. Avoid shampooing the tail or applying any kind of creme rinse or coat dressing to the mane or tail within a day or so if it is to be braided—it will make the hairs slippery and make it difficult to braid neatly or keep the hairs in the braids.

How to Shampoo the Tail:

1. You will need: warm water hose or two large buckets of warm water, large body sponge, shampoo, creme rinse or silicone coat dressing, towel. The horse should be tied in a wash stall or suitable area.
2. Wet down the tail, including the dock, with hose or sponge. If the horse is gentle, you may lift up the bucket and dunk the skirt to wet it. Be careful—when the horse feels the water on his tailbone, he may squat down and might want to kick.
3. Apply shampoo to the skirt and rub it well into the whole tail, working up a lather. Use the sponge to wash the skin of the dock.
4. Rinse out the sponge and use the warm water hose or the sponge to rinse the tail from the top down, making sure the hairs are rinsed until they "squeak." The skirt may be dunked and swirled around in the bucket to rinse it until no more soap comes out.
5. Wring the skirt hairs out gently and blot them with a towel. A creme rinse or hot oil treatment may be applied (follow directions on commercial products) or a silicone coat dressing may be sprayed on the damp tail hairs.

The tail can be washed in cold weather when it would be too cold to bathe the whole horse, especially if only the skirt is washed. While the mane can be shampooed in the same manner, this is not a good idea in cold weather as it will get the neck wet.

TICKS, LICE AND RUBBING

During grooming, the mane and tail should be carefully checked for signs of ticks, lice or rubbing. Ticks can be a problem in warm climates or in spring and summer, and often are found at the bottom of the dock. (How to remove ticks is explained on page 51.) Lice are less common, at least in stables where horses are well cared for; they are most often seen in winter or early spring when horses are kept in large herds without much individual attention, and on thin, run-down animals with long winter coats. The individual lice are hard to see, but the nits or eggs are more obvious, resembling tiny, pale-colored sesame seeds attached to the hair shafts and often found in the roots of the mane. Lice can be treated with Captan in dip or dust form, and the treatment will have to be repeated ten days later to kill those that hatch out later. In the meantime, the horse should be kept away from other horses and its blankets, brushes and tack kept separate and disinfected. Horse lice are not the same variety as those that infest humans, but they give most people the shudders, and precautions should be taken by disposing of clipped hair, disinfecting equipment and washing your clothes after dealing with this problem.

Once the mane and tail are clean, untangled and in good condition, it is important to protect them from damage from pulling out or rubbing. First, check the horse's environment. Anywhere you see a hair caught—on a splinter, a door latch or a handle of a bucket—is a spot where your horse's hair is being damaged. A dirty spot along the edge of a door or window may point to a place where your horse likes to rub his mane or tail. If there are thistles or burdocks in your horse's paddock, they should be cut down and removed. A favorite rubbing spot on the fence may need to be protected with a strand of electric fence wire.

The worst and most common cause of hair loss is habitual rubbing. In order to cure it, you must first find and eliminate the cause. Tail rubbing is often caused by pinworms; these thread-sized parasites live in the rectum and leave a telltale grayish or yellowish powdery discharge near the anus. Deworming with Ivermectin or another broad-spectrum wormer will eliminate these tiny pests. If your horse is found to have pinworms, it would be a good idea to have a fecal parasite egg count done by the veterinarian. He may also be infested with strongyles or other intestinal parasites as well.

Next, check the skin condition. If it is noticeably dry and flaky, dry skin may be causing itching. This can be due to too frequent or too harsh shampooing, or to a very dry environment. Shampooing with a mild, soothing shampoo and treating the skin with an ointment containing lanolin or aloe vera may help. Some people smear a large blob of Vaseline on the rubbed area, which often stops the rubbing. If the skin is broken or irritated, it may be a bacterial or fungus infection. (Fungus infections are common in damp or humid weather.) The affected area should be bathed with a mild, medicated shampoo, preferably one that is fungicidal as well as antibacterial. Fungisan, Micodex and iodine-based shampoos are all commonly used. The skin may be treated afterward with vitamin A and D ointment or a topical antiseptic cream containing cortisone to reduce the itching. If the skin irritation is severe or if it does not respond to simple treatment, it may be necessary for the veterinarian to see the horse to determine whether it is dermatitis, a bacterial infection, a fungus or perhaps a type of allergic or autoimmune reaction. Cortisone or other prescription drugs may be necessary to bring the condition under control.

Finally, some horses get into the habit of rubbing even after the physical reason no longer exists. This may be caused by boredom. The only answer in this case is to make it impossible for the horse to rub, either by covering the mane and tail or by eliminating whatever he rubs on. Stalls for tail-set horses are often equipped with a tail board—a horizontal board that projects inward along all four walls of the stall at the height of the horse's point of buttock. This prevents the horse from getting close enough to the stall wall to rub his tail. Sometimes a spot can be padded, or as a last resort, an electric fence wire may be run across that place, but if this is used, the horse must have plenty of room to move around without encountering the electric wire. A blanketed horse may wear a tail guard (a reinforced leather or plastic tail cover, often lined with fleece) or a tail bag that attaches to his blanket or sheet. (Tail bandages are not recommended for preventing tail rubbing, as they must be left on for too many hours at a time and can cause damage to the hair and even to the tissues of the dock.) Mane rubbers may wear a full hood with a silk lining, but the mane must be watched to be sure that it is not being worn away by constant contact with the hood. Sometimes more exercise, more turnout time, stall toys and less monotony may break up the boredom and cut down on the habit.

TAIL BANDAGES

The dock of the tail is sometimes bandaged for protection during shipping, or to flatten and shape the hairs at the top of the dock to make the top of the tail appear slimmer in the show ring. A braided tail is protected with a bandage whenever the horse is not showing.

There are two types of tail bandage: the shipping bandage and the bandage for shaping the tail or covering a braided tail. For shipping, the tail bandage must be very secure so that it will not slip off. It prevents the horse from rubbing the hair off his tail by leaning against the tailgate of a trailer or the wall of a van. A leather or plastic tail guard may be used for the same purpose, but this must be attached to a sheet or blanket. Tail bandages should never be used when shipping horses for long distances or by commercial carrier. If the bandage slips or begins to cut off circulation, as may happen when it is left on for many hours, the shippers may not notice the problem until serious circulatory damage has been done to the tail. This can cause the horse to lose the hair of his tail or, in severe cases, even to develop gangrene, requiring amputation of the tail!

How to Apply a Tail Bandage for Protection While Shipping:
1. Use a cotton stockinette bandage, not an Ace or elastic bandage. Do not dampen the bandage or the tail.
2. Anchor the bandage by taking one and a half wraps around the dock, two thirds of the way down the dock. Wrap snugly but not tightly enough to cut off circulation in the tail.

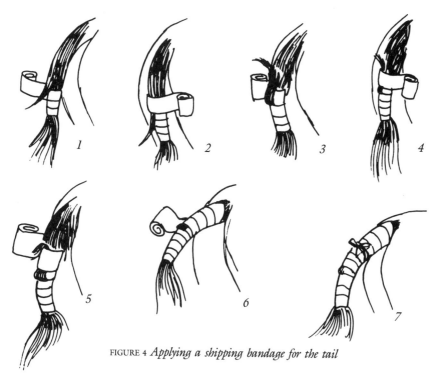

FIGURE 4 *Applying a shipping bandage for the tail*

3. Pull a section of hair (about 2 inches wide) from below the wraps and fold it upward. Take a turn or two of the bandage over the turned-up hair.

4. Turn the end of the hair section downward and continue wrapping over it and on up to the top of the dock. Keep the wraps snug and uniform, overlapping each time.

5. Wrap downward, back over the bandaged area, as far as the bandage lasts. Finish the wrap by securing with Velcro or with two safety pins. The fastening can be reinforced with elastic adhesive tape, but the tape must never be pulled tighter than the rest of the bandage, and only elastic tape should be used.

A shaping or finishing bandage is applied over a tail braid, for protection, or over the dampened hairs of the dock to smooth and flatten the upper hairs

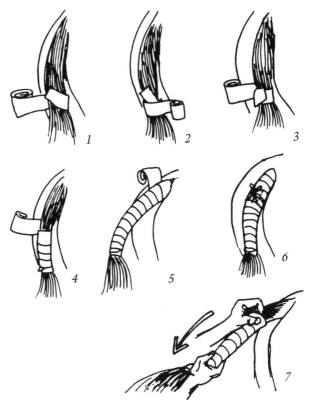

FIGURE 5 *Applying a finishing bandage to shape the tail*
Removing a tail bandage

of the tail. It should only be left on for an hour or two, though bandages over braids are sometimes left on longer. Remember to remove the tail bandage before your horse goes into the ring—it spoils your braiding and turnout efforts to forget this!

How to Apply a Finishing Bandage to the Tail:

1. Slightly dampen the hairs of the dock (never wet the bandage or it may shrink!).
2. Start the tail bandage about 8 inches down from the top of the dock. Pull the end of the bandage up in a 3- to 4-inch tab, then wrap one and a half times over it.
3. Pull the end of the tab down over the wraps, then continue to wrap over the tab, the previous wraps and on up the tail. The wraps should be firm and snug but not uncomfortably tight. Each wrap should overlap the one below it by half the width of the wrap.
4. At the top of the dock, wrap downward over the wrapped portion and on down to the end of the dock, overlapping each wrap and keeping the wraps snug.
5. Finish off the wrap by fastening it with Velcro, two safety pins or elastic adhesive tape. Never pull the fasteners tighter than the wraps.
6. To remove the wrap, hook two fingers into the top wrap and pull the whole wrap downward and off the tail. This removes the wrap without disturbing the hair.

A tail bandage over a braided tail is applied similarly, except that some grooms use an Ace bandage or elastic wrap. The bandage should never be pulled to full stretch, as it could cut off circulation and injure the tail. Once the bandage has been run up the tail and back down to the bottom of the dock, the next-to-last wrap is lifted and the remaining roll of bandage tucked beneath it. This bandage must be unwound, not pulled off like a finishing bandage.

MANE TAMING—HELP FOR PROBLEM MANES

While the mane hair may be worn short, medium or long, depending on the conventions of each breed and type of horse, we always want a neat, tidy mane that falls on one side of the neck. Certain types of show horses have conventions regarding the side of the neck to which the mane falls—

for instance, western horses are traditionally shown with a left mane and most English horses with the mane on the right. However, this is not mandatory in any class, and sometimes the trouble involved in training the mane to fall on the opposite side is not worth the effect, especially if the mane is neat, smooth and attractive and naturally lies all on one side. However, if the mane wants to stand straight up, fall to the opposite side in one section, or part down the middle and fall to both sides, you may have to train it to lie on one side.

Often a problem mane is very thick and wiry, or the hairs may be stiff and brittle. The shorter the mane, the more difficult it is to train it to lie down, so you should get the mane lying on the correct side before you start pulling or shortening the hairs. Wet the hair down thoroughly with water, and braid it into small, tight "pigtails" no more than 1 inch wide at the top. The hairs must be pulled across the crest of the neck and the braid started on the side, not on top. The pigtails may be fastened at the ends with rubber bands or they may be turned under and tied off as in braiding a hunter (see the chapter on braiding show hunters). Once fastened, the braids may be saturated with setting gel. (If you put setting gel on the hair before you braid it, it will be too slippery to hold onto.) Leave the pigtails in for several days, applying more setting gel each day if the hair has dried out. When you undo the braids, dampen the hair with setting gel and brush it over to the correct side of the neck. If the mane is relatively soft and not too short, this method will usually train it over in a few days.

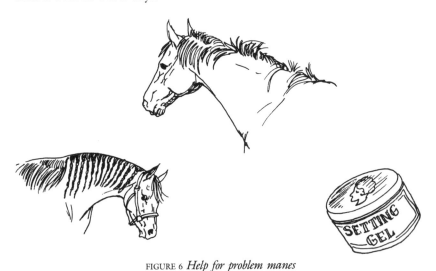

FIGURE 6 *Help for problem manes*

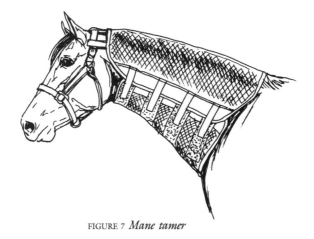

FIGURE 7 *Mane tamer*

A full hood, lined with silk, can be used to help train a long mane to stay on the correct side of the neck. The mane must be carefully brushed, dampened and laid down before the hood is applied. Watch the mane carefully for signs that the hood is rubbing the hair out, however.

A mane-tamer is a kind of equine hairnet, applied for an hour or two before a class to lay the mane flat on the correct side of the neck. The mane should be dampened and combed through with setting gel, and the mane-tamer fastened firmly down over it. This method is usually temporary, with the effect lasting just about long enough for a show class.

A mane that has been roached and is being grown out, or a part of the bridle path that has been cut too far back and is being grown out, is a special problem. Roaching or clipping closely shortens all the hairs to the same length, so as they grow out, the tendency is for all the hairs to stick straight up. Nothing can be done except to wait until the hair is long enough to be put into tiny braids, pulled off to the desired side and saturated with setting gel. As soon as the mane begins to lie over to the desired side, the hairs on the underside should be pulled as short as possible. It may be necessary to use pliers to grasp the short hairs on the underside to begin pulling the mane, taking only a tiny bit of hair from the underneath edge. This allows room for the remaining mane to turn toward the desired side and lie down. The mane cannot lie smoothly until the hairs from the far side grow long enough to cross over and lie flat on top and the middle and underneath hairs are thinned and shortened until they are shorter than the top hairs. It can take six months to a year for the hair to grow out enough to permit this, so keep this in mind when you decide to cut a bridle path or roach a mane!

Some long manes have a tendency to mat and tangle or to become "ropy." These can be protected by being kept in long, loose braids much like the skirt of a tail. The mane is divided into sections of 3 to 5 inches in width, and a piece of cotton sheeting can be braided into the braid as in tying up the tail. These braids are not turned under or tied up, but keeping the mane braided prevents it from becoming tangled. The braids should not be too tight at the top or they may cause the hairs to break off, creating an unsightly fringe. The condition of the hair, especially the hair at the top of the mane, must be watched carefully, and the mane should be unbraided and gently picked out once a week. If the hair seems dry or brittle, it should be treated with a conditioner or a hot oil treatment.

Long natural manes usually vary in thickness, with the hair being thicker at the upper end of the neck, where the crest and mane is widest, and thinner near the withers, where the mane is very narrow. Sometimes this results in an unattractive bushy look at the front that does not fit with the finer, thinner and sometimes shorter mane back near the shoulders. Cutting the bridle path a bit farther back eliminates some of the thickest mane, but a little judicious thinning and shortening near the front can improve the overall appearance of the mane. The long mane should not be all of one length, which looks unnatural, but should gradually grow longer toward the middle of the shoulder; from that point it gradually shortens again toward the withers. Any thinning and shortening should be done by pulling, never cutting with scissors.

Rubbed or ragged manes are another kind of problem. This condition usually results from the horse's habit of rubbing his mane under a fence board

FIGURE 8 *Basic trim for long manes*

or against the edge of his window or doorway. Sometimes a horse will lose a chunk of his mane when it is full of burrs or gets caught on a nail, or another horse may chew off a portion of the mane. The problem is to camouflage the damage for show purposes while the damaged portion grows out to match the rest of the mane. If the horse is of a breed that can be shown with a pulled mane, one solution is to pull the rest of the mane quite short. If a long mane is mandatory, it may be possible to create a hairpiece from tail hair or even from mane hair pulled carefully from a thicker part of the mane or from another horse. The hairpiece can be braided into the mane beside the damaged portion, and the nearby hair may be pulled slightly shorter if that helps to blend in the special effects; or it may be left as long as possible and combed over the edge of the hairpiece. In one case of a hunter that had reduced his mane to bald spots with a few short wisps by rubbing, artificial mane braids were made out of tail hair and were sewn on to the remaining short wisps. The horse looked presentable, but his rider had to be warned not to grab the mane over fences, lest she come out of the ring with the horse's "mane" all in her hand!

MANE PULLING

Hunters, sport horses, some driving horses and western horses may need their manes shortened and thinned for braiding, neatness or show conventions. The cardinal rule is that the mane must never be cut with scissors or clippers unless it is roached or hogged entirely. Cutting the mane shortens without thinning and results in an unnatural, squared-off "Dutch-boy" cut that is unacceptable for show purposes and which also makes neat braiding almost impossible. The mane must be as short and as even as necessary for the type of horse—but it must look like it grew that way. This appearance can be achieved only by pulling and thinning the mane by hand. Before pulling the mane, have the hair brushed out and free of tangles. A pair of thin gloves and a small metal pulling comb are helpful, although pulling can be done entirely by hand. Have the horse cross-tied and work where the wind will not blow the mane around.

Begin pulling at the longest spot in the mane. You should first make the mane even, then work along the whole length of the mane, shortening it only 1/2 inch or so at a time along its entire length. This keeps you from pulling the mane very short in one spot and then having to pull the rest of the mane to match it!

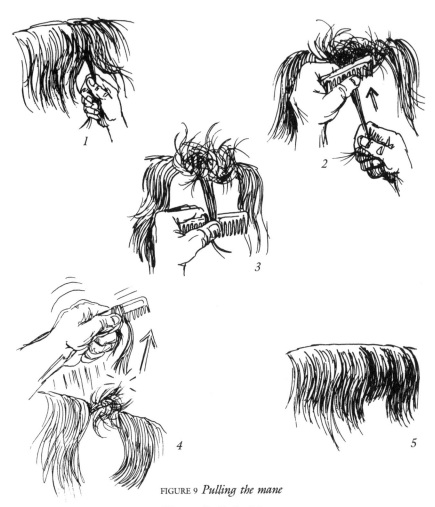

FIGURE 9 *Pulling the mane*

How to Pull the Mane:

1. Grasp a few of the longest hairs at the *underside* of the mane firmly between the fingers and thumb of one hand.
2. With the fingers of the other hand or with a small metal pulling comb, push the other hairs up toward the neck—like teasing hair. You should be left with a very few hairs—half a dozen or so—which should fan out to a section of neck about an inch wide.
3. Wind the long hairs around your fingers or around the pulling comb.
4. Pull the hairs out with a swift jerk *straight up*. (If using a comb, pull against the side of the comb, not against the edge. You want to pull hairs out, not cut them off with the edge of the comb.)
5. Comb down through the "teased" hair before picking up a new portion of hair.

As you work, feel for the thickest part of the mane and always pull the hairs from the underside. This allows the top hairs to lie down and thins the mane to a uniform thickness. You will find that some parts of the neck (especially near the head) have thicker hair and require more pulling, while other parts are finer and thinner, such as the hair back near the withers. If the hair is so fine and thin that you do not want to thin it any more, but you need to shorten it, you could try carefully trimming the hairs with a "thinner"—a wire-wrapped razor tool used in dog grooming. Be careful to use the thinner to produce a tapered cut—if you pull the hair straight across the blade you will produce a blunt "Dutch-boy" cut, just what you are trying to avoid. It is wise to practice with the thinner on some part of the mane that you will be pulling out anyway, until you are sure that you can use it skillfully enough that it will produce the tapered, natural effect you want.

Pulling the mane is not as painful as it sounds, because horses have fewer nerve endings in relation to their hairs than humans do. Nevertheless, some horses find it uncomfortable or downright painful. You should work below your horse's pain threshold—start by pulling only two or three hairs at a time and gradually increase until he lets you know that's enough by raising his head or shaking his neck. Once you know his limit, take fewer hairs so that he doesn't mind. Pulling straight up quickly is much less painful that pulling slowly downward (try it on your own hair!) Warming the skin of the mane with a hot towel makes the hair come out easier and feels good to the horse. If you pull only a few hairs from each area along the neck every day while grooming, staying under your horse's pain threshold, you can gradually thin and shorten his mane without taxing his toleration. One exception might be the horse that is extremely sensitive and that has been manhandled and forced to endure a long, painful mane-pulling session. Such horses may need to be tranquilized in order to pull their manes, as the tranquilizing drug raises their pain threshold as well as calming them. This is safer and more humane than fighting with a horse or coercing him to try to make him hold still while you hurt him, and several nonpainful sessions may break the pattern of tension and anticipating pain.

When pulling a mane, it takes some judgment to arrive at the correct length. If the horse is always braided when he is shown, the mane is pulled to the best length for braiding, regardless of how it looks when unbraided. This may be as short as 3 1/2 to 4 inches on some horses. However, if the owner cares more about how the horse looks in his everyday appearance and only rarely braids, his first priority may be to find a length of mane that is neat, lies flat on one side and flatters the horse's neck—often slightly longer than the ideal braiding length. A massive horse with a long neck (for example, a warmblood standing 17 hands or more) may need a much longer mane to look in proportion to his body than a smaller, finer horse or a pony. The shorter the mane is pulled, the more it tends to stand up and sometimes to curl over to the opposite side of the neck. Remember, it is always possible to take off a bit more mane, but if you pull it too short, you will simply have to wait until it grows out.

Five

TRIMMING AND CLIPPING

Trimming can make a wonderful change in a horse's overall appearance in just a few minutes. A horse in the rough has shaggy fetlocks and sometimes "feathers," or long hair, which obscure the tendons and lines of the lower legs; his ears are hidden in fuzz and his face and jaw may be so hairy as to make him look more like a billy goat than a horse! Long muzzle whiskers give him a comic appearance, and his mane and tail may be bushy, tangled and over-grown. With a little barbering, the country bumpkin looks like a city slicker, with a more refined head, face and muzzle, cleaner throatlash and more sculptured ears and slimmer-looking, cleaner legs. But before you start clipping, you should give some thought to how much and what kind of trimming your horse really needs.

All that extra hair serves a practical purpose, especially if a horse is turned out to pasture or must work outside in rain, mud or bitterly cold weather. While a little trimming makes a horse look nicer, it is unkind and detrimental to his well-being to go overboard in trimming him inappropriately. If he is to be kept stabled, carefully groomed and meticulously looked after, and especially if he is showing in a specialty that requires the ultimate in trimming, you may need to do the ultimate trimming job. But if you are cleaning up the old pony for a one-time appearance at the county fair, don't go too far and deprive him of some important natural protection he will need as soon as he's turned back out to pasture.

BASIC TRIMMING

Long fetlocks come to a natural point and help water to drain down the legs, away from the sensitive skin of the heels. If your horse works outside in all weather or is ridden in muddy conditions (such as foxhunting), you may trim his leg hair enough to neaten it but you should not remove his fetlock hair entirely nor clip his legs closely, or he may be exposed to mud fever or "scratches," a chapped and cracked condition of the heels and pasterns. If he's mostly stabled and kept as a show horse, he can be trimmed more closely and even "booted up," especially if he has white legs. The edges of the hair above the coronary band can be trimmed short so they don't become sticky with hoof dressing.

The chestnuts (horny, insensitive growths found inside and above the knees and inside the hocks) should be cut off close to the skin with a sharp knife. Since they are not sensitive and have no blood supply close to the surface, you will not hurt the horse if you cut them off carefully. They are easier to remove when they have been softened when the horse has a bath.

If you see botfly eggs on your horse's legs, shoulder or mane, they should be removed.

The mane is often thick and bushy at the top, near the ears; sometimes there is so much mane that it is hard to bridle the horse without getting tangled up in it. A short "bridle path" clipped just behind the poll makes it neater and more comfortable to put the bridle or halter on. The basic bridle path should be clipped no longer than an inch. While certain breeds of horse are shown with much longer bridle paths, if you cut it too long it will take six months to a year before the clipped part will grow out to match the rest of the mane. Check your breed specifications before you clip it too far!

The long hair under the horse's chin and lower jaw insulates him if he has to live outdoors in arctic weather, but most horses can do without it, and trimming it improves the shape of the head and the appearance of the face. The long hair between the jawbones and under the throat can be trimmed closely and makes a great difference in the appearance of quality about the horse's head.

Fuzzy ears have a purpose. In winter, the extra hair keeps the ears warm and wards off frostbite; in summer, it prevents gnats and biting flies from getting into the ears. To neaten the ears, you can trim the long hair around the edges, giving them a more sculptured look, and the inside hair can be trimmed level with the outer edges. Halter horses and high-level show horses usually have their ears clipped clean on the inside; a tiny "diamond" is left at the tip of the ear, to bring it to a natural point. If the ears are cleaned out, you should use a scrim ear cover whenever your horse is turned out and may be bothered by flies.

The long whiskers of the muzzle and above the eyes may look unkempt to some, but they serve an important purpose to the horse. He uses these

FIGURE 1 *Horse in the rough vs. basic trim*

whiskers as a cat does, feeling what is near his muzzle as he grazes and as an early warning system when something is coming close to his face or eyes, especially in the dark. If your horse is turned out most of the time, he probably needs his whiskers, especially those around the eyes. If he is kept primarily as a show horse, especially in high-level showing, it is customary to clip the muzzle hairs off. If you choose to clip the muzzle whiskers, they should be kept close-trimmed by clipping frequently. When the whiskers grow out to short "nubs," these are stiff and blunt and cause discomfort as they bump into things. *Never* clip the hairs inside the muzzle or the eyelashes—these are essential for the horse's safe functioning and comfort.

Some horses grow coarse, heavy hair on their faces. This acts as an insulator in cold weather and helps keep white-faced horses from getting sunburned. For high-level halter competition, the white markings or the face may be clipped closely, but it is important to leave enough hair so that there will be some protection from sunburn and so the area does not look "scalped." If a horse's face is clipped, it may be necessary to use a sunscreen highlighter or coat dressing when he is out in bright sun.

The basic trimming job ends with carefully picking out and neatening the mane and tail. The mane may need to be pulled, or it may be left long and natural, depending on the type and purpose of the horse. The tail is usually left as long and full as it will grow, but some horses and ponies with bushy tails look better when the top of the tail is thinned and pulled somewhat to make it more in proportion to the rest of the tail. The mane should be trained to lie smoothly on one side (see Chapter 4 on mane and tail grooming for instructions on pulling and training manes).

COSMETIC CHANGES

Some cosmetic changes can be made through clever clipping and trimming. A coarse, chunky horse can be made to look much finer, even when in winter coat, by clipping the face, head and throatlash and trimming the legs closely. If the coat is long, the clipped areas must be blended skillfully or they will stand out in startling contrast from the unclipped areas. Thick legs can be made to appear finer by trimming closely along the contours of the tendons, giving more definition and the appearance of quality to the leg. A thick throttle looks less gross when it is clipped closely underneath and when the horse has a slightly longer than average bridle path. Clipping the face and close-clipping the area around the eyes and muzzle makes the head look more refined and the eyes look larger, but this must be done skillfully and blended without a visible line. A blemish such as a thickened tendon or a large ankle can be minimized by clipping a little less closely over the blemish and carefully blending the clipped hair at the knee. White markings look whiter when clipped closely (but not so closely as to leave "clipper stripes" or to appear scalped), but clipping the lower legs closely may make big feet look even bigger by contrast. A less-than-perfect head can be flattered by judicious shaping and trimming of the mane and forelock—a Roman nose or big ears can be minimized by a larger forelock, and a thin neck may look more substantial with a little extra mane. If the horse's hind legs are less than perfect, leave the tail long and full to camouflage them; thinning and slimming the top of the tail can make the hindquarters appear wider.

CLIPPING MACHINES

Electric clippers are a great help in making a horse look presentable. Years ago, horsemen were limited to what they could do with scissors and comb, the singeing lamp or the old-fashioned, hand-cranked clipping machine. These methods were slow and tedious and could be unsafe, especially if a horse was uncooperative. Modern electric clippers cut quickly, evenly and without danger of hurting the horse. There are several types of horse clippers and many models, with prices ranging from about twenty dollars to several hundred dollars.

Large heavy-duty clippers—used for body clipping, roaching manes and trimming heavy, coarse hair around the legs. Because of their size, they are

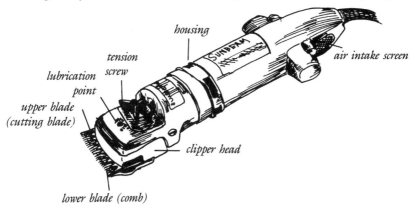

FIGURE 2 *Heavy-duty clippers*

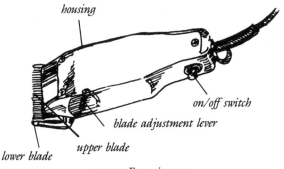

FIGURE 3 *Ear trimmers*

too cumbersome for fine trimming, and their loud noise makes them less desirable to use around the horse's head. One type has a variable speed control; it can be turned down to clip at a slow speed, greatly reducing the noise factor. Heavy clippers are air cooled and can be run for a longer period of time without overheating than can smaller and lighter models, and the larger motor has the power to cut through coarse and heavy hair. They cost about $120 and up.

Small ear trimmers—light, inexpensive (prices range from about $20) and nearly noiseless. They are designed to trim fine hair around the ears and muzzle accurately and quietly. They cut more closely than heavy-duty clippers and are not made to cut thick, heavy hair or to be run for long periods of time. Some models can be used to trim fetlocks if the hair is not too thick, but the very fine blades tend to leave unattractive "clipper lines" when used on thick hair. One useful type is a battery-powered or cordless rechargeable trimmer, which can be used in a stall or at a show where an electrical outlet is not available.

Small animal clipper or "groom clipper"—a clipper similar to those used in professional dog grooming shops, perhaps the most versatile and useful model for the serious show groom. This type is more powerful than ear trimmers but lighter and easier to maneuver than heavy body clippers. The blades snap on and off, allowing a wide range of different blades for different types of clipping. The blades are identified by number, with the most useful types for horse clipping being the #10 (coarse; equivalent to a body clipping blade), #15

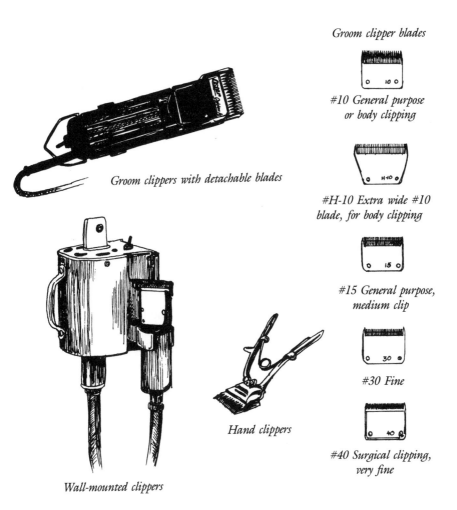

Groom clipper blades

Groom clippers with detachable blades

#10 General purpose or body clipping

#H-10 Extra wide #10 blade, for body clipping

#15 General purpose, medium clip

#30 Fine

Hand clippers

#40 Surgical clipping, very fine

Wall-mounted clippers

FIGURE 4

(medium), #30 (fine) and #40 (very fine, used for surgical clipping). While a wider-body clipping blade is available, this clipper is less satisfactory for body clipping than the heavy-duty clippers, especially if it is used for heavy-coated horses or if several horses must be done in a day. It can be used to body-clip a single horse if the coat is clean and not too coarse, or to finish a body-clipping job by clipping the head, legs, etc. This clipper is powerful enough to trim a number of horses' heads, legs, etc., in a day, and its smaller size and weight make it easier to use skillfully for a professional-quality trim. Small animal clippers cost about $100; blades about $12 per set.

Recently a line of clippers has come out that combines a more powerful motor, which may be wall mounted or attached to the operator's belt, with a flexible cable that transmits power to the small animal clipper head. This type combines the advantages of the small animal clipper, with interchangeable blades, with the power of a much larger clipper. The only disadvantage is its greater cost—about $300 at this time, with blades extra.

The main parts of a clipping machine, from figure 2, are:

Housing—the metal or plastic case that holds the electric motor. This must be free from cracks. The on-off switch is located on the housing.

Clipper head—the part that holds and moves the blades. There are screws or a snap-on arrangement for changing blades, and there may be oiling vents for lubrication.

Blades—a set of clipper blades consists of: *Lower blade or comb*—A fine- to coarse-toothed comb which glides over the skin and directs the hair into the cutting blade. The comb keeps the cutting blade from touching the skin. The coarser the comb, the longer the hair left after clipping. *Upper blade (cutting blade)*—a zig-zag-shaped blade that cuts the hair against the teeth of the comb with a scissorslike action. Only the upper blade is moveable. Some clipper blades come in a blade set, with both upper and lower blades held together by a spring and installed or removed as a unit.

Tension adjustment—found on some models; permits adjustment of the pressure between the upper and lower blades. Use the lowest tension that will produce a clean cut. The tension setting may be increased as the blades wear down, until they become too dull to cut even at the highest tension setting. Setting the tension too high will cause the blades to heat up and will wear them out faster.

Lubrication points—may be located on the clipper head, or on some models, only the blades are oiled.

Air intake screen—On air-cooled models, the screen should be kept free from hair. If it becomes clogged, the motor will run hot. Without the screen, hair and dirt will be sucked into the housing and may interfere with the motor.

Electric motor and cord—most American clippers operate on 15 volt AC current, although there are cordless rechargeable and small battery-operated models. It is strongly recommended that you use a grounded plug and use only UL-approved models to avoid shock to either the horse or the operator. Remember that when the clippers are plugged in, the cord is "hot" even if the motor is switched off. If the horse should chew on the cord or step on it, breaking the insulation, he could be badly shocked. Unplug the clippers whenever you stop for a break, and never operate clippers in a wash stall or on a wet surface.

Clipper blades are made of hardened steel so that they may be ground to a sharp edge. This makes them brittle, and if dropped on a hard surface, a tooth may break off. This leaves a ridge of unclipped hair behind if the broken blade is used. Most clipper blades can be resharpened (inexpensive clippers may require replacement of blades instead), but eventually they reach a point where they will not take a sharp edge and further resharpening is impossible. Any dull blades should be resharpened as a set; replacing only one blade of a set will not work.

One set of clipper blades can probably do several body clips if the horses are clean and the blades are kept clean and lubricated, but they will wear out on one clip if the horse is dirty, the tension is improperly adjusted or blade washing is neglected. Dipping the blades frequently in Blade Wash or kerosene will reduce the buildup of hair, scurf, and grease between the blades and keep the heat down; the blades and occasionally the clipper head should be lubricated with a light clipper oil at intervals. When clippers are put away, they should be cleaned free of hair, lubricated and kept in a clipper bag or a protective box. Keep the instruction manual handy with the clippers, and read it—it can save you a lot of frustration.

Using the Clippers

There are three basic ways to use the clippers: trimming, brushing and clipping; a fourth technique is called edging.

Trimming—refers to clipping "with" the hair, gliding the blades over the surface of the hair with gentle, even pressure and clipping off only the hair that sticks up into the blades.

Brushing—a technique sometimes used in trimming, in which the clippers are turned "upside down" and the edge of the blade is brushed along the tips of the hairs. This is sometimes useful when blending a clipped or trimmed area into an unclipped area.

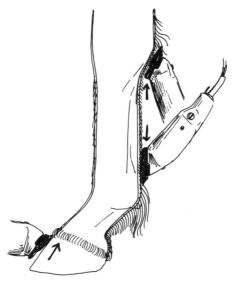

FIGURE 5 *Trimming, brushing and edging*

Clipping—running the clipper "backward," with the blades going against the hair. This shortens the hair to a uniform length, which is determined by the type of blade used. Clipping is used in body clipping and when a close, uniform cut is desired all over the area clipped.

Edging—a technique for evening up a line of hair, such as the hairline at the top of the hoof. The clipper blades are brought upward to the edge and slowly rocked upward, cutting the hair in a sharp, clean edge.

The clipper blades must be clean, sharp and properly lubricated to clip and especially when used for trimming, brushing or edging. Dull blades will not cut easily but may catch and pull out some hairs, causing discomfort to the horse. When trimming, the horse must hold very still. An assistant to hold the horse, steady his head or pick up a foot for you can be a great help.

When clipping, hold the clipper as shown in figure 6. The bulge at the back of the lower blade should glide easily over the skin with firm pressure, but you should not dig the edge of the blade into the skin or it will create welts. Keep the clippers moving directly against the direction of hair growth. Make long, slow strokes, keeping the lower blade evenly against the skin. Each stroke should overlap the last by 1/2 inch or so. When clipping over rounded surfaces, you will have to keep rotating the clippers to keep the blades flat against the skin and cut the hair evenly. On concave surfaces or loose skin,

FIGURE 6 *Clipping*

such as the skin of the throat or the flank, you may have to stretch the skin flat with your other hand in order to have a smooth surface to clip.

In clipping, the undercoat is exposed, which often makes the clipped area appear a lighter color than the surface hair. Chestnut horses appear light palomino when clipped and bays or brown are sometimes mouse-colored. Greys, roans and Appaloosas show the least visible difference between the clipped and unclipped coat color, so they are the best to learn to clip on—your mistakes won't show as much!

Introducing Your Horse to Clippers

A quiet and patient introduction to clippers can save untold time, trouble and even injuries later. Horses are naturally suspicious of any strange object that buzzes, and if they are forced to stand still while it is applied to their head, legs and body, it is no wonder that some become terrified or violently resistant. Most horses can be trained to accept clippers (and vacuum cleaners, hoses, spray bottles, etc.) if they are introduced to them patiently and quietly, and if they are neither hurt by the experience nor allowed to escape. Horses have a strong sense of association, however, and if they have learned that clippers are the signal for being hurt, being frightened or a fight, they will be on the defensive and ready for trouble at the first sign of clipping. A little extra time and patience in the beginning can make the difference between a horse that is easy to clip and trim and one that is difficult, annoying or downright dangerous.

The handler must be a good trainer, and above all he must have plenty of time and patience. Don't try to teach a horse to accept clippers when you are in a hurry to get the job done, or if you are already cross and impatient. It takes a handler who is calm, confident, sensitive to the horse's feelings and reactions and relaxed about the whole business to convey the same attitude to the horse. Anyone who helps you must also have the same attitude—a nervous or impatient helper is no help at all.

The first step in teaching the horse to accept clippers is to teach him to lower his head, calmly and confidently, at the request of his handler. This can be taught with a halter and chain lead shank (the shank is passed through the side ring of the halter, over the nose and out the other side ring and snapped to the top ring on the far side.) The shank is *not* used to "shank the horse down" or punish him, but to make a light, clear, insistent signal on his nose; it must be instantly relaxed whenever the horse makes the slightest move to lower his head. When the horse will lower his head, gently rub the top of his head and the base of his ears, partly as a reward and partly to get him used to having these parts handled comfortably. (If he's afraid of having his ears handled, he will be twice as scared when you try to run clippers over them!) Lowering the head is important not only for the convenience of the handler in clipping, but because a lowered head goes with an attitude of relaxation, trust and acceptance in the horse. A raised head goes with fear, resistance and flight.

One of the most helpful training methods is the T.E.A.M. techniques developed by Linda Tellington-Jones. T.E.A.M. work incorporates a system of unique touches and ground work to teach horses confidence, relaxation and acceptance in handling and riding situations. While describing this method goes beyond the scope of this book, T.E.A.M. training is available through clinics, articles, videotapes and Linda Tellington-Jones's book, *The Tellington-Jones Equine Awareness Method*. It is not difficult to learn and has many helpful applications beyond training to clip.

Once your horse has learned to quietly lower his head, you can introduce him to clippers. Hold him with the halter and chain shank; do not tie him. Bring out the clippers and offer them to him to sniff. If he raises his head or backs away, ask him to lower it again and continue only when he will keep his head down. Next, rub his neck, cheek and head with the clippers (still unplugged and with the cord wrapped up) as though they were a brush or

FIGURE 6-A *Introducing clippers quietly*

currycomb. If this doesn't bother him, unwrap the cord and let it dangle as you continue to rub him with the clippers. If he should tense up or try to get away, use the chain shank to ask him to lower his head and feed him a tidbit when he does so, then continue to work with the clippers until he is unconcerned.

When the clippers are accepted, it is time to let him hear them running. Plug them in and turn them on, but keep them down low at your side. (At this point, it may help to have an assistant to hold the horse.) If he becomes tense, stay where you are but do not turn off the clippers; you or your assistant should ask the horse to lower his head, reward him when he does and persist until he will stand quietly with head down while the clippers are turned on at a distance. Never rush this stage of training and do not permit the horse to get away. Don't turn the clippers off while he is resisting, or he will learn that that behavior works. Turn them off during a moment when he is standing quietly, with his head lowered.

Once the horse is unconcerned or merely interested in the running clippers, you can move closer. Move the clippers around; turn them on and off. Eventually you will come close enough to touch him. First, place your hand against his shoulder and hold the housing of the running clippers against the back of your hand. This muffles the vibration and reassures the horse. Work up his neck and down his legs, then back to his head until he has felt your hand with the clippers behind it on all the places you intend to clip. Keep asking him to lower his head if he gets tense; reward with praise, rubbing and a tidbit when he complies.

When the horse has felt the clippers through your hand, you can begin actual clipping or trimming. It often works better to trim the front legs first, then work up to the head or back to the hind legs. The assistant can remind the horse to lower his head whenever he gets tense or fidgety, and can help keep the horse still by holding up the opposite front foot while you trim the foreleg. Be careful not to jab the horse with the corner of the blades, and stop before the blades become uncomfortably hot. The blades must be sharp so that they will not pull the hair and hurt instead of clipping cleanly.

Often the training process goes better if spread out over several days or longer. Try working with the clippers a little bit each time you groom the horse, always insisting on lowering the head and finishing on a good note. Perhaps you can trim the front legs one day, the hind legs the next, then work on the head and jaw, and finally finish the bridle path and ears.

If you are body clipping, start on a less sensitive part of the body, such as the shoulder. Once the horse has become accustomed to clipping, you can proceed to more sensitive areas like the belly, flanks and head. If a horse has been trimmed on the head and legs without fuss, he will usually accept body clipping with less trouble.

HOW TO TRIM

To trim a horse, you will need electric clippers, hand clippers or a comb and a pair of sharp fetlock scissors with curved blades. Electric clippers are by far the easiest to do a good job with, but a fairly neat result can be obtained with scissors and comb and a lot of patience. Hand clippers are hard to operate and require much hand work; it is difficult to blend or taper off clipped areas, and often the blades are not sharp enough to make them worth the trouble. Don't try to trim a horse with ordinary scissors alone; first, it isn't safe—you can poke the sharp points into the horse easily if he moves or jumps—and secondly, you will have an uneven, amateurish-looking job when you finish. If you must use scissors, use a comb to lift the hair and snip it off; this will give a smoother surface and protects the horse from an accidental jab.

You will need a suitable place to work with good lighting and an electrical outlet and a way to restrain the horse. An assistant to hold the horse is very helpful, as it may not be safe to try to clip some horses while they are tied up or cross-tied. When clipping the head, a grooming halter or a halter which unsnaps at the throatlash is helpful. You will also need clipper oil, Blade Wash in a can and spray lube, plus a brush to clean the blades. The horse should be groomed and cleaned before you start to trim him, as wet, muddy or dirty hair is impossible to trim neatly. The clipper blades must be sharp or they will do a poor job.

Trimming the Legs

For trimming, use medium blades—#10 or #15.

1. Trim the excess hair from the lower legs by holding the clippers pointing down and running them down the leg, with the blades pointing in the direction of the hair growth. By pressing lightly and evenly, you will clip only the long outer hairs that stick out beyond the surface. Go over the surface of the leg several times, being careful to lift the blades gradually at the end of each stroke. Trimming this way thins the hairs and trims off the excess hair but does not change the color of the trimmed area. If you press the blades down or take them off the leg abruptly, you will leave a noticeable line on the leg.
2. Trim the fetlock by picking up the foot and running the clippers around and under the bulge of the fetlock joint. The ergot (a small, horny growth at the back of the fetlock, similar to the dew claw of a dog) may have to be snipped off close to the skin with scissors to allow you to trim the fetlock hair closely. Trim downward and backward, in the direction of the hair growth.

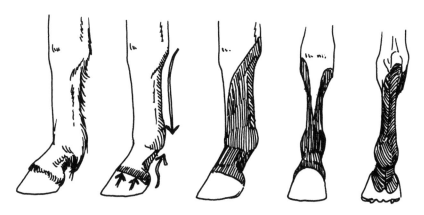

FIGURE 7 Front Leg: *trimming and booting up*

3. Reverse the clippers and trim the edge of the hair at the coronary band by clipping upward, making an even edge all around the foot.

4. If the horse has long hair or "feathers" at the back of the knee or hock, trim this by running the clippers downward, in the direction of hair growth. Blend carefully!

Booting Up the Legs

"Booting up" means clipping the hair of the legs closely, clipping against the hair growth instead of trimming by running the blades over the legs and downward. This makes the hair shorter and gives the legs a finer appearance, but may change the color of the hair by exposing the undercoat, sometimes resulting in a raw, "scalped" appearance. White legs are often booted up to shorten the hair so that it will not pick up ring dust. The clipped area must be carefully blended at the top, following the contours of the lower edge of the knee or hock and leaving a **V** down the front of the cannon bone. When booting up, fairly coarse blades (equivalent to body-clipping blades) should be used, such as #10. Too fine blades will leave "clipper stripes" where the skin shows through and will leave the legs looking as though they have been shaved for surgery instead of trimmed for show!

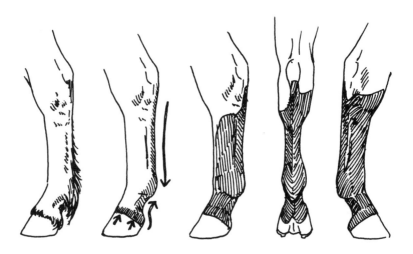

FIGURE 8 Rear Leg: *trimming and booting up*

FIGURE 9 *Untrimmed head*

Trimming the Head

You will need #10 blades for general clipping; #15 for finer clipping and #40 (surgical blade) if you want super-sharp trimming of the ears.

1. With the #10 blades, trim the hair from the sides and underside of the lower jaw. Work in the direction of the hair growth, with the blades held in the "trimming" position. You may also hold the blades in the "brushing"

FIGURE 10 *Trimming the face*
- A. *Basic face trim—ears, muzzle, jaw, around eyes*
- B. *Full face trim—ears, jaw, throttle, muzzle, around eyes. Face is clipped to edges of inverted* **V** *of forehead*

FIGURE 11 *Details of trimming the face*
A. *Close clipping under jawbones*
B. *Trimming and blending around eyes and outside ears to edge of bone*
C. *Trimming down a bushy forelock*

position (see diagram) to trim hair around the tendons and indentations of the lower face and jaw. Turn the blades around into the "clipping" position and clip closely along the bottom edge and between the bones of the lower jaw, clipping upward, against the direction of hair growth.

2. If you plan to clip the muzzle hairs, use the #10 blades to trim them off close to the skin. Check the muzzle from all angles to see if you have left any hairs untrimmed. The muzzle hairs can be clipped even closer by switching to #40 blades, or by finishing with a Flicker safety razor. Be careful not to clip the fine hair of the muzzle as you clip the whiskers—it will leave noticeable lines and marks if you do.

3. To clip the ears, hold the ear in one hand and clip along the outer edges. You will have to clip downward on the upper part of the ear and upward along the lower curve of the ear. Do not clip the tips of the ear; leave a natural point. The inner ear hair can be clipped off even with the edges of the ear to give it a neater appearance without removing the inner ear hair. The #40 blades give the sharpest line.

4. If you plan to clip the inside of the ear clean, first place a large piece of cotton in the ear to deaden the noise of the clippers and to keep hair from falling down inside the ear. Use the #40 blades to cut the hair down to the skin. Brush the inside of the ear clean before removing the cotton.

  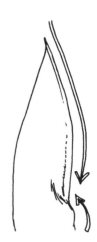

FIGURE 12 *Trimming the ears*

5. Clip the bridle path by clipping forward, from the starting point of the bridle path, to just behind the bump of the poll. The basic bridle path is no more than 1 inch. Clipping forward helps prevent the bridle path from getting longer each time it is trimmed, as might happen if you clip back toward the mane. The #40 blades give the closest, neatest trim.

6. If you plan to clip the face, put in the #10 blades (finer blades will remove too much hair, giving the face a bald, scalped appearance). Clipping against the direction of hair growth, clip the sides of the muzzle and lower face up to the edge of the cheekbone. Do not clip the cheek or jowl, or it will change the color of the hair too obviously. Blend the clipping upward as you approach the edge of the nasal bone. A more extensive facial clip involves clipping the face up to the inverted **V** formed by the frontal bones and the muscles of the forehead, and up to the eyelids. The skin above the eye may be trimmed or clipped closely, but careful blending is essential. The clipping must be smooth and even, without lines of longer hair or scalped places or it will look worse than not trimming the face at all. When clipping near the eye, put your thumb over the eye, gently holding it closed. This protects the eyeball from the clippers and stretches the skin so it is smoother and easier to clip. The #15 blades can be used to clip the area around the eyes and down to the cheekbones, but the clipping must be very smooth and even. This makes the skin appear darker and the horse's eyes appear larger. *Never* clip the eyelashes or the hair inside the nostrils!

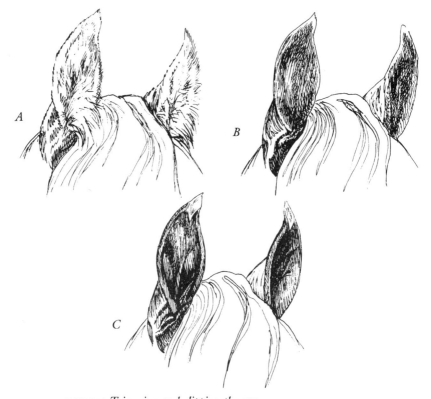

FIGURE 13 *Trimming and clipping the ears*
    A. *Untrimmed ears*
    B. *Edges trimmed and hair trimmed level with edges*
    C. *Clipped clean, leaving diamonds at tips*

The Full Head Clip

The full head clip is used for halter classes when it is not feasible to body-clip the whole horse but the head and neck must appear at their finest. It is useful when showing foals or weanlings who may be fuzzy-coated, or when a horse in winter coat needs to have its head and neck shown off to best advantage.

The full head clip starts as in clipping the face above, but the entire front of the face is clipped and the sides of the jaw and cheeks. The clipping is extended up to the ears, including the outside of the ears, and across the forehead to the foretop. The clipping is extended a short distance down the front of the neck (usually less than half the length of the underside of the neck), and a V is made by clipping along the jugular groove and up to the back

FIGURE 14 *Full head clip*

of the jaw. A longer **V** can be extended as far down as the chest and the full length of the jugular groove; this shows off the underline of the neck. Sometimes this clip is combined with a low trace clip, strip clip or other modified body clip.

CLIPPING THE DIFFICULT HORSE

Some horses have not had the benefit of a quiet, patient introduction to clippers and have already made up their minds that they want nothing to do with the procedure. These horses can often be improved by going through the procedure for introducing a green horse to clippers, but they have built-in responses of fear and resistance. Sometimes you will have to apply a restraint in order to protect yourself, your helper and the horse and to get the job done.

One of the easier restraints to apply is holding up a front foot. This helps to keep the horse from restlessly picking up the leg you are clipping every time the clippers touch it. To hold up a front foot, pick up the foot normally and then take a toe hold. Pass the palm of your hand over the sole of the foot, with your fingers gripping the toe. In this position, if the horse leans on you or tries to take his foot away, you can flex his ankle a bit more and move with him; if you have to let him go, you can safely get out of his way.

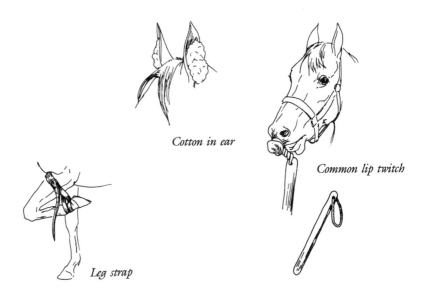

Cotton in ear

Common lip twitch

Leg strap

FIGURE 15 *Restraints for clipping*

A front leg strap is useful when you have no assistant to hold a front leg or if the leg must be held up for a longer period of time. An English stirrup leather works well; it is passed around the pastern, crossed and buckled around the forearm. When using a front leg strap, be sure that the horse is on level and secure footing and give him time to adjust to balancing on three legs so that he does not struggle and perhaps fall.

The most commonly used restraint for clipping is the lip twitch. It was long thought that a twitch quieted a horse by distracting it from clipping or veterinary procedures by focusing its attention on pain in its lip. It has recently been discovered that horses release endorphins (the body's natural painkillers) into the bloodstream when a twitch is properly applied, so the calming effect may have more to do with the body's chemistry than the threat of pain. Most horses become calm when a twitch is applied; there are some that become tense, agitated or even violent, so it should be applied with judgment and care. Certainly it is better to apply a twitch humanely than to have a horse jump and get hurt by the clippers.

A lip twitch should have a long handle, so that the operator can stay out of reach of the front legs. The loop of chain (or better yet, rope) is placed over the upper lip and tightened by twisting the handle toward the lip. So-called humane twitches are made like a pair of aluminum tongs—these are squeezed on the lip and then snapped to the halter. A safe "one-man" twitch

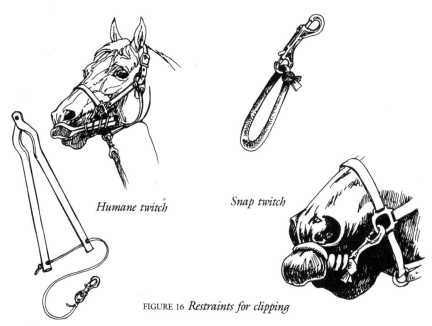

Humane twitch   Snap twitch

FIGURE 16 *Restraints for clipping*

can be made by snapping a large double-end snap into a 6-inch loop of light, soft rope. The rope loop is tightened around the lip by twisting the snap, which can then be snapped to the side ring of the halter.

If you must use a twitch, apply it quietly, remove it as soon as possible, and rub the horse's lip after removing it so that he does not learn that every time you handle his muzzle you put a twitch on it! *Never* apply a twitch to any part of the horse except the upper lip. Besides being brutally painful, using a twitch on an ear or elsewhere can cause permanent injuries.

Many horses are easier to clip if a generous wad of cotton is stuffed gently into each ear. This helps deaden the noise of the clippers and also prevents hair from falling down into the ears when clipping that area. A handler can take a firm hold on the base of the ear, squeezing it shut to deaden the noise and steady the head but *not* twisting it or hurting it. A hand cupped over the eye may also help when clipping near that area, and protects the eye from being bumped by the clippers if the horse should toss his head.

If, despite your best efforts and patience, a horse will not stand for clippers with a simple restraint humanely applied, it is a better idea to tranquilize him than to look for a more potent restraint. Tranquilizers are best administered by your veterinarian, who can give the correct dose safely and so that it acts quickly. It is not "chickening out" on training to use a tranquilizer to clip a difficult horse; it saves him and you stress, trouble and perhaps a bad experience, and he may in time become easier to clip. Be sure that if you use a tranquilizer to clip, you do so well in advance of any show you plan to compete in—if the drug remains in his system and he is drug tested with a positive result, you could be severely penalized. It is safest to allow at least five days between the use of a tranquilizer and competing in a show.

BODY CLIPPING

Although the horse's long natural coat serves him well when he lives a natural outdoor life, it can be a handicap to a hard-working horse and a problem for his groom. The long winter coat is designed for warmth and insulation, not cooling; when a horse works hard, his long hair becomes soaked with sweat and is heavy, clammy and uncomfortable. The wet coat quickly conducts heat away from the body in cold weather, exposing the horse to chills and perhaps pneumonia and may take hours to dry. In warmer weather, the sweat mixes with the extra scurf of the long coat to produce a thick, gummy lather that does not dry rapidly or cool the body efficiently, so the horse tires more quickly and is in danger of overheating. The heavy winter coat is difficult to groom, as the body brush does not penetrate thick winter hair well, and the dandy brush only brings more scurf and dandruff to the surface. If your horse sweats excessively in ordinary work and remains wet long after he has cooled out, he might be better off with some type of body clip.

Clipping shortens the coat to a bit below its summer length. It permits quicker evaporation of sweat, more rapid drying and easier grooming, besides making the horse more comfortable while working and improving his appearance. While clipping will save some time and effort in grooming, it will require that you keep the horse blanketed according to the temperature, and clipping sometimes temporarily changes the coat color.

If you use your horse for fast work during the winter (such as foxhunting), if you regularly ride him in an indoor arena and work him hard or if you follow the show circuit during the winter, you will very likely need to clip your horse. Horses that move from a cool climate to a warm one, and sometimes event horses or endurance horses may even be clipped during the summer, as clipping makes it easier for a horse to radiate away excess heat and can improve his performance or his ability to acclimatize to hotter weather. Older horses sometimes shed out very late or may even retain a coarse, winterlike coat throughout the year; they may suffer in hot weather but never shed out sufficiently to be comfortable. During the spring and

Full body clip   *Hunter clip with stockings and saddle patch*

Trace clip   *High trace clip or racing clip*

Blanket clip

Strip clip

FIGURE 17 *Types of clips*

fall, many riders are quite active, but the horse that is shedding out too slowly or growing his winter coat may be overheating on warm days and taking much too long to dry. If you are an instructor who must see that six lesson horses are properly cooled out and put away after each lesson, you will be grateful for the benefits of clipping.

Body clips range from the *full clip* or all-over body clip usually done on show horses to partial clips that leave the horse with much of his natural cold-weather protection but shorten the coat over the places that sweat the most. A *hunter clip* is used on field hunters, pleasure horses and event horses that must work outdoors over rough country. The body and head are clipped, but the long hair is left on the legs and on a "saddle patch" in the shape of the saddle, which protects the skin of the back. A *trace clip* is a partial clip that covers the bottom of the belly and the chest up to a line at about the height of the traces of a carriage, which was popular in the days of harness horses. A trace clip may be extended to include part or all of the head and neck, or along the lower edge of the hindquarters. A *high trace clip* includes at least part of the neck and shoulder, and brings the line of the clip higher up on the belly, with a "keyhole" running up into the flank and hindquarters. A *blanket clip* removes the long hair from the neck, chest and belly and sometimes the legs, leaving a neatly squared-off "blanket" of long hair that protects the muscles of the back and loins. Finally, a *strip clip* is the most conservative; only a strip of the underside of the neck, chest and belly are clipped, leaving the horse with almost all his winter coat, but allowing him to cool faster. The main benefits of the strip clip, trace clip and other partial clips are that the horse has most of the protection of his winter coat and may not always need to be blanketed, but he does not get as hot and dries more quickly than if left unclipped. The long hair over the loins also protects the back and hindquarter muscles from chilling when the horse is worked outdoors at slow gaits, and the long hair left on the legs helps them withstand mud, brush and thorns. Horses that are given a high trace clip or blanket clip will probably need to be blanketed, and those that are hunter clipped or given a full body clip will need the most blanketing and care.

If you plan to body-clip your horse, you will need at least one warm winter blanket, a sturdy sheet, a cooler or walking cover and probably a turnout rug with leg straps. A trace-clipped horse can sometimes go without blanketing, but may need a sheet or a light blanket if the weather turns extremely cold. A horse with a strip clip will probably not need any blanketing, but an anti-sweat sheet is useful in reducing the time it takes for an unclipped or partially clipped horse to dry after work.

For best appearance, and so that you will not have to repeat the clip again too soon, it is best to wait until the horse's winter coat is well established and the summer coat is shed. If you clip a bit early (which may be more convenient for fall competitions or because the horse is overheating during early fall weather), you may need to clip a second time after the coat finishes growing. In the spring, the last clip should be done before the horse begins to shed much, or you will clip the ends of the ingrowing summer coat and it will not be as rich and glossy a color. A full clip will usually grow out completely in about three months, although this varies from horse to horse and according to the climate.

To body-clip your horse, you will need large, heavy-duty body clippers with newly sharpened blades, a can of Blade Wash or kerosene, clipper oil for lubrication, and Spray Lube to cool the blades. A drop light on a long cord is helpful, and you will want to clip in a well-lighted area with a grounded electrical outlet—not in a wash stall or on a wet surface! Wear old clothes and a cap or bandanna to cover your hair; coveralls with a slick surface that will not pick up the loose hair are a great help. Have a sheet or blanket handy to cover the horse while you work, and do not clip on an especially bitter-cold day. The horse should be as clean as possible; if weather or heated facilities permit, he should be given a bath, or if not, thoroughly groomed, vacuumed if possible, and cleaned with a hot towel all over. Of course, he must also be thoroughly dry.

A novice should learn to clip on a patient, quiet horse that is unconcerned about clippers. (A grey or Appaloosa is ideal, as these colors won't show any mistakes as much as a bay or chestnut.) If possible, have someone experienced to help you.

If you are planning to do a trace clip, hunter clip or any of the partial clips, the edges of the clipped area must be marked out first. Even if you plan to do a full clip, it is wise to start with a trace clip, extend it to a hunter clip and then finish by clipping off the rest of the legs, etc. This way, if the clippers should break down or you encounter problems, you will still be left with an acceptable clip. To mark out an area, you can use a felt pen (watercolor, not permanent ink!), but masking tape is easier and does not leave marks on the hair after it is removed. Use strips of masking tape to mark the edges of the stockings (the long hair left on the legs), the border of a trace clip or a strip clip. For a hunter clip, place your saddle on the horse's back and use masking tape to mark around it; this will make sure that your saddle patch is properly placed and conforms to the shape of your saddle. When you clip, make the saddle patch a couple of inches smaller than the actual outline of the saddle;

FIGURE 18 *Taping out a clip*

this way it will not show when the horse is saddled. Use the tape to outline an inverted **V** at the top of the dock. Before clipping around the hindquarters, you may want to tie up the horse's tail and cover it with a tail bandage, so that it will not accidentally be switched into the path of the clippers and spoil its looks.

When you actually start to clip, begin on a less sensitive area like the shoulder. Turn the clippers on and draw the machine backward down the shoulder several times to get the horse used to the vibration. Once he accepts it, you can begin to clip. Keep the bottom blade pressed evenly and lightly against the horse's skin, so that the hair is cut closely; use the same pressure for every stroke, or you will leave some areas of longer hair. Don't dig the edge or corner of the blade into the horse's skin—this is uncomfortable and will raise a welt, although the moving blades will not reach his skin. Make long, fairly slow and steady strokes, overlapping each stroke by about an inch. The clippers must always work directly against the direction the hair grows—you will have to turn the clippers to follow the swirls and contours of the horse's body. If an area of longer hair is left, or if there is a ridge of unclipped hair, simply go over that place again until it is clipped evenly.

Stop frequently to dip the blades into the can of Blade Wash or kerosene (*don't* dip the motor!). Run the clippers for a moment to allow the hair and

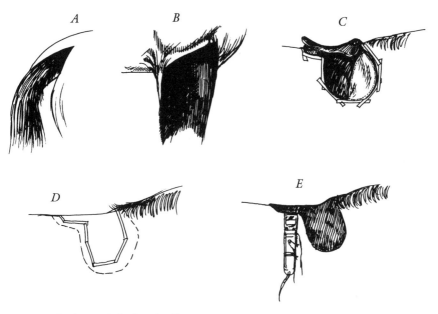

FIGURE 19 *Taping and clipping details*
   A. *Inverted* V *at top of tail*
   B. *Top of stocking follows line of arm muscle but drops down below elbow at back*
   C. *Saddle patch—tape around saddle*
   D. *Make saddle patch smaller than saddle*
   E. *Finish by edging with clippers*

Blade Wash to drip away, then turn them off and wipe them dry with a rag. An occasional spraying of the blades with Spray Lube will help to keep them cooler and lubricated. A high-pitched, laboring noise indicates that the blades are becoming clogged with hair and debris and need cleaning. Keep the air intake screen free from hair as you work, or the motor may begin to run hot. If the blades do not cut efficiently, try tightening the tension a quarter turn at a time until you find the tension at which they produce a clean cut. New blades do not need too much tension, but the tension screw will need to be tightened as they wear down. Overtightening the tension will cause the blades to heat up and wear down quicker. When the blades will no longer produce a clean cut even with the tension at its tightest, they are too dull to clip and need resharpening. Newly sharpened or new blades should go through about three body clips if the horses are clean—one dirty horse will wear out a set of blades!

   If the clippers suddenly stop cutting well, a wad of hair may have become

FIGURE 20 *Direction of hair growth*

stuck between the blades. Unplug the clippers, clean the blades and, using a heavy screwdriver, remove the bottom blade. If you discover a wad of hair, remove it and wipe the blades clean, then replace the bottom blade exactly as it was. Usually this will solve the problem quickly.

If you notice that the blades are beginning to heat up, stop clipping, clean them and put the machine aside for a while before continuing. Hot blades are uncomfortable for the horse and do not cut efficiently. Besides, both you and the horse may be glad of a rest.

The most efficient way to clip is to work in sections, usually from back to front. Clip each section completely, brush it off with a body brush and then use the drop light to check your work. If you see "railroad tracks"—ridges of longer hair left by uneven pressure or careless overlapping of strokes—or patches of longer hair, simply go over them again, carefully working against the lay of the hair, until they are as closely and evenly clipped as the rest of the area. By clipping each part thoroughly, you will avoid discovering mistakes and missed spots later after you have finished.

When clipping the head, much patience and care is needed. If you have small animal clippers available with #10 blades, you may find it much easier to manipulate these around the planes and hollows of the face. *Never* try to clip the head with ear trimmers or finer blades, however—they will leave scalped-looking spots and ugly clipper tracks which will take a long time to grow out! Clip upward along the jaw to the edge of the cheekbone and the ridge of bone that extends backward between the eye and the ear; in some cases, the clipping can end at this spot and still look presentable. Clip up to the base of the ear and the muscles of the top of the neck behind it. For an ideal clip, the face, forehead, temples and the outside of the ears should also be clipped, but be very careful not to clip into the forelock when clipping the forehead and near the ears. Putting cotton in the ears may help the horse accept clipping of his head better, but the bones of the skull transmit sound, and for some horses, the vibration and noise is a real trial. It helps to have a competent assistant to help hold the horse for you; even so, you may find it necessary to apply a twitch in order to finish the head, even on a gentle horse.

When you clip along the top of the neck, have your assistant place his arm over the mane so that it will not fall into the path of the clippers. Be very conservative about clipping too close to the mane, as any mane hairs you clip will eventually stand up like a roached mane when they grow out. When clipping the area around the tail, be careful to leave a large enough inverted V that you do not clip any of the tail hairs.

To clip the throat, have an assistant hold the horse's head as high as he can and turn it away from you. You may also have to stretch the skin with your fingers to give the clippers a taut surface to clip over.

When clipping the flank, first clip down the center of the "swirl." Then, move the clippers in an arc toward the center of the clipped area. Hold your hand behind the loose skin at the bottom of the flank and stretch it taut with your fingers.

To clip the girth area and the inside of the foreleg, have your assistant hold up the horse's foreleg by the cannon bone and stretch it well forward. This stretches the skin behind the elbow and allows you to clip the girth area. While the leg is held up, you can also clip the inside of the opposite forearm and the area directly underneath the horse's chest.

When clipping stockings, the edge of a trace clip or a saddle patch, you may mark out the edge of the area by clipping in a single slow, smooth stroke. In other areas, you may have to use the technique of "edging." The clipper blades are run slowly and carefully up to the line of tape, then kept there and carefully lifted to cut a sharp, neat edge. Each stroke is brought up to match the edge of the last. When clipping stockings, the top line of the stocking on the hind leg may be slanted, straight across or slightly rounded. On the foreleg, the edge of the stocking should follow the contour of the arm muscles.

FIGURE 21 *Tips for clipping difficult areas*

When clipping, stop frequently to give your horse a rest and a pat and brush the clipped hair away from the area you have been working on. This is the time to check your work and catch any mistakes that need reclipping. Keep the horse covered except for the part you are actually working on; he feels the loss of his winter coat keenly and can easily catch cold. Remember that a clipped horse is more vulnerable to drafts than to simply low temperatures, and treat him accordingly.

After clipping, your horse's coat will show a mousy look because any remaining dandruff and scurf is now close to the surface and visible. Fine-skinned horses sometimes show "clipper welts" caused by the edge of the machine turning up the hair, but these do not seem to cause discomfort and quickly disappear. A good grooming and a hot towel treatment will quickly clean the coat right down to the skin, or if you have a heated wash stall, you can follow up on the clip with a bath and a hot oil treatment to restore the shine and softness of the coat. Wisping and rubbing will also help to remove the excess scurf and bring up the shine in a newly clipped coat.

Six

THE FINAL TOUCHES

Whether turning out a show horse for the ring or presenting a horse for the inspection of the public or a prospective buyer, the little things can make the difference between a first-class appearance and an ordinary one. While you cannot change the horse's basic structure or make up for a complete lack of preparation, there are many small extras that can give you an advantage. In many cases, a rather ordinary looking horse can appear to be really outstanding through really good grooming and presentation. Attention to details is the hallmark of the topflight stable, showman and groom.

It should be evident that a show horse should be immaculately clean before being brought out, and should be correctly trimmed and/or braided according to his breed or type. Clipping and trimming ideally will have been done recently enough to appear clean and sharp, but long enough before the event to allow the trimmed areas to grow out enough to regain their shine and soften the newly clipped appearance. The tack should be clean, supple and shining, with metal polished and all parts correctly adjusted, and saddle pads or any washable items should be freshly laundered. The horse should be posed correctly for his breed or type when led out in hand.

COAT

The coat should be clean and well groomed, but may be enhanced with a silicone coat spray such as Showsheen. The silicone is sprayed on the clean coat after grooming, or it may be applied after a bath while the coat is still damp. Spray the coat thoroughly, allow it to dry and then brush lightly with a soft brush to lay the hair in place. Silicone should not be used beneath the saddle pad, as it can make the saddle more likely to slip. It can be applied to

Pick out and polish feet
Apply highlighter to face
Wipe off mouth and bits
Lexol tack and rider's boots

Apply fly repellent
Powder white socks
Polish coat

FIGURE 1 *Applying the final touches*

the face with a dampened rag, as most horses hate to have anything sprayed on their heads.

Fly repellent should be used, especially if the horse must stand for a Halter class or for a photo session. There are silicone coat products that contain fly repellent; these are better than the oily type, which will pick up dust.

FACE AND SKIN

The face, muzzle, eyelids, ears, and any other places that have fine hair and show the skin should be carefully cleaned with a sponge or damp towel. Highlighter applied to these areas will cause the skin to appear darker and finer, will reflect light, and will enhance the expression and refinement of the head. Highlighters are available in clear, brown or black. Only clear highlighter should be used on white face markings, but black will make the eyes appear larger and accents the contours of the face more dramatically on horses with dark skin. Brown is best on chestnuts or horses that fall between the extremes of very light and very dark.

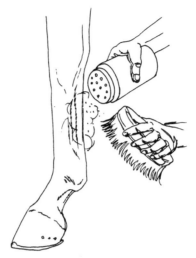

FIGURE 2 *Powdering white legs*

To apply highlighter, rub it on the face, muzzle, eyelids and ears (including inside the ears, if they have been clipped) with a rag dampened with the highlighter gel. Wait five or ten minutes for it to dry, then wipe off any excess with a clean towel. Highlighter is preferable to baby oil or Vaseline, as it does not pick up dust and dirt like oily preparations do.

The fine skin beneath the tail and under the belly should also be cleaned. The chestnuts should be cut off level with the skin and may be rubbed with highlighter or Vaseline, or darkened with foot polish if the leg around them is dark. Any cuts, scars or blemishes should be treated so as to minimize them. On dark-coated horses, a touch of gentian violet on a scrape will darken it as you treat it and will minimize the problem, but on a grey or a Palomino it would make the defect more noticeable. Don't use scarlet oil to treat a wound before a horse is shown—it looks like blood. Scars or scabs can have a very light touch of Vaseline, which helps to soften the scab and also minimizes the blemish.

STAIN REMOVAL AND WHITE MARKINGS

White markings should appear dazzling white and spotless. They should be shampooed during grooming if necessary, and carefully dried. A shampoo with a whitening agent, such as Quick Silver, helps to get whites perfectly clean. White legs or face markings are sometimes clipped closely so that the hair will pick up less ring dust and appear whiter, but this should be done far enough in advance that the hair is slightly grown out and shows no clipper tracks.

White leg and face markings can be made their whitest by dusting them with cornstarch, baby powder or French chalk just before showing. The powder is dusted onto the leg and sifted into the hair with the fingers, working against the lay of the hair. The excess is then lightly brushed off with a soft brush. Whitening sprays are also available for white legs, but use whitening agents sparingly, especially on the body. It can be embarrassing to have your horse leave his white markings all over the judge's hand!

MANE AND TAIL

The mane and tail should be neatly braided or picked out by hand until the hairs are untangled and free of dust, bedding or other debris. The roots of the mane and tail should be clean, especially on horses that are braided, as each braid exposes the skin and roots of the hair.

Arabians sometimes have a rather thin, fine tail that needs more body. The tail can be made to look fuller by braiding it into tiny pigtails or "crochet-

FIGURE 3 *Picking the tail by hand*

155

ing" small strands into figure-8-shaped loops and then treating the hair with setting gel or hair spray. The braids or crocheting is removed just before show time, and the tail hair carefully picked and separated. This has the same effect as setting human hair—it gives the tail more body, with a wavy look.

When a horse is presented with an unbraided mane, the mane should be "laid" on the correct side by brushing the roots with a damp brush. Setting gel can be used to make cowlicks or fly-away areas lie down. A mane-tamer may be applied for an hour or so before the class, with the mane wet down with setting gel to lay it flat and smooth on the desired side.

The forelock should be picked carefully and smoothed into place. Some horses look best with the forelock tucked down neatly beneath the browband; others are flattered by a free forelock.

The top of the tail should appear smooth and slimmer than the skirt. On sport horses and some western horses, a tail bandage may be applied to the dampened dock for an hour or so before showing, to lay the hairs of the dock and shape the tail. Don't forget to remove the tail bandage before the horse is shown!

FEET

Hoofs should be cleaned out just before going into the ring and hoof dressing or hoof polish may be applied. Dirt may be scrubbed from the outer hoof wall with a nail brush, but *do not* sand the feet or attack them with a wire brush. This removes the periople (the natural outer covering of the wall) and can damage the feet, causing them to crack and dry out. Another old-time method of cleaning the outer wall is to scrub it with a cut onion.

The type of hoof dressing or hoof polish used is partly a matter of convention according to breed or type, and determined partly by what looks best on the individual horse. Hoof dressings are usually oily; they give the feet a dark, uniform appearance and have long been preferred by hunter and sport horse exhibitors. One disadvantage is that the oil is quickly obscured by mud, dirt and dust; the feet must be painted anew before each class. Hoof polishes are similar to nail polish. They are painted onto the clean, dry hoof wall and allowed to dry. Hoof polishes come in clear, black and brown, and give the hoof a higher shine than oil dressings. They do not need to be renewed for each class, but may last for a day or even longer. Hoof polish is more commonly used on saddle and harness horses, Arabians, Morgans and in breed halter classes; it has often been used by western showman, but some western showmen now use oily hoof dressings instead. Appaloosas should be shown with clear hoof polish, as their striped feet are a breed characteristic and should be visible. Horses with light feet usually look best with clear polish—black polish beneath a white leg sometimes makes the hoof appear larger and gives the impression the horse is wearing galoshes! Using brown polish on the feet of a chestnut tends to minimize the size of the feet and draw attention away from them. When a horse has one white foot and one dark one, it should usually have both feet darkened. Sometimes the contrasting coloration can make the stride appear uneven. The best idea is to try both colors at home and use the one that looks the best for that individual.

After showing, hoof polish should be washed off (but avoid abrasive scrubbing). Hoof polish removers are available that make the job easier. The hoof can then be treated with a good moisturizing hoof dressing. Today's hoof polishes are formulated for use on horse's feet; they do not dry and crack the feet as did the shoe polish that was used in the past. Most drying and cracking is due to overenthusiastic scrubbing or sanding of the hoof wall in an effort to make the hoofs look cleaner.

Hoofs that have cracks or blemished places can be improved cosmetically by filling the gaps with epoxy glue or with acrylic putty. While this will not make the hoof stronger, it does present a more even appearance, and when covered with hoof polish, the crack or defect will be hidden.

QUARTER MARKS

Quarter marks are sometimes used on formally turned out hunters, sport horses or driving horses. They call attention to a well-turned croup and wide, well-muscled hindquarters, as well as pointing up the gloss of the coat. Quarter marks look especially nice under the lights in an indoor class at night.

Quarter marks should be made only on horses with especially good conformation of the croup and hindquarters, as they draw attention there. They act as artificial dapples, and are best used on solid-colored horses. In order to make quarter marks, the hair must be very clean, shiny and short. Quarter marks are usually made in a checkerboard pattern, which may be square, triangular or another simple design. The pattern should start above the point of the hip and should not extend too far back and down the side; it should make the hindquarters appear wider and fuller.

Square pattern

Hourglass pattern

Triangle pattern

Four-leaf-clover pattern

FIGURE 4 *Quarter marks for hunters and sport horses*

How to Apply Quarter Marks Using a Comb:

1. Break off a 1-inch section of fine-toothed comb.
2. Wet down the hair of the croup, using a sponge or body brush dipped in setting gel. Sponge or brush straight backward, in the direction of hair growth.
3. Starting along one side of the center line of the croup, comb downward, across the direction of hair growth, for exactly the width of the comb section to form a square. Skip a section of exactly the same width, then make another square. Continue along the line of the croup.
4. Start the next line by making squares in alternate sections along the bottom of the first line to form a checkerboard pattern.
5. The pattern should be placed in a triangular area that lies between the center line of the croup, the point of the hip and the hip joint. Don't place it too far back.

Plastic templates are available to make quarter marks with checkerboard, triangle or rounded patterns. To use a template, first wet down the hair and brush it toward the tail. Place the template firmly over the wet croup, and using a body brush or a water brush, brush straight downward across the direction of hair growth. Carefully remove the template and the design will be left on the hair.

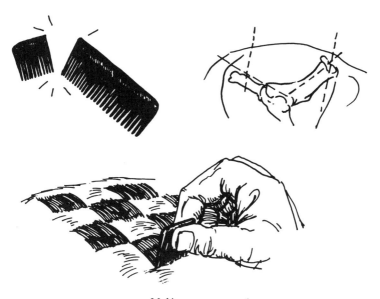

FIGURE 5 *Making quarter marks*

TACK

The bridle, saddle, girth, breastplate or martingale and the rider's boots (including the soles of the boots, as these will be visible) should be clean and shiny when the horse goes into the ring. The groom can wipe over exposed leather parts with Lexol (however, don't overdo wiping the reins, as it can make them slippery). The rider's boots should also be gone over with Lexol and a rag, and any mud wiped off the stirrup tread. If the horse's mouth is foamy, the bits should be wiped off, except in dressage competitions, where foam is a desirable sign of acceptance of the bit. Check to be sure that all parts are correctly adjusted and that all strap ends are secured by their keepers. A last-minute check should also be made of the rider's clothing and hair, and the number should be firmly secured and easily visible to the judge.

Seven

THE WESTERN SHOW HORSE

The purpose of western trimming styles is to show off the characteristic features of the western horse and to contribute to the best overall picture of horse and rider.

The old-time cowboys trimmed their horses purely for practical reasons when they trimmed them at all. The tails of working cow horses were shortened to keep them from picking up a stray piece of cactus, which could have immediate and violent consequences. The mane was roached to keep the rider's rope or fingers from getting tangled—an accident that could cost a cowboy a finger when roping. The roached or shortened mane made it easier for the reined cow horse to respond to the "rustle of the rein" along his neck. Trimming also allowed a cowboy to tell at a glance whether a horse was broken to ride or unhandled. The vaqueros of California cut a single tuft of mane at the withers to indicate a finished horse that worked "straight up in the bridle"; two tufts indicated a green horse, still working in a hackamore, and an untrimmed mane meant an unbroken horse. While few of today's western show horses ever see a cow, western tradition still influences our thinking about what looks right on a western horse.

The outstanding characteristics of the stock-type horse are full, broad and well-muscled hindquarters; a compact and powerful appearance without extreme height or legginess; clean and athletic legs and feet, and a neat, wedge-shaped head radiating intelligence and cow sense. In recent years, the conformation and type of the western show horse has evolved into a taller, slimmer, more refined and longer-legged horse than the early "bulldog" type. The roached mane and shortened tail that was traditional for the shorter, stouter horses of years past is not as flattering to the taller, more streamlined modern western show horse. In addition, many western exhibitors also show their horses in English classes such as Hunter Hack in pursuit of "All Around"

FIGURE 1 *Western horse, trimmed for show*

awards; here a roached mane or short tail looks inappropriate. Hence current styles favor a long, full tail and a shortened, pulled mane or a long natural mane with a medium-long bridle path. Roached manes are seldom seen today except on working ranch or rodeo horses.

TRIMMING

The finer points of the stock horse head can be emphasized by careful trimming. All long hair should be removed from the lower jaw, and the whiskers should be trimmed off closely. The characteristic "fox" ear of the Quarter Horse and related breeds is emphasized by closely trimming the hair of the outside edges and clipping it clean inside. For top-level halter competition, the inside hair is completely removed, sometimes by using a depilatory cream such as Nair. A tiny "diamond" is left at the inside tip of the ear, which gives it a natural sharp point. (Since this removes the horse's natural protection from flies, he must be protected with fly repellent and sometimes a scrim ear net.) Horses that grow a heavy hair coat may have their muzzle, jaw and face clipped closely, but the hair on the jowl is left natural except for trimming the lower edge. This looks best on greys, roans or Appaloosas, which show less obvious color difference where the hair is clipped. Large white markings such as a wide blaze or bald face are often clipped to make them appear whiter

FIGURE 2 *Western horse head, showing trimming*

and finer, but they should not be cut so closely that they appear pink and "scalped." The #10 clipper blade usually works best. Since clipping the muzzle and face removes much of the horse's natural sun protection, he should have sunscreen ointment applied to the white areas to prevent sunburn.

A well-trimmed bridle path sets off the head and neck of the western horse. Western bridle paths are usually longer than those of hunters, averaging about 6 to 8 inches. A large horse or one with a heavy throat looks more refined with a longer bridle path, but don't extend the bridle path too far or the mane will appear out of proportion, as if it started halfway down the neck. If the horse is to be shown in English classes as well as Western, you should compromise with a shorter bridle path—the braids should start as close to the ear as possible to give a long, smooth unbroken line of the neck. A 4- to 6-inch bridle path is more acceptable in this case.

The mane is usually pulled to a length of 3 1/2 to 6 inches. The length should complement the length and shape of the neck of the individual horse, and the type of hair should be taken into account. The mane should be long enough to lie smoothly all on one side. It will need careful pulling (as described in the chapter on mane and tail grooming) to make the mane appear even yet natural and thin enough to present a refined appearance. A very short, fine mane makes the neck appear longer and more refined; a massive neck can carry a longer mane, which would be out of proportion on a thin, slim neck. Western performance horsemen, especially those competing in reining, barrel

FIGURE 3 *Appaloosa, showing pulled mane*

racing and speed events, sometimes prefer the look of a longer mane, which accents the line of the neck when the horse is working at speed. Those who show Arabians, Morgans, Palominos and other pleasure breeds in Western classes generally adhere to the norm for these breeds, which is a long, natural tail and a full mane grown as long as nature will allow, with a 6- to 8-inch bridle path. One exception is the Peruvian Paso and the Paso Fino breeds, which are shown with full, natural manes and tails and either a very short bridle path or no bridle path at all.

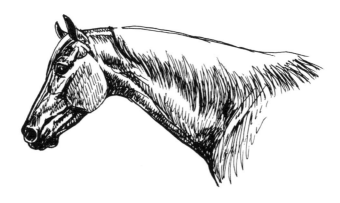

FIGURE 4 *Palomino, showing longer mane*

THE MANE, FORELOCK AND TAIL

It is traditional for a western horse's mane to fall to the left side, originally to prevent it from getting in the way of the rope, which is handled on the right. English manes usually fall to the right, which leaves the versatile horse caught in the middle! However, changing the side to which the mane falls is difficult, especially if the mane is pulled short. Where the mane naturally lies smoothly all on one side, it is often neater and easier to leave it on that side. If part of the mane crosses over or if a cowlick stands up, this part must be trained to lie down on the correct side. Few judges today take much notice of which side the mane falls on, as long as it is well pulled, neat and lies smoothly all on one side.

Some exhibitors use a butane-heated curling iron to turn the mane under on the desired side. This works well on very short manes of 3 to 4 inches, and is one way to make a wiry mane lie down neatly. The mane should be curled under and hair spray or setting gel applied to keep it flat during the class. Do not use too hot a setting or apply the iron for too long or it may damage the hair and make it brittle.

Another alternative is to "band" the mane. The hair is wet down and neatly parted into small segments about 1/2-inch wide. Each segment is combed and pulled down flat against the correct side of the neck and a rubber band is wound around it close to the roots. The band should match the color of the mane, and the banding must be done evenly and with uniformity. The bands can be applied several hours before showing, and the mane soaked with setting gel; they can be removed just before showing and the mane lightly brushed out. Banded manes have become acceptable for showing, too.

The forelock should be in proportion to the horse's head. For a fine-headed horse, the forelock should be fairly thin and not too long. A horse with a large, plain or Roman-nosed head usually looks better with a longer, fuller forelock—a very thin, short forelock emphasizes a convex profile, giving the horse the sloping-forehead look of a Neanderthal man! If a horse's forelock is excessively thick and bushy and pulling it does not solve the problem, you can carefully clip a strip of half an inch or so from each side and from underneath, leaving a reasonable amount of forelock. This clipping will have to be repeated at least once a week or it will form an unsightly stubble as it grows out. The horse must be held very still when clipping—if he tosses his head, you could remove his whole forelock!

Some exhibitors like the look of a braided forelock, especially when the horse has a fine head and a pretty face marking or small, shapely ears. The

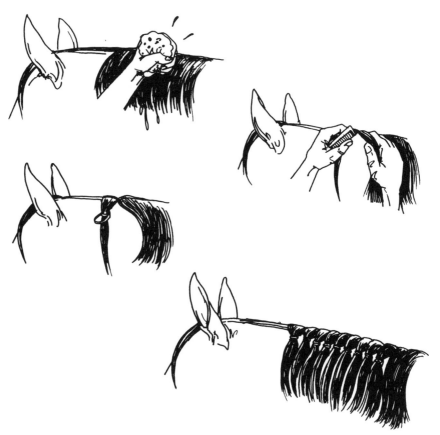

FIGURE 5 *How to band a mane*

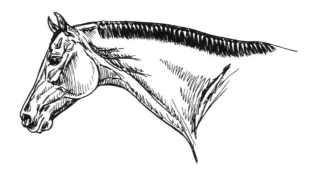

FIGURE 6 *Banded mane*

FIGURE 7 *Roached mane with forelock and wither lock*

dampened hairs are gathered into a single braided pigtail and fastened with a single rubber band of a color to match the mane. Sometimes the end is fastened with a tiny silver barrette in the shape of a concho. You should check your breed rules, however—Quarter Horse rules prohibit braiding of any kind in halter or showmanship classes.

The modern western horse is shown with a full, natural tail grown as long as possible. (Indeed, some exhibitors carry the length to such an extreme that accidents can happen, such as a horse stepping on his tail when asked to back up or a competitor stepping on his tail when working in close quarters on the rail.) The skirt of the tail should be long and full; the hair of the dock should be flat and smooth, not bushy, to emphasize the width of the hindquarters. A little careful thinning can be done along the upper dock to reduce the thickness of a bushy tail, but the hair should not be noticeably shortened. A tail wrap applied over the dampened hair of the dock for an hour or so before showing will make the hair of the dock lie flatter and trimmer. The skirt should be well picked out, clean and full. To make the skirt fuller and slightly wavy, it can be braided into several pigtails or a single braid and sprayed with hair spray or setting gel; when unbraided and carefully picked out, it will have more body and have a slight crimp or wave.

Since the long, full tail is prized today as one of the chief beauties of a western show horse, the skirt of the tail should be protected by keeping it clean, conditioned and protected by a braid, bandage or tail sack when

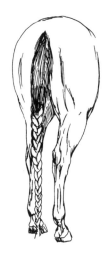

FIGURE 8 *Western horse with tail braided for protection; long tail unbraided*

the horse is not showing. Some exhibitors simply keep the skirt in a single long braid; others double up the skirt braid and bandage it, or they may use a special tail sack or tail cover that attaches to the sheet or blanket. The braid or tail cover cannot make the hair grow faster or longer, but it preserves the hairs so they do not break off or pull out as they naturally would if unprotected. Since a single tail hair can take several years to grow to ground length, it is important to take all possible measures to prevent loss and breakage of the tail hair. (For directions on tying up tails and more about tail care, see Chapter 4.)

LEGS AND FEET

The western horse should have clean, well-defined legs without an excess of hair. Chestnuts should be cut off close to the skin and smoothed with Vaseline, or darkened if the color of the leg is dark. The fetlocks and any hair at the back of the knee and lower leg should be trimmed closely, clipping with the hair so the hair is thinned and shortened evenly but no obvious clipped zone of a different color is visible. The coronary band should be trimmed evenly, and the ergot may have to be cut off close to the skin so that the fetlocks may be trimmed closely. White legs or horses that grow heavy hair on the legs may be booted up using a #10 clipper blade, but the clipping must

168

be very neat and even, without scalping, leaving clipper tracks or clipping so closely that surface scratches are visible.

The hoof wall should be cleaned with a nail brush or a vegetable brush before hoof polish or hoof dressing is applied. Horses with white feet usually look best with clear hoof dressing, as black makes the hoof look larger. Appaloosas should wear clear hoof polish, as their striped feet are a breed characteristic which should be visible to the judge. Horses with dark legs may use black, brown or clear hoof polish or a dark oil hoof dressing. Brown hoof polish may look better on a chestnut or sorrel, as it provides less contrast than black and does not make the feet appear as large. If the hoof wall has cracks or other surface defects, these can be filled in with acrylic putty; an opaque hoof polish will hide the repairs. Some western exhibitors have adopted the dark hoof oil dressing long preferred by hunter exhibitors; this type of dressing gives the foot a dark but natural-looking shine and is good for the hoof's condition, but it picks up dirt and must be repainted just before each class. Hoof polish gives a more even, opaque and glossy finish, which some feel looks artificial. It should be washed off using hoof polish remover after the show. Whatever kind of dressing is used, the hoof wall should not be sanded to clean it, as this destroys the hoof's natural outer varnish or periople and can damage the feet.

SHOW HALTERS

When showing western horses in halter or showmanship classes, a leather halter is used, usually trimmed with silver. It should fit in such a way as to follow the contours of the face and jaw and flatter the head. The throatlash is rounded and shaped to lie along the back edge of the jaw, outlining it; the cheekpieces should lie just below and parallel to the upper edge of the cheekbone. The noseband lies high on the face, within one to two finger widths of the point of the cheekbone, and it should be buckled snugly beneath the jaw without a large gap. A noseband fitted high and closely makes the head appear shorter and more wedge-shaped; a low and loose noseband gives the illusion of a longer and less refined head. The center stay (which runs from the chin ring to the throatlash) should be adjusted so that it fits closely under the jaw without hanging loose.

Show halters come in a range of sizes, widths and prices. The width of the leather and the type of decoration should flatter the individual horse. A horse with a massive, plain and solid-colored head can carry a wider, heavier and more ornate halter than a horse with a finer, smaller head or a horse with flashy markings. When the halter has been custom fitted, extra length should be cut off the ends of the straps so that they will tuck neatly into their keepers without excess length sticking out.

A western show halter typically comes with a matching leather lead shank with a chain end. The chain may be doubled through the central chin ring or may be run through the left side ring, under the chin and snapped to the right ring. If this leaves too much chain on the left side, the chain can be passed through the right side ring and run along the right cheekpiece to fasten to the upper ring. The shank should always be held by the leather portion, not by the chain, so an excessively long chain is a nuisance. A chain over the nose is usually frowned upon in showmanship classes, although it is preferable to have complete control of a rank or bully horse.

Eight

THE PLEASURE AND VERSATILITY BREEDS

Arabians, Morgans, Pintos, Palominos and grade horses and ponies often present a trimming problem because of their versatility. How does one correctly trim a horse that may be shown in halter, western pleasure, English pleasure, driving classes and perhaps in trail classes or over fences too? Owners of pleasure horse breeds such as the Arabian, Morgan and Half-Arab point to the versatility of these horses with pride. But while the owner-rider may become a quick-change artist in switching from English to western in three minutes or less, he cannot change his trimming or braiding styles as easily as he changes his tack!

THE TAIL, MANE AND FORELOCK

The answer is a basic universal trim for pleasure horses that is acceptable in both English and western classes and in breed shows and classes as well. A long, natural mane and tail, with a medium to long bridle path, is the norm for pleasure breeds, especially when shown in western and saddle seat or pleasure driving classes. It is not much help for the exhibitor who also wishes to show his horse as a hunter, for the short, pulled hunter mane is not appropriate for an Arabian Park Horse class, for example—but then, few horses are that versatile anyway! Breed association rules specify a long, unbraided mane for Arabians, Morgans and most of the pleasure breeds. While the long mane is unconventional in a hunter class, it can be braided by sewing in and doubling the braids (see Chapter 10 on hunter braiding), or the mane can be left free.

The pleasure breeds are shown with the natural mane and tail as long as they can be grown. The tail must be carried in a natural position without the

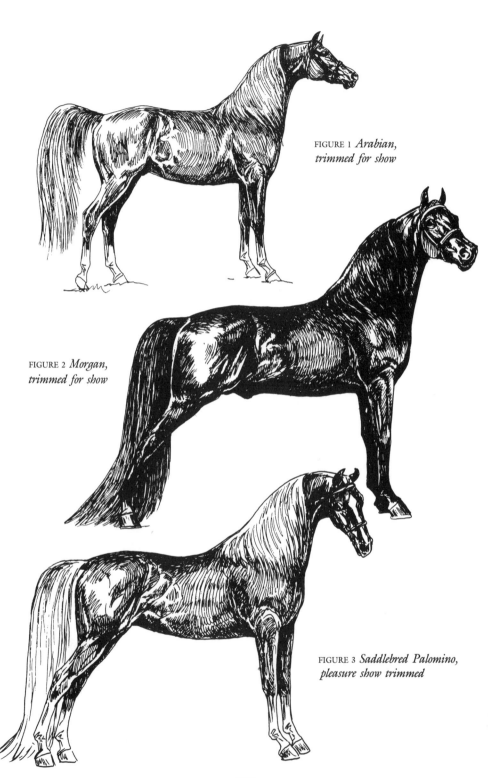

FIGURE 1 *Arabian, trimmed for show*

FIGURE 2 *Morgan, trimmed for show*

FIGURE 3 *Saddlebred Palomino, pleasure show trimmed*

help of tail sets, ginger or artificial appliances. The horse's natural tail carriage is considered as a conformation point in Arabians especially, and any interference with Nature in this area is considered an illegal and unfair practice in showing. Neither the mane nor the tail is braided when showing these breeds, except when competing in a hunter, jumper, dressage or roadster class in which braiding is customary.

The mane and forelock are grown long and should be shortened only if necessary to give the mane a graceful slope from the front of the neck to the longest point above the point of the shoulder. It then tapers back up toward the withers. The mane should all lie on the same side, usually the right. A mane that tangles easily may need to be kept in long braids to protect it (see Chapter 4 on mane and tail care). The forelock can be quite long but is sometimes thinned if it appears too thick and bushy to complement the head. Since a long forelock is usually considered beautiful in a pleasure horse, it should not be shortened. A narrow strip (about 1/2-inch wide) can be clipped closely along each side to reduce the bulk of the forelock, but this must be done very carefully to avoid clipping too much, and it must be trimmed closely every week or it will grow out into unsightly stubble.

FIGURE 4 A. *Bridle path clipped 6 to 8 inches*
B. *Longer bridle path—acceptable*
C. *Bridle path cut too far back*

The bridle path is usually medium to long. One way to measure the bridle path is to follow an imaginary line about 30 degrees back from the line of the back of the jaw. The point where this line intersects the crest is where the bridle path should begin. This will usually be no more than 6 to 8 inches from the poll on the average horse. The bridle path may be cut slightly shorter or longer to flatter the individual horse, but remember that a bridle path cut too far back breaks up the line of the crest and gives the impression that the horse is missing half his mane. The bridle path should be trimmed very closely, using #30 or #40 blades. Do not trim the hair coat next to the bridle path with such fine blades, as they will remove the hair right down to the skin!

The tail is kept as long as it will grow, and a full and slightly wavy tail is considered a beauty. The skirt of the tail should be kept shampooed and treated with conditioner to strengthen and smooth the surface of the hairs so that they do not tangle or catch on things and break off. The skirt hairs are kept in a braid or a tail sack when the horse is not showing; the braid is usually doubled up and protected with a Vetrap bandage or with a cotton tube sock that is taped to keep it in place. Before showing, the skirt may be put up in several pigtails and treated with hair spray or setting gel to make it more wavy and full when the braids are removed. The long hair of the tail and mane should be carefully hand-picked, never combed or brushed. Spraying the long hair with silicone coat spray or conditioner will make the hairs slippery and makes it easier to pick the tail clean of bedding and tangles without breaking off or pulling out hairs. (For more on care of the long mane and tail, see Chapter 4 on mane and tail grooming.)

Some horses, particularly Arabians or Half-Arabs, have very fine tails that may appear limp and stringy. The tail hair can be done up in "rings" and treated with hair spray or setting gel, much like women setting their hair. When the "rings" are picked out and the tail carefully picked free and teased a little, it gives the appearance of more fullness and body.

To Put in "Rings" for More Body in the Skirt of the Tail:
1. Part several strands of hair from the skirt of the tail and make a loose overhand knot. The "ring" you form should be about 3 inches in diameter.
2. With the long end of the hairs, make a second 3 inch ring intersecting the first. Make a third ring by passing the next ring through the second. Continue on until you reach the end of the strand.
3. The entire skirt is treated this way, making a series of rings from the dock down to the end of each strand. The smaller the rings, the more full and fluffy the skirt will be.

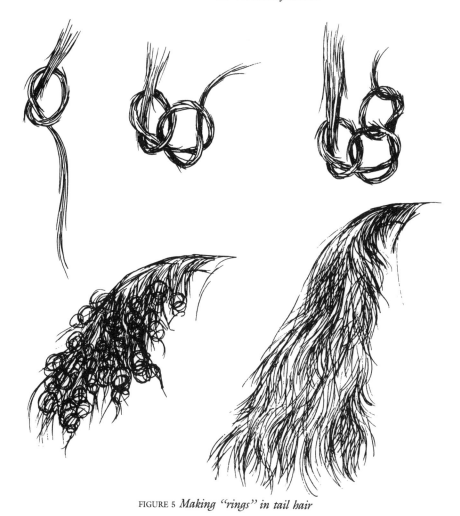

FIGURE 5 *Making "rings" in tail hair*

4. Spray the chains of rings with hair spray. Another method is to put in the rings while the hair is wet. The chains and rings may be left in for an hour or more, until the hair spray is dry.
5. Carefully undo the chains and pick out the tail. The skirt will be full and fluffy. If it is too full, spraying it with a little water will remove some of the curl.

If a horse's tail is too thick, bushy and wiry, it can be tamed by applying a conditioner and by wrapping it with a bandage (over the dampened hair) for an hour before showing.

TRIMMING AND TOUCHING UP

The pleasure breeds usually have small, refined and expressive heads. Good trimming around the head, ears and muzzle is important to emphasize the short face, chiseled head and expressive eyes and ears. The muzzle, jawline, face and eye area should be clipped closely, using # 15 blades on the fine-skinned areas around the eyes and #10 blades on the hair of the face, jaw and muzzle. The hair above and below the eyes is clipped closely to give the impression of a larger eye, but the eyelashes themselves should never be cut. The outside edges of the ears are trimmed closely, and the inside hair is removed and clipped clean. While #40 blades will give a razor-sharp line to the hair at the edges of the ear, the clipper must be handled smoothly or it will leave irregularities. The inside hair of the ears can be removed by applying a cream depilatory such as Nair, and the bare skin inside should be treated with Vaseline to protect it from flies. A small "diamond" is left at the tips of the ears to leave a sharp natural point.

The muzzle and face may be clipped closely, or if the horse has a broad blaze or other extensive white markings, they may be clipped with #10 or #15 blades to make them appear finer and whiter. The underside of the jaw and the first few inches of the throat may need to be clipped closely in order to give a clean, sharp appearance, but if clipping would show an obvious color contrast, it is better to trim with the hair instead. Keeping a jowl wrap or a hood on the horse will help to keep the hair and skin of the face fine and shiny.

The legs should also be closely trimmed, removing all long hair from the lower legs, fetlock joints and coronary band. The legs are often booted up to make them appear cleaner and more slender and to keep white markings from picking up ring dust. Booting up must be carefully blended so that it does not show a dividing line between the clipped and unclipped hair. The chestnuts are cut off close to the skin and smoothed with Vaseline or darkened with hoof polish if the leg is dark colored.

When they are shown, pleasure horses have highlighting gel applied to the fine skin of the muzzle, face, eyelids, ears and bridle path. The highlighter dries to a shiny, reflective but soft coating that makes the details of the face stand out. Clear highlighter should be used on white or light-colored hair, but brown or black can be used to emphasize the dark skin of the eyelids, muzzle and ears—this makes the eyes appear larger and the nostrils look thinner and finer. Silicone coat spray or a light oil dressing may be applied to reflect light from the body, muscles and coat. Spraying the lower legs with silicone coat spray will help them to repel dust, stains and ring dirt, keeping white markings whiter.

The hoofs should be scrubbed clean before hoof polish is applied. It has been customary for grooms to scrub the hoofs clean with steel wool, a wire brush or even sandpaper in order to make them white and even, but this practice removes the hoof's natural protective coating (the periople) and can damage the feet. A better method is to scrub the hoof clean with a nail brush or a vegetable brush. When the hoofs are clean and dry, the horse should be stood on a mat or a piece of cardboard while his hoofs are painted with hoof polish. If he stands on a dirt surface, the polish will pick up dust before it dries.

Light hoofs are usually painted with clear hoof polish, and black or brown polish is used for black or chestnut legs. Black polish under a white leg makes the hoof appear larger. However, a horse that has one white leg and one dark leg may give the impression of an uneven stride—here, it may look better to use black polish on both feet. The polish dries to a high gloss and can remain on the hoof for the duration of the show. A touch-up with extra polish or a polish enhancer gives an extra gloss before showing. After the show, the polish should be washed off with hoof polish remover.

(For more on care of the mane and tail and trimming, see Chapters 4, 5 and 6 on mane and tail, clipping and trimming and final touches before showing.)

SHOW HALTERS

The pleasure breeds, when shown in halter or in-hand classes, may be handled in a show halter, an in-hand bridle or a riding (show) bridle with a curb bit. Mature horses shown in saddle seat attire usually wear their show Weymouth bridle, fitted as for riding. The curb reins are brought over the horse's head and the horse is handled on the curb. The bradoon sliphead, including the bradoon (snaffle bit) and snaffle rein are usually removed for in-hand classes. Alternatively, the bradoon may be left in place and the snaffle rein left up over the horse's neck, resting across the withers. The horse is always posed, run out in hand and controlled with the curb reins.

A show halter usually consists of a noseband and headstall with a matching browband. A throatlash is required so that the horse cannot slip out of the halter during a class. Show halters for Morgans, Arabians, National Show Horses and the color breeds often employ colored vinyl or patent-leather browbands and nosebands with a contrasting bead around the edges, like the cavesson and browband sets popular for saddle-seat Weymouth show bridles. The chin strap is formed by a fine chain that passes from the halter ring under

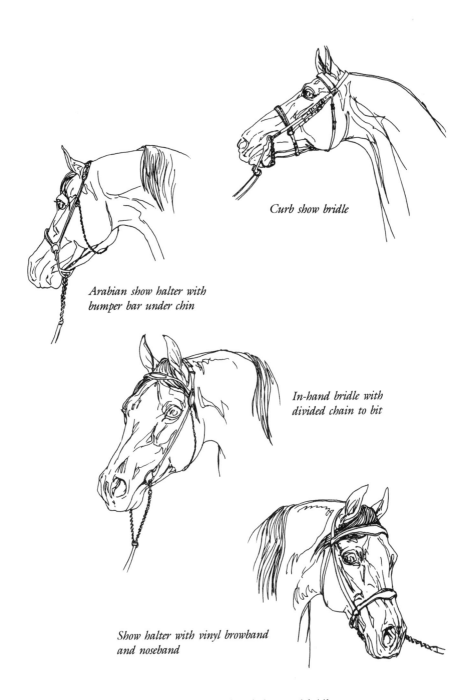

Curb show bridle

Arabian show halter with
bumper bar under chin

In-hand bridle with
divided chain to bit

Show halter with vinyl browband
and noseband

FIGURE 6 *Pleasure breed show halters and bridles*

the jaw to the far ring. A show halter should fit the lines of the horse's face, with the noseband lying high and close to the point of the cheekbone and the cheekpieces parallel to the line of the cheekbone. The browband should complement the size and shape of the head; the forelock is usually tucked back under one side of the browband. All billet ends should be confined in keepers and any excess length cut off so that it does not hang loose and distract from the clean and elegant appearance.

Arabian show halters are sometimes made ultra-fine, using a narrow but strong cable covered with leather, vinyl or a metallic finish to enhance the line of the head. A fine chain may form the throatlash, and the halter is held together by a silver or jewelled concho. The chain underneath the chin gives control and keeps the halter securely in place.

An in-hand bridle is a fine headstall with a snaffle bit. The lead shank chain is run through the bit rings, or a divided chain may be snapped to both bit rings to equalize the pressure on the mouth. An in-hand bridle usually does not have a noseband and may or may not have a browband, but a throatlash is mandatory. It is most popular on Arabians, National Show Horses and Half-Arabs.

Nine

THE SADDLEBRED, WALKING HORSE, PARADE HORSE AND OTHER SET-TAIL HORSES

The show ring saddle horse or fine harness horse exhibits the height of formality and elegance in show grooming. Even in formal hunter classes a workmanlike appearance is expected, but the saddler is all "show biz" while being shown, even using wigs, glitter and makeup! Gaited riding and fine harness driving evolved from formal riding and driving parties often held as social events in the Gay Nineties; saddle-seat attire for evening classes is patterned after the tuxedo, and ladies driving in Fine Harness classes wear long formal gowns. Tennessee Walking Horses, racking horses and parade horses are presented in a similar style, as are Shetland ponies and long-tail harness ponies. The combination of horse and rider or driver should always present an impeccably groomed, elegant, but somewhat dramatic appearance.

While any riding horse can be called a saddle horse, the term is used more specifically to refer to horses ridden in the saddle-seat style, especially the American Saddlebred. Morgans, Arabians, National Show Horses and other breeds are ridden saddle seat, but the Saddlebred is the prototype of this style. In the past, Saddlebreds were shown as three-gaited horses (which perform only the walk, trot and canter), five-gaited horses (performing the walk, trot, canter, slow gait and rack), as fine harness horses or in hand. Today they may compete in several pleasure divisions, including Country Pleasure, Show Pleasure and Western Pleasure. Saddlebreds shown as pleasure horses are required to wear a long, natural mane and natural, unset tail; they must be shod without artificially built-up feet to enhance the action. Tennessee Walking Horses have a Plantation Walking Horse division that has similar requirements. Show trim for horses showing in a pleasure division is covered in Chapter 8. In this chapter, the term "saddle horse" is used to refer to the three-gaited, five-gaited or fine-harness show horse or pony, whatever his breeding.

FIGURE 1 *Show trim for Five-Gaited, Walking Horse, Fine Harness and Shetland ponies—long mane, braided forelock and first lock of mane, set tail with long hair*

TRIMMING

Like other show horses, the saddle horse is trimmed to accentuate its special conformation points and performance style. Saddle horses are ridden in high collection, with a lofty head carriage and highly arched neck. The refinement and expressiveness of the head and the line of the neck contribute to the high "front" and showy appearance. Hence perfect trimming of the head and bridle path are very important. The characteristic high action is pointed up by clean, sharp trimming of the legs and polishing the feet. A highly arched and flowing tail balances the high head carriage, and the mane and tail may be lightened or dyed or have extra hair added to match or contrast with the color of the coat.

A medium to long bridle path of 6 to 8 inches accents the line of the crest and the shape of the ears on horses shown with a long mane (which includes all types of saddle and fine harness horses except three-gaited saddle horses). The forelock and the first lock of the mane are braided into two long, slim braids using colored braiding ribbon. Tennessee Walking Horses and parade

FIGURE 2 *Show trim for Three-Gaited Saddle Horse—roached mane and forelock, set tail with clipped dock*

horses may have fancier braids for some classes, sometimes adding bows, bangles or metallic ribbons in the braids. The three-gaited saddle horse has the mane and forelock completely roached off, which draws attention to the clean outline of the neck and head.

The trimming of the saddle horse is much the same as for the pleasure breeds; the jaw, muzzle, eyelids and ears are clipped closely, using #15 or #30 blades and carefully blending the clipped areas into the unclipped hair so there is no visible line. The ears are completely clipped inside and along the edges, leaving tiny diamond-shaped tufts at the tips to give the ears a sharper appearance. If the horse is in winter coat, the entire head and face may be closely clipped, blending into the regular coat at the back of the ears, where the tell-tale dividing line will be covered by the bridle. Another method is to clip the head and partway down the front of the throat, blending the line of the clipping along the jugular groove. This gives the horse a clean line of the jaw and throttle and makes the head more refined and expressive. If the horse's head is clipped in cool weather, he will need to wear a hood or the long hair will soon grow back in.

The legs are trimmed cleanly, with chestnuts cut off close to the skin and

FIGURE 3 *Built-up shoe and hoof with band and quarter boot*

smoothed with sandpaper. Legs may be booted up for a more refined appearance, but the clipper blades must be very sharp and a careful job done in order to avoid "stripes" or clipper tracks; #15 blades usually work well.

The hoofs of a saddle horse or fine harness horse are usually built up with weighted shoes and leather pads. Heavy shoes may be held in place by a metal band that passes across the front of the foot as well as ordinary clinches. The weight and angle of the shoes are critical to producing the horse's best action, but they can cause problems if the horse trips, stumbles or throws its legs about when playing or on uneven ground. Horses with built-up feet are usually worked in protective boots or polo bandages and may wear quarter boots to protect the inside of the coronary band from blows from the opposite foot. Roadsters and five-gaited horses work at speed with high action and are hence more vulnerable to injuries. The groom must notice any loosening of the shoe or nails or roughness of the clinches before a shoe can be cast, an accident that can break off so much wall that it is very difficult to nail the shoe back on securely. Because the sole of the foot is covered with a leather pad, it would be easy for thrush to get started in the cleft of the foot or around the frog, as it cannot be picked out and exposed to the air. To avoid this, the horseshoer usually packs the foot with a protective packing, but meticulous stall cleaning and daily attention to the feet are still necessary. For showing, the feet are usually painted with a dark hoof polish—black for black legs and brown for chestnut legs. White feet may be scrubbed clean with a nail brush and painted with a clear hoof polish, as black polish beneath a white leg makes the feet look bigger. However, if the horse has one white foot and one dark one, it may look better to darken both feet. The contrasting legs can sometimes create the illusion of an uneven stride.

MANE BRAIDING AND TRIMMING

The bridle path (or the whole mane and forelock on a three-gaited horse) should be freshly trimmed the day before a show, using #40 blades. When roaching a mane, it is easier to clip it closely using heavy-duty body clippers or #10 blades and then to finish it with #40 blades.

The forelock must be very fine and thin in order to be braided neatly. If the forelock grows thickly, it should be closely clipped in a U shape beside and below the forelock until a fine, narrow strip of forelock remains.

When a long-maned horse is to be braided, the ribbon color should be selected to match or coordinate with the color of the browband, the horse's color and the rider's outfit. A solid-color horse may be braided with two contrasting colors; a horse with a broken color or a flashy face marking may look better with solid-color braids. To braid the mane, you will need 5/8-inch-wide satin braiding ribbon and sharp scissors.

How to Braid the Mane and Forelock for Saddle and Harness Horses:
1. Cut three 2-foot lengths of braiding ribbon for each braid.
2. Wet down the hair and divide the forelock into three segments. Place the three ribbons over the forelock hairs, with about 3 inches of each ribbon protruding above the top of the hairs. An assistant places a finger over these ends, holding them securely as you begin the braid.
3. Begin to braid, incorporating one of the ribbons into each braiding strand. Roll the ribbon so that it completely encloses the hairs each time you braid.
4. After the hairs end, keep braiding until the braid is about 18 inches long. At the end of the braid, loop one ribbon end around the others and pull it through, forming a slip knot.
5. Cut the ends of the ribbons into a "swallowtail" about 1 1/2 inches long. Open out the ends to form a bow. The upper ends of the ribbon are treated in the same way.
6. The first lock of the mane (about 1/4 to 1/2 inch of hair) is treated in the same way as the forelock.

The mane should be long, free and clean. If the horse's natural mane is not long enough or is thin or uneven, a switch or wig can be added.

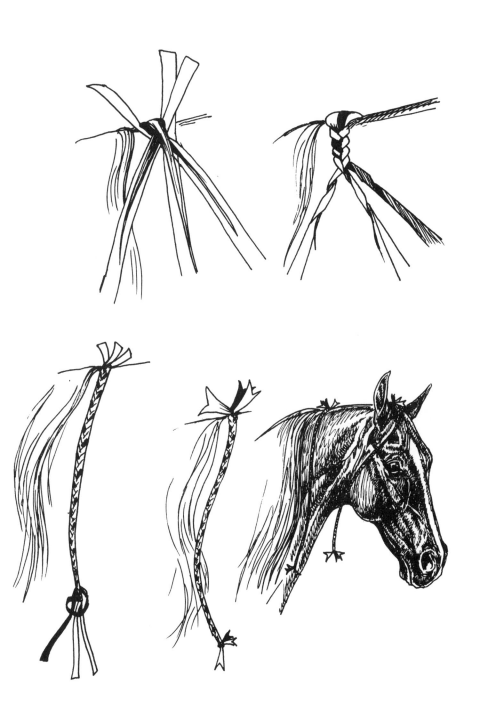

FIGURE 4 *How to braid the Saddle Horse's mane and forelock*

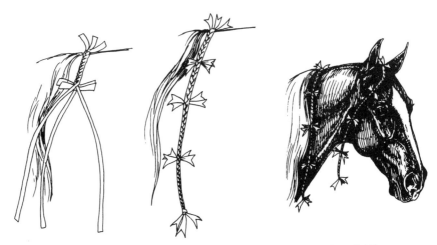

FIGURE 5 *How to add bows to braids for Walking Horses and Parade Horses*

This is applied underneath the natural mane and is usually braided into the underside of the hair to hold it in place. Chestnuts often have the mane or tail lightened to provide a dramatic contrast with the coat, and darker hair that has a dull or rusty color can be touched up with hair coloring. White manes are often treated with a rinse that whitens and removes yellowing, similar to the products used by some gray-haired people. If the hair is treated or colored, it should be treated with a conditioner and cared for like human hair. If the horse's natural mane and tail color and texture are good, you may simply spray the hair with silicone coat spray to prevent it from tangling and make it float freely. Picking the hair with a little brilliantine on the fingers will add shine to the mane. The mane should be picked carefully by hand, never combed or brushed, to avoid breaking or pulling out hairs.

The bridle path or the roached mane and forelock should be clean, shiny and free from dandruff or scurf. This can be rubbed clean with a hot towel and treated with highlighter gel or brilliantine.

If the mane is very soft and prone to become tangled or damaged, it can be kept in braids when the horse is not being shown. This gives the mane a wavy look when the braids are undone. To put the mane into protective braids, simply braid it as for show, using much larger sections of hair (about 2 to 3 inches per braid) and wide strips of cloth torn from an old bedsheet. The sheeting strips are rolled to cover the hair as in show braiding, but the braiding is somewhat looser. The braids should be undone and the mane carefully picked out every week or two when not showing.

CARING FOR THE SET-TAIL HORSE

Tail setting is a highly controversial subject. This operation and the care and trouble to horse and handlers it entails are virtually required for some breeds and types of horses, but it is heartily condemned by many people. I do not propose to debate the question of whether or not tails should be set; the fact is that if you show or groom Saddlebreds, Tennessee Walking Horses, Hackneys, Shetlands or fine harness horses or ponies, the chances are that you will have to deal with the care of a tail that has been set. (When shown in their respective pleasure divisions, these breeds are shown with natural, unset tails.) Remember that the results of nicking and tail setting are artificial at best, and that an improperly adjusted or neglected tail set can become a source of constant pain to the animal, as well as spoiling his appearance. If you cannot keep the horse clean, protected from flies and the tail set comfortably adjusted, you have no business handling a tail-set horse.

Several methods are used to obtain the desirable high tail carriage of the saddle or fine harness horse. The tail is not broken, as many people think; instead, the operation of nicking is performed. The horse's tail is anesthetized and the retractor muscles on the underside of the dock are divided or "nicked." Once the incisions heal, the horse is unable to clamp his tail down closely, but the tail will not have the desired high carriage unless the muscles are trained by keeping the tail in a supporting harness and crupper, called a tail set. The tail set is kept on all the time except when the horse is being worked or shown. In the show ring, ginger salve is usually applied to make the horse hold his tail upright for the duration of the class. If the tail set is not used for a matter of months, the tail will gradually return to a natural position, as the muscles are no longer supported by the crupper.

Another method of obtaining a high tail carriage is the use of a humane tail brace or a spoon crupper. These devices are used to support the tail in the desired position while showing and do not require nicking or tail setting. Their use is limited to horses shown with long hair at the top of the tail, which is necessary to hide the brace. A special tail brace may also be required if faulty nicking or setting has disfigured the tail by causing the horse to carry it off to one side.

Tail sets come in several styles and patterns; they generally consist of a bellyband and back pad, breast strap, and crupper with adjustable side straps to balance the tension on the tail. The tail set is usually worn over a sheet or blanket and additional padding may be necessary under the back pad for some horses. A tail tie-down net is worn over the top of the tail to keep the hair

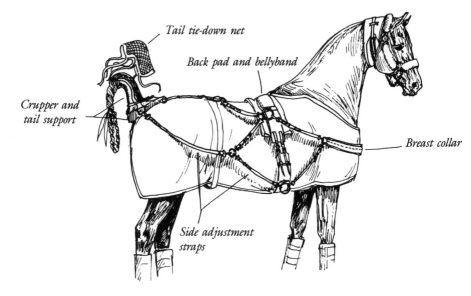

Tail tie-down net

Back pad and bellyband

Crupper and
tail support

Breast collar

Side adjustment
straps

FIGURE 6 *Tail-set*

of the dock in place, and the hair of the tail is kept up in a braid or an old nylon stocking.

When fitting the tail set, comfortable adjustment with the right amount of support is most important. The skin of the dock area must be clean and smooth; it may be treated with baby powder. The sheet, blanket or fly sheet is put on first. Next, buckle the bellyband and back pad around the horse's girth as you would when harnessing for driving. The girth must not be too tight and the back pad must not press on the withers. Next, fasten the breast strap across the chest so that it does not press against the base of the windpipe or drop down across the point of the shoulders. Slip the crupper under the tail, being careful not to leave stray hairs between the crupper and the skin of the dock. Some horses may need soft cotton padding for comfort. The crupper is attached to the back pad and the side straps are attached to crupper, back pad and bellyband, taking care to keep the tension even on both sides. The tail set should fit comfortably without any points of excessive tension or strain, but firmly enough to provide support and to prevent shifting. If adjusted too tightly, the tail set can cause painful pressure sores; if adjusted unevenly or too loosely, it may shift out of place when the horse lies down or moves around.

The tail set should be removed, cleaned and readjusted daily, with special attention to the inside surface of the crupper, girth and any other parts that touch the horse's skin. The skin of the dock should be checked daily for irritation and sponged clean and powdered before the tail set is replaced. The skirt of the tail may be kept braided in cloth strips and protected by a bandage or tail sack; it should be taken down and picked out by hand every two weeks or so when the horse is not showing. The top of the tail is protected by a tail net, which is placed over the tail and tied underneath after putting on the tail set.

When presenting the set-tail horse in the ring, an upright position of the dock with a crimp or break-over at the end of the dock is desired. This can be achieved by a tail brace or by tying the tail with a shoelace. Since there are several models of tail brace, you should follow the directions for applying the particular brace you choose; first-hand instruction from an experienced groom is essential to get the best results. Tying the tail is simpler.

To tie the tail, you will need a long shoelace or a piece of cloth tape in a color to match the tail. One piece is wrapped around the base of the dock, keeping the wraps flat and not too tight, as the root of the dock expands when the horse raises his tail. The tape is tied in a square knot and the ends are left hanging free. Another lace or tape is applied at the tip of the dock, beneath the long hairs, care being taken not to pull the tape tight enough to cut off circulation but fastening it securely. The ends of both laces are tied together and the excess cut off. The tie should be just comfortably snug when the tail is raised. It will be hidden by the hair at the top of the dock.

 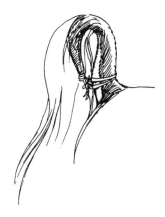

FIGURE 7 *How to tie the set tail*

FIGURE 8 *Braiding in a tail switch*

Since a set tail doubles up the dock and raises it, it tends to make the skirt look too short. To improve the appearance of length and fullness, a tail switch or wig is often used. The hair may match, blend or contrast with the color of the natural tail hair. The wig or switch is attached by braiding a shoelace, which is attached to the top of the wig, into the underside of the tail hair and tying it securely with a tail tie as described above. The natural tail hair is teased and combed over the hair of the wig. It is essential to fasten the wig securely, as nothing is more embarrassing than to have your horse suddenly lose most of his tail in the middle of a class!

On long-maned horses, such as fine harness horses and five-gaited horses, the hair at the top of the dock is left long. This covers tail ties, tail braces and the attachment of a tail wig or switch. Three-gaited horses traditionally have the first 4 to 6 inches of the dock (up to the breakover point) clipped or pulled short. The hair may be roached closely with clippers, but this should only be done on a horse that carries his tail perfectly and should not be continued too far down the dock, or it may expose any defects of tail carriage and give the look of a mule's tail. When roaching the dock, it is best to use #10 blades or heavy-duty body clippers and to trim downward, in the direction of the hairs first until the length of the hairs is reduced to an even, short length. If clipping against the hair, use coarse blades that will leave a little extra length. A "feathered" tail has the upper hairs pulled slightly shorter than the long tail, but left long enough to hide a tail brace or tail tie. This style is more flattering to the horse that needs a little extra help to keep the tail in place or that has a less than perfect breakover.

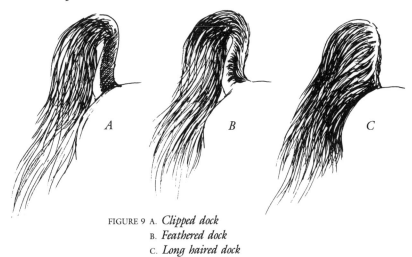

FIGURE 9 A. *Clipped dock*
B. *Feathered dock*
C. *Long haired dock*

When the horse is prepared for showing but is being warmed up or is outside the ring, the extra-long hair of the wig or switch should be loosely knotted to keep it from dragging on the ground. When the switch is removed, it can have an old nylon stocking pulled over it to keep the hairs from tangling.

PARADE HORSES

The parade horse is trimmed the same as a five-gaited saddle horse, with the mane and tail left as long and full as they will grow. A 6- to 8-inch bridle path is cut, and the forelock and first lock or two of the mane are braided with ribbon. Often metallic ribbon is used for extra emphasis, and small bows or bangles may be added to the braid every few inches. Similar braids are sometimes added to the top of the tail to fall with the long tail hair. The tail should be full, long and slightly wavy. The full and wavy effect is sometimes enhanced by braiding the skirt of the tail into many small pigtails and treating it with

FIGURE 10 *Parade horse prepared for the ring*

setting gel; when unbraided, it will be much fuller, with a wavy "crimp" that comes from setting the hair. The skirt of the tail may also be done up in "rings" (see Chapter 10) to give it more body without obvious crimping, or it may be carefully back-combed. Using a blow drier on the wet tail can give the skirt more body and fullness.

The parade horse's feet are cleaned, painted with hoof polish and sprinkled with glitter while the polish is wet. The glitter and polish is removed later by using polish remover. Glitter may also be lightly dusted over the horse's croup.

Saddle horses are usually presented in hand in a show bridle with the bradoon sliphead, snaffle bit and snaffle rein removed. They are handled on the curb rein. Young horses may be shown in a show halter, which usually has a colored vinyl or patent leather browband and noseband similar to the cavesson and browband sets found on a show bridle. The noseband of the show bridle or halter should be adjusted high up close to the cheekbone and buckled snugly. This makes the bridle or halter fit the contours of the head closely and gives the look of a shorter, more refined head.

Ten

THE SHOW HUNTER

Today's show hunter is usually a Thoroughbred or of Thoroughbred type. In the early days of hunting, Thoroughbreds were usually braided, both in the hunting field and when racing, while cold-blooded hunters had their manes hogged or roached off. Hence braiding came to denote "blood" or quality. Today braiding is used to point up and emphasize the line of the neck when the horse is presented in hand, moving on the flat or using his neck well when jumping. The lines of the Thoroughbred are long, smooth and clean, and his trimming, braiding and turnout should emphasize and reflect these qualities.

FIGURE 1 *Show hunter—formal turnout*

194

Like any quality show horse, the hunter should have all long hair trimmed from his fetlocks, lower legs, jaw, face and muzzle. Ears should be trimmed outside and the inner hair trimmed short and neat if not completely removed. It is not mandatory to braid either the mane or tail when showing hunters, but it is customary to braid at least the mane. The horse may have only the mane and forelock braided and the tail left free, but if the tail is braided, the mane and forelock must be braided also. The tail is sometimes put up in a mud knot (less formal but permissible on muddy days), a mud braid or a braided stick—a braided tail with the skirt braided and tucked up inside. The last style is more formal and sometimes is used to show off good hindquarters even when it is not muddy.

Whether the mane is braided or not, it should be pulled to a short, even length of about 3 1/2 to 4 inches, and should lie evenly on the off side of the neck. A shorter mane will produce smaller, neater braids; a slightly longer mane looks better when unbraided and is less likely to stick straight up. The mane should always be pulled by hand, never cut. This is necessary for a natural appearance when unbraided, and to provide the right length and thickness for neat braiding. The mane is always braided on the right side of the neck, regardless of which side the hair tends to fall on, so hunter grooms usually train the unbraided mane to lie on the right side. The forelock should be fairly short and thin so that it makes a neat braid that is not excessively bulky.

A hunter's bridle path should be very short—only long enough to remove the hair that lies beneath the crownpiece of the halter or bridle—about 1 inch.

FIGURE 2 *Pulled mane*

The first braid, or the edge of the mane when unbraided, should begin as close to the poll as possible and continue in an unbroken line as far back as possible. This gives the impression of a long neck and long, well-set-back withers, which go with a sloping shoulder. If the bridle path is clipped too long, it breaks up the line of the neck and gives the illusion of a shorter neck. If the mane is removed or left in an unbraided fringe at the withers, it not only makes the neck look shorter but gives the impression of high withers and a straight shoulder.

The tail is usually left as long as it will grow, or it may be banged off (cut off square at the bottom of the skirt) at the height of the pasterns. Some tails look better with a natural point (a "switch" tail), especially those that are rather thin. The hairs at the top of the dock, especially those at the edges, should not be broken off or shortened, as these will be used in braiding the tail. While it is permissible to show a hunter with a tail pulled as for a dressage horse, this is uncommon in this country and makes it impossible to braid the tail, as the braiding hairs are pulled short. This is more commonly seen on show jumpers and event horses than on show hunters, although it is an alternative to consider if the tail hairs have been so damaged that braiding is impossible.

BRAIDING THE MANE

Hunters' manes are customarily braided to display the line of the neck and to keep the mane from blowing and tangling in the reins and the rider's hands. Braiding is not mandatory—in fact, certain horses may look better with a well-pulled and unbraided mane, especially those with a large head and a thin or ewe neck. However, braiding does show that the exhibitor cares about his turnout, and good braiding can flatter good conformation or subtly play down defects. A short neck can be made to look longer by using many small braids, and an excessively long or heavy neck can be balanced by using fewer and larger braids.

The number of braids varies with the size of the horse or pony and the length and thickness of the mane, but a good average number is about thirty braids. Good mane pulling will result in a mane of even thickness, tapering slightly at the ends, which can be put up into uniformly spaced braids of about the width of a cigarette. Slightly heavier braids are acceptable if neatly done, especially on large horses. Very thin braids are harder to put in and often do not lie straight. The segments from which the hair is gathered for each braid should be about 1/2 to 1 inch and evenly spaced, which will mean that it is rare to put in fewer than twenty braids. While the traditional custom in England is to make seven to nine larger plaits, American hunter show customs call for many more and smaller braids. Purists claim that the number of braids should be odd for a stallion or gelding and even for a mare, but few judges have the time or patience to count the braids!

While the braids can be fastened with rubber bands or sewn in with thread, yarn is universally used in top-class hunter shows today. Yarn is easy to apply and tie, holds securely without breaking off hairs and is easy to remove; it is available in all colors. It is always correct to use yarn the same color as the mane; some exhibitors prefer a subtle color contrast such as dark blue or hunter green for a black mane, light blue for a gray mane, or dark brown for a light chestnut mane. Keep in mind that any color contrast draws attention to the braiding and to the neck—it must be extra neat and used only on a neck with excellent conformation. Some judges dislike contrasting yarn, considering it flashy and untraditional, especially when red, yellow, bright green or white is used. Since the object is to make a correct and classic appearance, it makes sense to be conservative.

To braid the mane, you will need a comb to part the mane, a sponge to wet it down, a braid puller or latch-hook to pull the yarn ends through, a clip to keep the unbraided hair out of the way, and scissors. A seam ripper is

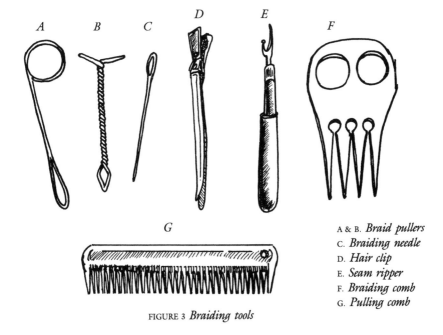

A & B. *Braid pullers*
C. *Braiding needle*
D. *Hair clip*
E. *Seam ripper*
F. *Braiding comb*
G. *Pulling comb*

FIGURE 3 *Braiding tools*

FIGURE 4 *Cutting yarn for braids*

Wet down mane

Part one-inch section

1 INCH

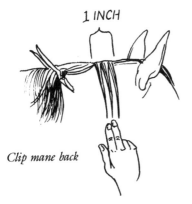

Clip mane back

Beginning to braid

FIGURE 5 *Beginning to braid*

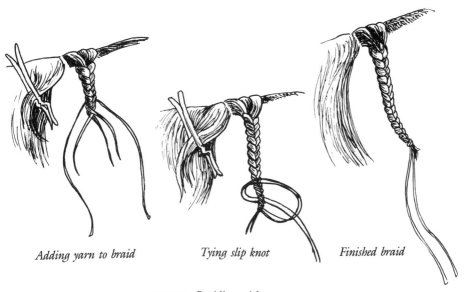

Adding yarn to braid   *Tying slip knot*   *Finished braid*

FIGURE 6 *Braiding with yarn*

necessary for taking out the braids without cutting the hair, and you will need a bucket of water and a stool to stand on. The horse should be cross-tied in a well-lighted area. It is helpful to have an apron with pockets or a small braiding kit that attaches to your belt to keep your equipment within easy reach.

To cut your yarn to the proper length, wind the yarn around your hand and elbow about twenty times. Slip the wound-up yarn off your elbow and cut it at the top and bottom. If you want longer yarn pieces, cut only once. You will need about 35 yarn pieces 12 to 16 inches long.

To Braid a Hunter Mane Using the Basic Yarn-braid Method:

1. Part a section of mane about 1/2 to 1 inch wide, using a comb to part it straight. Wet down the section with warm water.
2. Use a beauty parlor clip to keep the unparted mane out of the way.
3. Divide the section into three equal strands and begin to braid. Pull the hair across the neck and braid down from the side of the neck, keeping the braiding very tight.
4. When you have braided an inch or more, place the center of a 12- to 15-inch piece of yarn behind the braid. Add each end to one of the braiding strands and continue braiding to the end of the strand.
5. At the end of the braid, separate the tiny ends of the hairs, pinching them

tightly, from the two yarn ends. Pass the yarn ends around the braid and pull them through, creating a doubled slip knot around the end of the braid. Usually the entire mane is braided this way before pulling up and tying off the braids.

6. To pull up the braid, push the loop end of the braid puller or latch-hook down through the hair at the top of the braid, keeping it close to the skin of the neck. Double the yarn ends and push them through the loop of the braid puller, then pull them through so the end of the braid is tucked tightly under, against the edge of the crest.

There are two basic methods of tying off braids—the basic method and the "knob" method, which is preferred for dressage braiding. The basic method is quick and easy to put in and works best on a very short mane; the knob method is extra secure and works best on a mane that is slightly longer.

To Tie Off Braids Using the Quick and Easy Method:

1. Separate the yarn ends above the crest and bring them down on each side to cross beneath the braid.

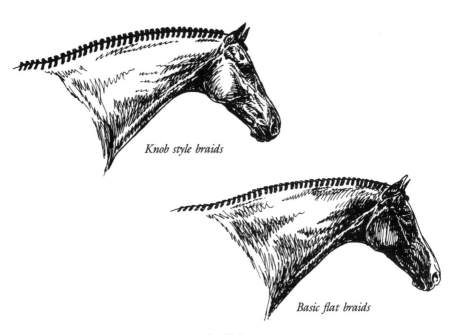

Knob style braids

Basic flat braids

FIGURE 7 *Braided mane*

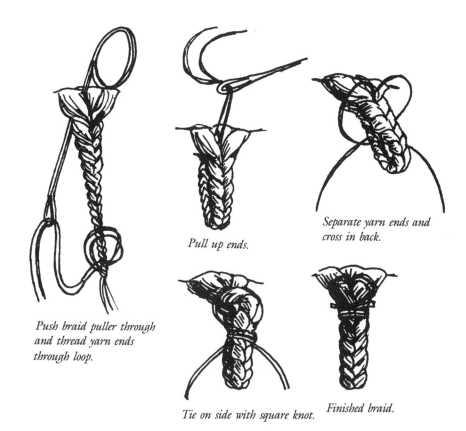

Push braid puller through
and thread yarn ends
through loop.

Pull up ends.

Separate yarn ends and
cross in back.

Tie on side with square knot.

Finished braid.

FIGURE 8 *Tying off braids—basic flat braids*

2. Bring the ends to the front of the braid and press the braid with your thumb
   to make it "turn the corner" at the crest.
3. Tie the yarn ends in a square knot about 1/2 inch down on the side of the
   braid. (If you give the first wrap of the knot an extra twist, it will form a
   "surgeon's knot," which holds more securely. The second part of the knot
   is tied as an ordinary square knot.)
4. Cut off the ends of the yarn, leaving about 1/4-inch ends to prevent the
   knot from coming untied.

To Tie Off Braids Using the "Knob" Method:
1. Separate the yarn ends above the crest and bring one down on each side
   of the braid to cross behind the braid.
2. Bring the ends to the front of the braid and press the braid upward with
   your thumb to make it turn the corner of the crest and create a knob that

sticks up about 1/4 to 1/2 inch. Cross the yarn ends below this knot, keeping the yarn tight.

3. Cross the yarn ends underneath the braid again, then tie them on top of the braid, just above the knob. Pull the ends very tight and tie them in a square knot or a surgeon's knot (see above).

4. Cut off the ends of the yarn, leaving them about 1/4 inch long.

The finished braid should always lie flat against the neck. The knobs should be uniform and should not stick up high above the crest. This method results in a line of colored yarn that is visible from both sides, so it must be very neatly tied off.

The forelock is braided whenever the mane is braided. There are two basic methods of braiding the forelock. The simplest way is to part the forelock hairs into three sections, braid to the end and pull the braid under and tie off as for a mane braid. This looks fine if the forelock is fairly short and thin. For a bushy forelock, a French braid (similar to a miniature tail braid) will contain the hair all the way down and create a neater and fancier effect. The French braid can be done in either the "outside" or "inside" style, just as in braiding a tail, but the "outside" braid looks fancier.

To Braid the Forelock with an "Outside" French Braid:

1. Divide the topmost 1/2 inch of forelock into two equal strands. Cross the right strand over the left.

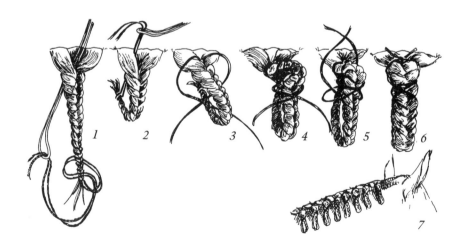

FIGURE 9 *Tying off braids—knob style braids*

2. Separate another strand on the right side below the first. Bring it into the center behind the end of the left-hand strand.

3. Bring the topmost strand (upper left strand) around behind and into the center. Part another section (about 1/4 inch or less) from the left side and add it to the strand just braided, from behind. Keep the strands tight.

4. Continue to braid by braiding the topmost strand around the back and into the center, adding an extra 1/4-inch strand from the same side each time you braid. This will result in a raised, braided ridge that gathers in the hair from the sides of the forelock.

5. When you reach the end of the forelock, divide any remaining hair among the three braiding strands and continue to braid. Place the center of a 15-inch piece of yarn behind the braid and add one end to one of the braiding strands. At the end of the hair, tie off the braid in a double slip knot as described in mane braiding.

6. Push the braid puller down underneath the French braid from the top. Double the yarn ends and push them through the loop of the braid puller, and pull the braid up until it is the same length as a mane braid. (The braid can even be pulled up inside the French braid if it is too long.) Tie off and trim the yarn ends as you would for a mane braid.

Sewn-in braids or button braids were more popular in the past and are not seen as often on show hunters today. They are more time-consuming to put up and to take out, but they are very secure and the tiny round "buttons" are flattering to some horses, especially those with a rather thick crest. Button braids are sometimes used when the rider is apt to grab the mane, as they are the most secure type of braid. They are also one way to put up a long mane (such as a Morgan's or Arabian's) into an acceptable hunter mane, although the braids will be larger than usual. This is useful for the long-maned horse that must make an occasional appearance in a hunter class, particularly a hunter class for his own breed, but which cannot have the mane pulled short enough for conventional braiding. To sew in button braids you will need heavy braiding thread (button and carpet thread will do) in a color to match the mane, and a large-eye metal or plastic needle. A yarn needle (available in knitting shops) works well, or some tack stores sell braiding needles.

To Make Sewn-in Button Braids:

1. Separate, wet and braid a section of mane to two-thirds of its length, as you would for a conventional yarn braid. Place the center of a 15-inch piece of thread behind the braid and add it in, as you would add in a piece of yarn. Tie the ends off with a double slip knot, as in using yarn.

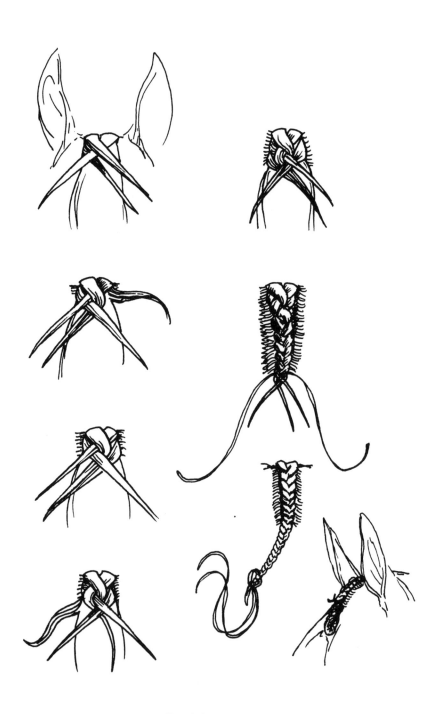

FIGURE 10 *French braiding the forelock*

2. Thread the ends of the thread through the braiding needle. This is easier to do if the ends are cut off together.
3. Use the needle to pull the braid up, stitching up through the braid at the crest of the neck.
4. Stitch back down through the braided loop, using large stitches. The thread ends should come out the end of the braided loop.
5. Turn the doubled braid under again and stitch up through, close to the crest. Bring the thread around the braid to the right and stitch up through the braid again.
6. Bring the thread around to the left and stitch up through the braid once again.
7. Unthread the needle and separate the thread ends. Cross them behind the braid and wrap them around the braid once or twice, tying them in a square knot about 1/4 inch to 1/2 inch down the braid on the side, then trim the ends short. The finished braid should be short, tight and rounded, resembling a braided button.

Another method of braiding hunter manes is the scalloped mane. This is not as common as conventional yarn braids, but is sometimes seen on

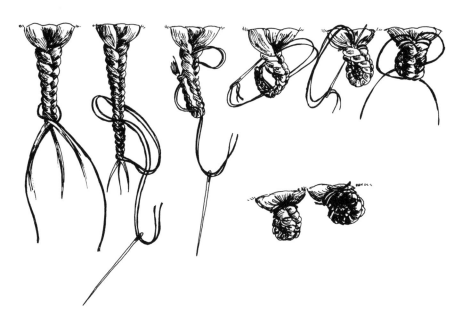

FIGURE 11 *Sewn-in button braids*

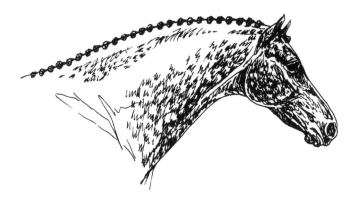

FIGURE 12 *Mane braided with button braids*

formally turned out conformation hunters in Canada as well as in the United States, and has even been used by the Olympic team. It draws attention to the line of the neck and can make a thick crest appear thicker, so it should only be used when the horse's neck conformation is particularly good. Scalloping looks especially nice when the mane contrasts with the color of the neck, and it works best with a mane that is a bit longer than usual—about 4 to 5 inches. Scalloping is acceptable in any hunter or equitation class, and can be used for jumpers or dressage horses as well.

To Make a Scalloped Mane:

1. Braid the mane into individual braids, using sections about 1 to 1 1/2 inches wide, with matching color yarn or thread braided in.
2. The first braid of the neck is passed behind the second and pulled up underneath the base of the third braid. This can be done with a braid puller or using thread and a braiding needle. The ends are separated, crossed underneath the third braid and tied in a square knot on the top, about 1/4 inch down on the side of the braid. The ends are trimmed short.
3. The next braid is passed underneath the one next to it and pulled up and tied off under the next braid. This is continued down the neck. The scallops will look best if the braid is given a slight twist so that it turns and lies flat.
4. At the end of the neck, the last braid is looped under and fastened as a regular mane braid. The last two braids are fastened underneath this braid.

Braiding with rubber bands is quicker than sewing in yarn or thread, but it is not as acceptable for high-level competition and it will break off hairs and

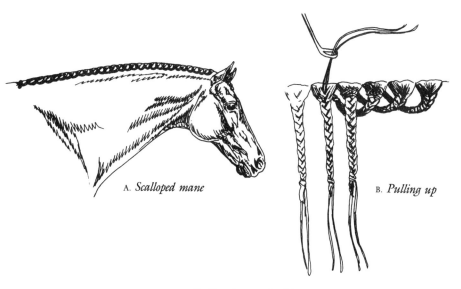

A. *Scalloped mane*   B. *Pulling up*

FIGURE 13 *Scalloped mane braids*

damage the mane. Rubber band braids should be reserved for times when it is necessary to put a mane up in a hurry, or less formal occasions. The rubber bands should always be the same-color as the mane hair. Rubber bands in black, white, gray, brown and chestnut are available in most tack stores. Because the hair is easily broken off or pulled out when using rubber bands, they should be removed by cutting the band with a seam ripper—don't try to save the bands, save the hair!

To Braid a Mane Using Rubber Bands:

1. Part and braid a section of mane about 1/2 to 1 inch wide. Braid all the way to the ends of the hairs. The mane should be wet down before braiding.
2. Fold the end of the braided strand upward, with the ends of the hairs on top, pointing up toward the neck. Fasten a rubber band around this tiny loop, wrapping it around until it is tight.
3. Turn the braid under, up against the underside of the braid and the edge of the neck. Use a second rubber band to fasten it, bringing the rubber band up higher with each twist.
4. The final twist of the rubber band is dropped down about 1/4 to 1/2 inch on the side of the braid to make it "turn the corner" and lie flat against the neck. This can create the effect of a "knob" if you push the top of the braid up a bit before starting to wrap the braid with the second rubber band.

FIGURE 14 *Rubber band braids*

Neatness is all important when braiding. If each braid is not started tightly and kept tight, it will loosen and spread out when it is fastened with a sloppy, bulging appearance. This can happen when the braider pulls out away from the neck while braiding, thinking he is keeping the braid tight. To make a tight braid, each strand must be pulled tightly against the last instead of pulling outward on the whole braid. The braids must be evenly spaced and of a uniform size. This requires good mane pulling as well as good measuring when braiding. An uneven mane or poorly divided hair sections results in uneven spacing of braids, with some braids too large and others too thin. Good tying off makes a great difference, especially if the braids are large or thick. The braids should lie down tightly against the side of the neck—if they are tied on top or fastened loosely, they will stand out as if caught in a stiff breeze and will bounce and flop with every stride. Stand up on a stool or hay bale when braiding—not only is it tiring to work upward, but this often causes the mane to be tied off improperly so the braids stick out. Don't take too much in one braid, especially if the mane is stiff and wiry, but don't make the braids so tiny that they look like little wiggly wires. If the mane is too thin, you can add yarn of a matching color right at the beginning of the braid; you can even add double yarn strands to give the braid some body. Remember that American hunters are *always* braided on the right side—a mane braided on the left is a sure sign of a greenhorn!

Ideally, the mane should be braided on the day of the show. Sometimes it is necessary to braid the night before, but the braids will not be quite as neat and bedding may get into the hair. A possible compromise is to braid the mane but not to pull the braids up or tie them off until the next morning. Professional braiders always braid the day of the show and take the braids out as soon as the horse's last class is over, as the longer a mane is braided the greater the

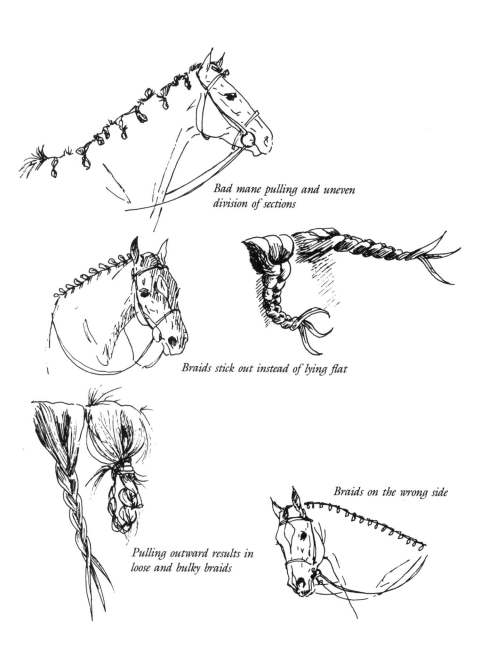

Bad mane pulling and uneven division of sections

Braids stick out instead of lying flat

Pulling outward results in loose and bulky braids

Braids on the wrong side

FIGURE 15 *Bad braiding*

risk of breaking off the braiding hairs. If even a few hairs are broken off each time the mane is braided, the horse will soon have an unsightly fringe of hairs too short to braid that sticks up above and around the braids. For this reason, professional grooms braid only when the occasion is formal enough to require it, in order to preserve the mane for the most important championship shows at the end of the season, and they never leave a mane braided overnight.

When taking braids out, it helps to wet the mane down thoroughly first. This stretches and loosens the yarn and makes the hairs uncrimp, so the horse will not have a kinky mane when the braids are removed. Use a seam ripper instead of scissors to cut out the yarn, as it is easier to cut accurately without accidentally snipping some hairs. To cut out a braid, first clip the tied portion at the side of the braid, then lift the braid up and cut the X formed by the yarn or thread where it crosses underneath. When the braid is extended, slip the blade of the seam ripper through the slip knot, cutting outward. This frees the hairs; if they are still tightly braided, the back of the seam ripper (the noncutting edge) can be used to pick the braid out until it unravels freely. Rubber-band braids are easily removed by clipping the band with a seam ripper; sewn-in thread braids require careful cutting of the thread until they can be straightened out.

BRAIDING THE TAIL

A braided tail is the final touch to a formal turnout for a show hunter. The custom originated in England, where hedges and thorn fences were common in the hunting field and tails were either cropped short or braided to keep them from picking up brush or thorn branches in the dock area. The slim, braided dock is an extension of the spine and draws attention to a horse that uses his back well over a jump or when moving on the flat, and the slender dock makes the width and muscling of the hindquarters more noticeable. Tail braiding is not required in hunter classes, but it is customary to braid the tail for formal occasions. The tail may be put up in a mud knot or mud braid, sometimes over a braided dock, to keep the skirt of the tail from becoming soiled on a wet day. Sometimes a mud knot over a braided tail or a braided "stick" (in which the skirt of the tail is braided and tucked up inside the braid) are used to emphasize the muscling of the hindquarters even when conditions are not muddy. The mane should always be braided if the tail is done.

The upper hairs of the dock should be left as long as they will grow if the tail is to be braided. Braiding breaks off and pulls out a few hairs each time,

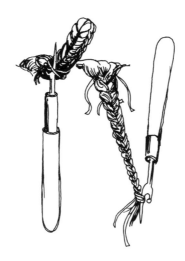

FIGURE 16 *Taking out braids with a seam ripper*

so it is preferable to braid the tail only on formal occasions that warrant it, saving the tail hairs for the most important shows at the end of the season. If a tail has had many hairs broken off short from tail rubbing, excessive braiding or other causes, it may be too short to braid neatly. Horses with brittle tail hair can have a hot oil treatment and other conditioners applied to condition and strengthen the hair, but this must be done at least a week or two before braiding, or the hair will be too slippery to hold and braid. If the hair is so short as to make braiding impossible, the tail can be pulled in the manner of a dressage horse, but this means that the hairs will be too short to braid for at least a year.

Before braiding a tail, it should be clean, as the underside of the hairs will be exposed. The tail should be shampooed a day or two before the show—if shampooed or conditioned the day you braid, the hairs will be too slippery. The tail should be brushed or hand picked out so that all the hairs are free and there are no tangles.

A hunter's tail is braided in a French braid for the full length of the dock. The three basic strands are braided down the center of the dock, with small strands added from each side of the dock each time a strand is braided. The tail is wrapped up in its own hair. This makes the center braid grow larger as the braid progresses, so the strands should be quite fine with only a few hairs added each time. Ther are two methods of making the French braid: the overbraid or "inside" braid, in which the braiding strands are passed over and into the center, with the braid on the inside, and the underbraid or "outside" braid, in which the braiding strands are braided under each other to produce a braided ridge on the outside. The over method is easier to learn, as it is more closely related to the way most people braid rope, twine or hair. Learning the under method is confusing at first for some people, but the resulting braid is more attractive and sometimes more secure.

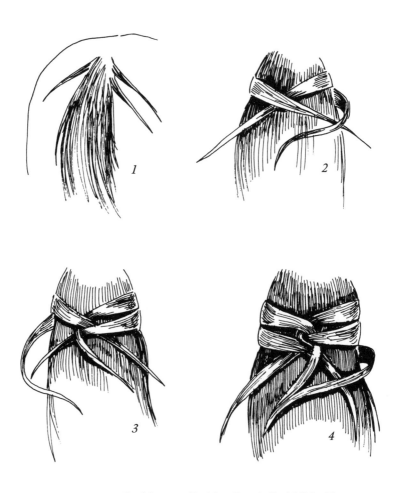

FIGURE 17 *Braiding a tail with a French "inside" braid*

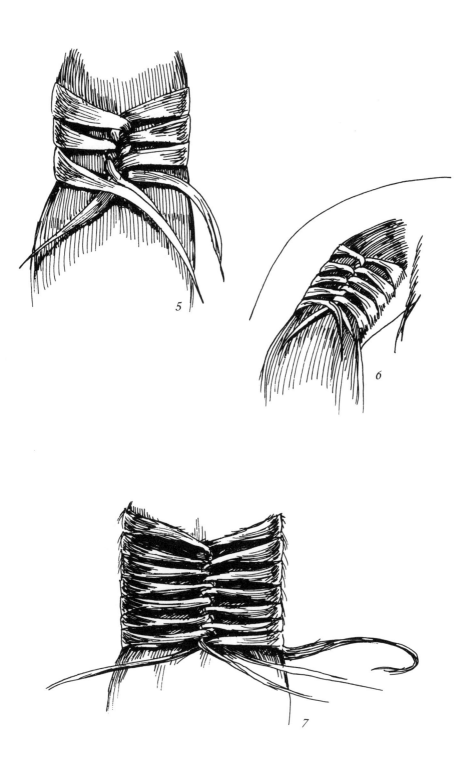

5

6

7

213

To Braid the Tail Using the "Over" Method, for an "Inside" French Braid:

1. Part one strand from the left top of the tail and two strands from the right.
2. Bring the left strand across the tail between the two right-hand strands.
3. Braid the topmost strand (the upper left strand) into the center *over* the middle of the next highest strand. Part a strand from the left (about 1/4-inch wide) and bring it *over* into the center, adding it to the strand just braided.
4. Continue braiding the topmost strand (upper right will be next) *over* and into the center, parting and adding a strand from the same side each time you braid.
5. Continue down the tail, keeping the braiding hairs pulled tightly across the tail. The strands added from the side should stay horizontal, and the tail should be tightly wrapped with an even center braid. Keep the strands you add small and thin, so that the center braid does not grow too large.
6. You are wrapping the tail in its own hair, holding the hairs together by braiding them down the center of the tail. You will begin to see the center braid, which is on the *inside* of the wrapping hairs.
7. An example of an actual-size braid. The braids are neat and tight; strands from the side are even and horizontal, about 1/4 inch wide at the edge. The center braid is inside, even and not too large.

To Braid a Tail Using the "Under" Method, for an "Outside" French Braid:

1. Part one small strand from the top left of the tail and two strands from the right.
2. Bring the left-hand strand across the tail between the two right-hand strands.
3. Begin braiding by bringing the topmost strand (upper left) into the center by passing it around *behind* the middle of the next topmost strand. Keep it pulled straight across the tail and very tight.
4. Part another small strand from the left side of the tail and *add* it to the strand just braided, passing it *behind* the middle of the next topmost strand.
5. Braid the next topmost strand (upper right will be next) by bringing it around *behind* the center of the next highest strand, and *add* a strand from the same side each time you braid. Keep the strands added from the side small (about 1/4 inch), as the center braid will grow as you work down the tail.
6. You are wrapping the tail in strands of its own hair, holding that hair by

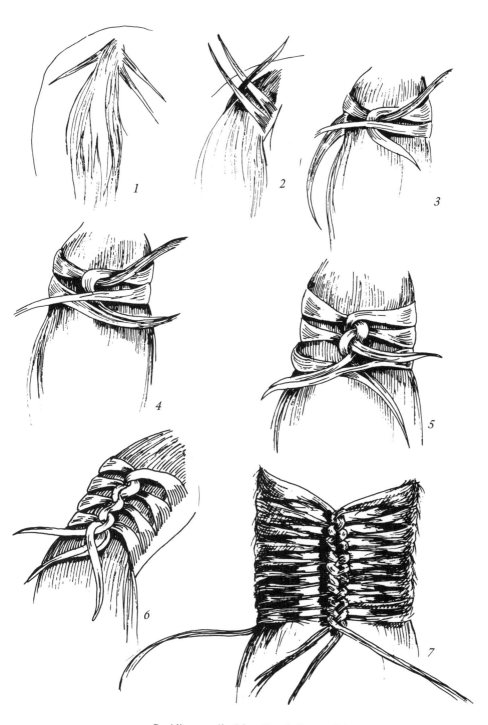

FIGURE 18 *Braiding a tail with a French "outside" braid*

braiding it down the center. Because you are twisting the hairs *under* the braid, the braided ridge is on the *outside* of the strands that wrap the tail.

7. An example of an actual-size braid. The center braid is neat and tight and should be about the width of a pencil. The strands are small (about 1/4 inch) and are pulled horizontally, not up or down at a slant, which loosens the braid.

When braiding by either method, it is fairly easy to keep the braid tight on the upper part of the dock, where the tail is bald underneath. When you reach the point where hair grows from the bottom of the tail, it becomes harder to part the hairs from the back and keep the braid tight and neat, with the wrapping strands horizontal. Be sure to keep an even tension on both sides as you braid—if you pull harder on one side than the other, the center braid will begin to slant off to one side. Remember to add a strand from the side each time you braid and to braid the strands in order—right, left, then right again—as a missed strand will throw you off your braiding. The tail should be braided all the way to the end of the dock, or you can stop an inch or two above the end of the dock, but don't braid for only a few inches at the top of the dock. Only yearlings and draft horses are shown with a partially braided dock, so you might be implying that your horse belongs in front of a cart if you only braid partway down! When you reach the end of the dock, simply stop adding strands from the side and continue braiding the central braid for 5 or 6 inches before finishing the tail off.

There are several methods of finishing the braided tail. The quick and easy method uses two rubber bands; the sewn-in pinwheel is the most formal. If you want to tuck the skirt up inside for a braided stick, it will have to be braided into two pigtails, which are then pulled up inside the French braid. If you plan to wrap the skirt up in a mud knot over the braided tail, a simple rubber-band fastening is best. Some people braid the central braid out to the end of the hairs and then sew the resulting long braid back up to the French braid; this works well when you have used the over-braiding method and the braided ridge is inside the wrapping hairs. You should not leave a long braided loop hanging below the dock, as this detracts from the neat appearance of the braid and can catch on things.

To Finish a Tail Using the <u>Quick and Easy</u> Rubber-band Method:

1. Braid out about 5 or 6 inches. Double the braided end up, with the unbraided hairs on top, pointing up toward the dock. Fasten a rubber band around the braided loop at the end.

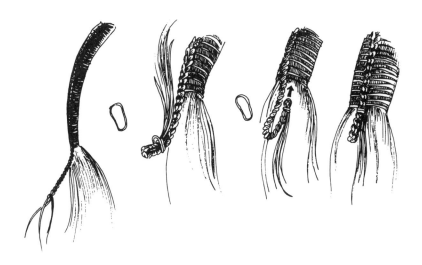

FIGURE 19 *Finishing a tail with rubber band method*

2. Turn the braid under and push it up underneath the French braid until the loop that remains is about the size of a mane braid. The unbraided part of the hair will blend with the skirt of the tail.
3. Fasten a rubber band around the small loop at the bottom of the French braid. To remove the braid, find the short unbraided hair ends and pull them; as the braid straightens out, the rubber bands will pop off.

To Finish a Tail Using the Pinwheel Method:

1. Braid the central braiding hairs out to the ends. About 2 inches from the ends, add in a 15-inch strand of braiding thread in a matching color. Tie off the end with a double slip knot and thread the ends through a large-eye needle.
2. Roll the braid back up toward the dock, keeping it very tight. At each complete turn, take a stitch through the center of the braid.
3. When the pinwheel is rolled up against the dock, take a stitch through the center of the pinwheel and through the French braid. Tie it off to the central braid and trim off the ends of the thread.

To Put Up the Skirt of the Tail in a Braided Stick:

1. Braid to the end of the dock, keeping the braid slightly looser than usual but not so loose that it will not hold the braid. At the end of the dock,

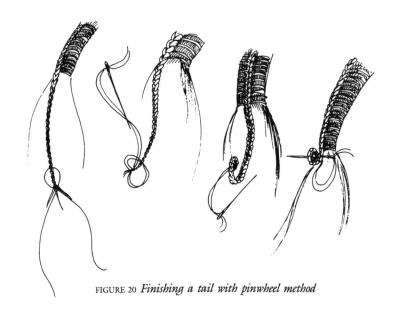

FIGURE 20 *Finishing a tail with pinwheel method*

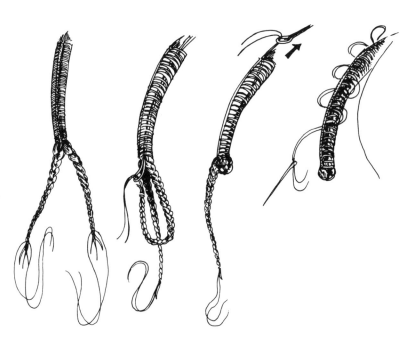

FIGURE 21 *Putting up a tail in a braided stick*

218

divide the skirt hair in two equal sections. One section is separated into three equal strands and braided along with the central braid hairs to the very end. The other section is divided into three segments and braided similarly. Each braid should have a piece of strong thread or yarn about 30 inches long, in a matching color, braided into it and used to tie off the end.

2. An extra-long braid puller is worked carefully down the length of the dock underneath the right side of the braiding strands. Thread the yarn ends through the braid puller and carefully work the braided pigtail up underneath the right side of the French braid.

3. Repeat with the left-hand braid, working it up under the French braid.

4. Thread the yarn ends into a large-eye needle. Stitch from the top down to fasten the skirt braids to the center braid, and tie off at the bottom of the dock.

A braided tail should be protected with a tail bandage until the horse is ready to show. A tail bandage can be applied over slightly dampened hair, or setting gel can be applied to the short hairs at the side of the tail to make them lie down with the braided hairs. Never wet the bandage—it may shrink into the tail and cause tissue damage. A soft cotton stockinette or "track" bandage is the safest type to use on a tail, but some professional grooms prefer an Ace bandage. If you use an Ace bandage, do not apply it at full stretch. The next-to-last wrap is lifted up and the extra roll of bandage can be tucked underneath to secure the bandage. Don't forget to take the tail bandage off before the horse goes into the ring!

A tail should not be braided until the day of the show, and should be taken down as soon as possible to avoid breaking off the braiding hairs. It is not a good idea to try to keep a tail braided overnight, even if the braid is covered by a bandage. Keep the horse protected from flies by using a scrim fly sheet and fly repellent, so that he will not need to switch his tail incessantly, which can loosen the braid. If he is wearing a tail wrap, check it for comfort from time to time—a bandage that is shrinking or wound too tight can cut off circulation in the dock in a matter of hours, leading to great discomfort if not permanent damage.

If you show on a muddy day, you may want to keep the skirt of the tail clean, especially if your horse has a light-colored tail. A mud knot keeps the skirt of the tail up out of the mud. It also keeps the horse from switching a muddy tail and covering his hindquarters, his tack and you with mud. If you are foxhunting, competing over a cross-country course or just hacking out on a wet day, you may want to put the tail up in a mud braid, which is more secure

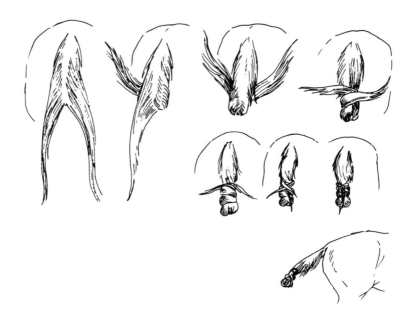

FIGURE 22 *Putting up a tail in a mud knot*

although it does not look as formal. The mud braid is derived from the method used to fasten up polo ponies' tails so that they will not spoil a player's aim by switching their tails into the mallet.

To Put the Skirt of the Tail Up in a Mud Knot:

1. Divide the hair of the skirt into two equal sections.
2. Pass the right-hand section around behind the dock.
3. Pass the left-hand section around behind the dock, crossing it over the right-hand section.
3. Give each section a twist to make it into a rope; continue wrapping each section alternately, crossing at the front and the back of the dock. Wrap up the dock until the hair is too short to go around again.
4. Separate one of the strands into two sections and pass the other single strand into the center between them. Braid the three sections very tightly to the ends and fasten with a rubber band or braid in a piece of yarn and tie off.

220

5. The small braided tab can be tucked down inside the last wrap of hair. A piece of plastic tape in a color close to that of the tail hair (black, white or brown) should be used to reinforce the mud knot, especially if it is needed to stay in for a long time.
6. To release the skirt of the tail, release and unbraid the small braid and give the dock a shake. The skirt will fall free.

To Put Up the Skirt in a Mud Braid or Polo Tail:
1. Divide the skirt into three sections.
2. Braid to the end and fasten with a rubber band.
3. Tuck the braid up under the skirt, turning the end under. Alternatively, the braid may be folded up on top of the dock.
4. Fasten the braid up with 3 to 5 pieces of plastic tape or elastic adhesive tape. Electrician's tape and plastic mending tape work well and are available in black, white or brown. Do not pull the tape so tight that it indents the skin of the dock.

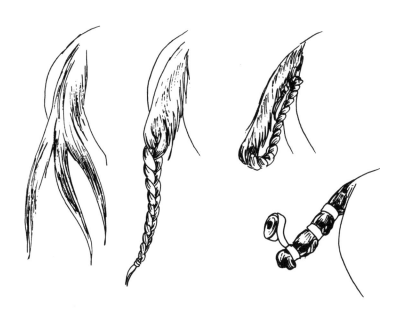

FIGURE 23 *Putting up a tail in a mud braid or polo tail*

Hunters are shown in Model or In-Hand classes in a regular bridle, usually with a full-cheek snaffle bit with keepers. The bridle should be carefully fitted, with the noseband high on the face and snug and with no loose ends to distract the eye. If a full-cheek snaffle bit is used, it should have leather keepers to secure the upper cheeks. The bridle may be plain, raised or stitched, but no white or colored trim should be used on hunters. The horse is handled with the regular snaffle reins, and a short crop is sometimes carried.

FIGURE 24 *Hunter shown in hand in a snaffle bridle*

Eleven

SPORT HORSES: DRESSAGE HORSES, SHOW JUMPERS AND EVENT HORSES

Sport horses include horses competing in the three equestrian Olympic disciplines: dressage, show jumping and combined training. Even though the occasion may be a small local Pony Club competition, the styles and turnout expected in these disciplines reflect the international influence, particularly that of Europe.

Sport horses are often massive, especially the European warmbloods that have become popular in these sports. Good trimming and attention to details is necessary to make a good impression. While a good horse looks beautiful in action, the heavier legs, larger feet and often Roman-nosed head can make the warmblood appear gross and coarse if he is not well trimmed. A clean, sharp turnout and trimming and braiding can make even a heavy, massive horse look impressive. Finer-boned horses also benefit from a careful presentation as well.

In Europe, it is not customary to trim muzzle whiskers, ears or even bridle paths as it is in this country; frequently the legs are left untrimmed also. The mane is braided on the side to which it falls—either the right or the left—and the braids are usually larger and fewer in number than would be acceptable in an American show stable. The top of the dock is pulled or sometimes clipped with electric clippers, which can make it uncontrollably bristly as it grows out. While the European look is becoming more common as more horses are imported, American show ring standards prefer a cleaner look with more attention to trimming and fine details. The influence of the hunter show ring is evident in the presentation of American show jumpers and event horses, and is felt to some extent in the turnout of dressage horses.

FIGURE 1 *Dressage horse correctly turned out for show*

TURNOUT AND BRAIDING FOR DRESSAGE

Dressage competitions are the epitome of formality, the direct descendant of command performances before royalty in the courts of Europe. Horse and rider are judged on the perfection and purity of each movement, so turnout and braiding should never distract or be disturbing to the eye. Besides, most dressage judges are conservative in outlook and are unfavorably impressed by an untidy or flamboyant turnout. In dressage competitions, the rules prohibit ribbons, bangles or any kind of decorations except for a properly braided mane, which may be accented with white tape. An impeccably turned out horse, sparkling clean and with every item correctly fitted, along with a rider equally well presented, will make the best impression.

Dressage horses should be trimmed as neatly as any other breed, with fetlocks and lower leg hair closely trimmed and the coronary band hair trimmed to an even line. The legs may be booted up, especially if the horse has heavy leg hair or white markings, but close-clipped areas should be carefully blended. The long hair should be trimmed from the jawline and the first few inches of the throat, and a short bridle path should be clipped (1 to 2 inches). The outside edges of the ears may be trimmed to give them a neater appearance, but it is not necessary or even advisable to remove the hair from the inside of the ears. If the inner hair is removed and the horse is bothered by flies or gnats attacking his unprotected ears, he may start tossing his head and spoil a performance. Horses with large ears are not flattered by removing the inside hair, anyway—this can make the ear appear larger. In this country the muzzle hairs are usually clipped closely, but this practice is not followed in Europe and some American dressage competitors choose to leave the muzzle and eye whiskers natural.

The mane of the dressage horse is pulled to a uniform length of 3 1/2 to 5 inches and is usually braided for competition. The braids may be done as hunter braids, knob-style braids or sewn-in button braids. Dressage braids are often thicker than hunter braids and may be fewer in number, averaging about twenty to twenty-five braids instead of the thirty or more usually used on a hunter mane; however, some exhibitors prefer more smaller braids. Unlike hunter braiding, the forelock may be left unbraided, which sometimes is more flattering to a horse with a large or Roman-nosed head. In this country it is more usual to braid the mane on the right, but in Europe the mane is braided on either side, and this custom is acceptable although less usual in American competitions.

The mane braids may be accented with white tape, which is either wrapped around each braid on the side, over the yarn fastening or around the "knob" so that it is visible above the neck from both sides. The tape should be no more than 1/4-inch wide and only white should be used. Plastic mending tape works well but must be cut down to 1/4 inch; narrow white plastic tape especially for braiding is available in tack shops. If the forelock is braided, it should also be taped.

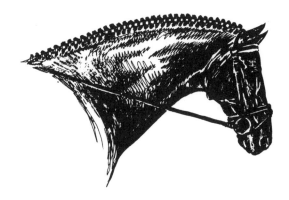

FIGURE 2 *Taped braids with knobs*

FIGURE 3 A. *Taping around side of braid*
B. *Tape around knob*

Most dressage grooms braid with yarn as for hunter braids and then apply tape over the yarn. If the mane is to be taped, the yarn should match the color of the mane. The mane may also be braided using white yarn, which gives a little less noticeable effect than white tape. The tape can be applied over the white yarn or left off, which can be a time-saver when the schedule is busy.

While taped braids are the most commonly seen, other styles are permissible for dressage shows. Scalloped braids such as those used on hunters are acceptable—these should not be taped and the color of the yarn or thread should match the mane so that it is not noticeable. Scalloped braids look especially nice when the color of the mane contrasts with the neck. Sewn-in button braids are also appropriate and look nice whether taped or not. They can be used to put up a longer, unpulled mane such as that of an Arabian or Morgan when shown in Dressage classes. (For instructions on basic braiding, hunter braids, knob braids, scalloping and sewn-in button braids, see Chapter 10.)

While it is customary to pull the manes of dressage horses, long-maned horses like Arabians and Morgans may show in dressage without pulling the mane. They may put the mane up in doubled and sewn button braids or leave it free and natural. However, there are two special mane styles that work well for long-maned horses.

The French braid is a long, single braid that runs along the crest of the neck. It encompasses all the hair much like a tail braid, except that the strands are added from one side only. One disadvantage of the French braid is that it may loosen and buckle as the horse flexes and stretches his neck.

To Put the Mane Up in a French Braid:

1. Part three strands at the front of the mane, with each strand about 3/4 inch wide. Cross the center strand over the right-hand strand.

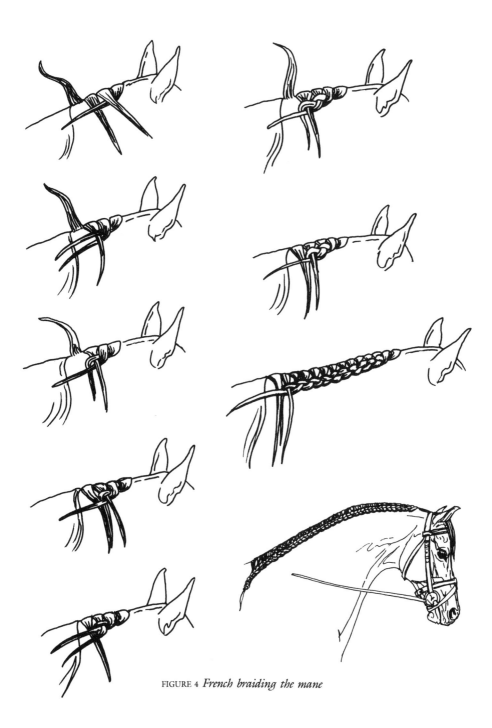

FIGURE 4 *French braiding the mane*

2. Bring the third strand (left-hand strand) behind the end of the first strand. (The first strand is "sandwiched" between the second and third strands.)

3. Bring the highest strand (the end of the first strand) down behind the end of the second strand. This begins the braid.

4. Part another strand about 3/4 inch wide from the edge of the mane and add it to the strand just braided, passing it *underneath* the braid. Keep the braiding tight and close against the neck.

5. Bring the strand at the far right around behind the braid and into the center.

6. Continue to braid by bringing the highest strand (upper left) around behind the braid and into the center, then parting and adding a strand from

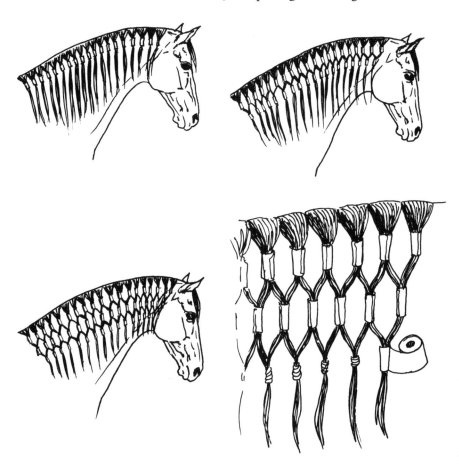

FIGURE 5 *Continental braid*

the edge of the mane. Then bring the upper right strand around behind and into the center.

7. Keep the braid tight and well up against the crest of the neck. Continue along the crest to the withers. The thickness of the strands may need to be adjusted to keep the strands perpendicular to the neck and the braid even.

8. At the end of the neck, stop adding hairs from the crest and braid the remaining hairs out into a short pigtail. This can be fastened with a rubber band or turned under and fastened with yarn as in a hunter braid.

The Continental braid (sometimes called the macrame braid) is sometimes seen on Arabians, Morgans, Andalusians and other long-maned horses. It does not really involve braiding, but creates a striking pattern of diamond shapes by parting, banding and reparting the mane. It looks particularly attractive when the mane color contrasts with that of the neck.

To put the mane up in a Continental braid, you will need braiding bands and plastic mending tape 1/2-inch to 1-inch wide. The tape may be either white or black, but colored tape is not appropriate for dressage competition.

To Put Up the Mane in a Continental Braid:

1. Part the mane into 1-inch segments. Apply a rubber band around each segment about 1 inch below the crest, keeping the mane pulled down against the side of the neck. The bands should all be the same distance from the neck.

3. Cover each band with a piece of tape. (Do not try to tape the mane without securing it with a rubber band first, as the tape will not hold securely alone.)

4. Part each segment below the tape into two sections. Band each half-section to the half-section beside it. This forms the first row of diamonds. Cover each band with a piece of tape.

5. The end sections are not divided, but are banded to the half-section next to them.

6. Continue the process as above to make two or three rows of diamonds, depending on the length of the mane. Too many rows distract the eye from the top of the crest and can distort the diamond shapes. The hair below the bottom row of diamonds is allowed to hang free.

The tail of the dressage horse is important, as it is an extension of the spine and its carriage gives the judge an indication of how well the horse uses its back. Braiding the tail is permissible under the rules, but braiding can cause

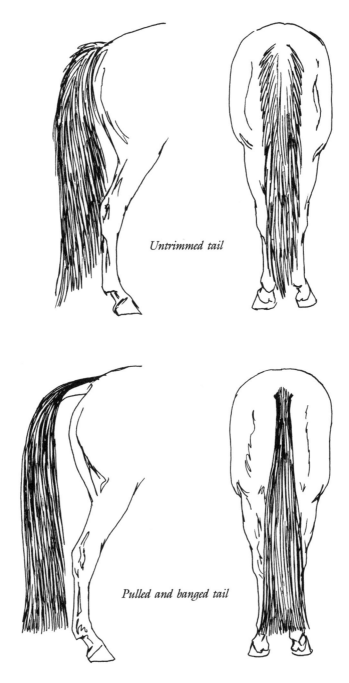

Untrimmed tail

Pulled and banged tail

FIGURE 6 *Banged tail*

a horse to carry its tail stiffly and hence lose points. Therefore, tails are seldom braided for dressage in this country. Instead, the hairs at the top of the dock are pulled or trimmed with clippers to slim down the line of the dock to the point where the dock turns over when the tail is carried in motion. The skirt of the tail may be banged off square or left in a natural point. While English grooms tend to favor a shorter tail, banged off level with the bottom of the hocks, in this country a longer tail, reaching to the bottom of the fetlock joint, is preferred. When banging off a tail, always have a helper raise the tail to the angle at which the horse carries it when he is moving. The skirt is then cut straight across at a slight angle, so that the bottom of the tail hangs level when the horse is in motion. A bang tail is not a requirement; horses with a thin skirt may look better with a natural switch tail.

The upper part of the dock may be pulled or trimmed to give it a slimmer appearance, which emphasizes the tail carriage. The hair is pulled short along the sides of the dock for a distance of about 4 1/2 to 6 inches, depending on the size of the horse and his natural tail carriage. The pulling or trimming should taper to an end just before the "turnover point" of the tail, and it should be done mostly along the sides and hardly at all on top. If the pulling is extended too far down the dock or the hair is pulled too short, the contrast between the short-haired dock and the long hair of the skirt gives an ungraceful "broom-handle" appearance. A well-pulled tail looks natural when it is carried in motion, but the lower side hairs have been thinned and shortened so that they do not obscure the underline of the dock.

When pulling the tail, you can use a metal pulling comb or your fingers. Pliers may be used to pluck out short hairs that are too short to grasp with the fingers. Work from the top of the dock down the edge, pulling the hair very short for a 1/4-inch strip, but taper the strip off at the point of turnover. When you have pulled a 1/4-inch strip from each side for about 6 to 8 inches, begin at the top and pull another 1/4-inch strip, blending this strip in a little earlier. Continue until the hair at the sides of the dock is shortened but not completely stripped bare, and stop to hold up the tail and check your work frequently. The pulling should not extend up onto the top of the tail, and it should not be obvious when looking at the tail from the side. It is better to leave the hair a little too long than to pull it too thin and have the tail look bald.

An alternative method is to trim the sides of the dock with clippers. Use #15 or #30 blades, which must be very sharp. Starting at the top edge of the dock, run the clipper blades downward with the hairs, pressing lightly and evenly to thin and shorten the side hairs for only about 5 or 6 inches. Taper

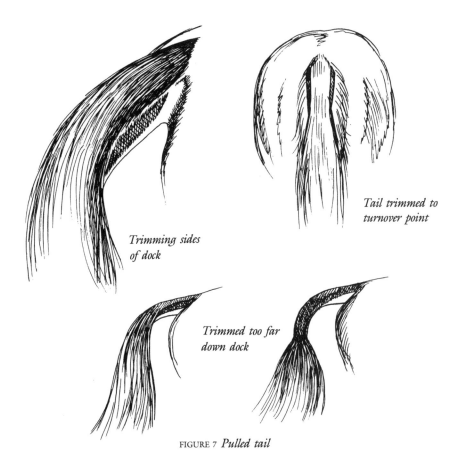

*Trimming sides
of dock*

*Tail trimmed to
turnover point*

*Trimmed too far
down dock*

FIGURE 7 *Pulled tail*

the trimmed area smoothly under the hair just above the turnover point. Trim the sides of the dock until they are even with the width of the tailbone, but do not use the clippers on the upper side of the dock. The trimming will have to be repeated every two weeks, or whenever the trimmed hair begins to get too long.

Electric clippers also make a neat job of squaring off the bottom of a banged tail—run your fist down around the hairs to the bottom of the skirt and hold it firmly—you can trim the ends of the hairs level with the clippers. Be sure to have a helper hold up the dock to the level at which the horse carries it in motion, or the banged tail will look too short when the tail is carried naturally.

Some horses do not enjoy having their tails handled, much less pulled, and a horse can register a very effective protest! If you pull only a very few hairs at a time and pull them out with a swift jerk straight out (not a long pull down or sideways), most horses will not object. If the horse is sensitive, pull only a few hairs each day until you get the tail sufficiently short, or use the clippers to trim him instead of pulling. When pulling tail hairs, you may see tiny points of blood on the skin. This is not painful and is harmless, but it should be wiped away with a clean, damp rag.

Horses that have had the tail pulled or trimmed should have a tail wrap applied to the dampened hair of the upper dock for an hour or so before their class. The bandage is removed just before entering the ring, leaving the upper tail smooth and slim. The groom must be sure to remove the tail bandage, as the rules forbid all bandages, including tail bandages, in competition. Should you forget to remove the tail wrap, the entry would be eliminated.

Pulling or trimming the top of the dock is not mandatory. Some horses, especially Arabians and others with a naturally high tail carriage, or horses that carry their tails crookedly, look best with a natural, untrimmed tail.

Dressage horses should be cleaned and finished off as other horses before entering the ring, but with one exception—do not wipe the foam from the horse's mouth or the bit. In dressage, foam is considered a desirable sign of a relaxed and responsive mouth; in fact, some dressage riders feed their horses sugar before warming up to encourage the horse to chew the bit and make foam.

Some additional final touches include applying silicone coat spray to the coat and the skirt of the tail; putting on dark hoof oil or hoof polish, and using highlighter gel on the face, muzzle, eyelids and ears. Fly repellent should be used on the face and ears, but be sure that it is not strong enough to burn the fine skin of the head. Since the horse must remain obedient, attentive and on the bit throughout his test, the distraction of flies or gnats can be a hindrance to his performance.

Dressage and sport horse breeds such as Hanoverians, Trakehners and other warmbloods are usually presented in hand in a snaffle bridle. A thick, hollow mouth eggbutt or loose ring snaffle is preferred, as it is less apt to damage the sensitivity of the mouth. A flash noseband is often used so that the horse cannot open his mouth and let the bit slide sideways when he is being run out in hand; many exhibitors consider the flash noseband more flattering to the horse's head than a drop noseband, which tends to make the face look longer and accentuates a Roman nose. A standard cavesson is also acceptable. The browband and noseband may be raised, stitched or lined with white or tan leather to accent the horse's color and the lines of the head. Brass-trimmed browbands ("clincher" browbands) or browbands with a raised,

FIGURE 8 *Sport horse shown in hand in snaffle bridle with flash noseband*

colored center bead are currently popular, and black bridlework may be used to accentuate a horse's color. Since many warmbloods are very large with massive heads, their bridles are usually made in a heavier weight than most show bridles. The handler may carry a dressage whip, and usually wears running shoes instead of riding boots in order to keep up with the extended trot of a big, athletic sport horse.

TURNOUT FOR SHOW JUMPERS AND EVENT HORSES

Show jumpers and event horses are judged solely on their performance, and their turnout is not judged specifically as long as their equipment is legal under the rules of competition. Nevertheless, any serious competitor will want to appear well turned out as a courtesy to the audience and the judges, and to reflect his pride in his horse, his stable and sometimes his team. While perfect braids or a clean coat won't make a horse jump higher, these and other points of turnout indicate the rider's and the stable's attention to detail—or lack of it. The best competitors get all the details right!

The standards for trimming and braiding show jumpers and event horses are similar to those for dressage horses. Show jumpers are often braided as hunters, with many small braids put in with yarn. The braids are not taped for show jumping; the forelock may be braided or left unbraided. Show jumpers' tails, especially Thoroughbreds, are sometimes braided as a hunter tail. Some jumpers are shown with a slightly longer mane—about 5 to 7 inches—and are left unbraided, but most will have their manes pulled to the shorter length appropriate for hunters: about 3 1/2 to 5 inches. If the tail is never braided, it may be pulled like the tail of a dressage horse, or it may be left natural. Some warmbloods have large, thick docks and thick, coarse tail hair; their tails are usually pulled short as they do not braid as easily or look as nice when braided as most Thoroughbreds.

Event horses are usually pulled and trimmed as for dressage. For the dressage phase of a combined training event, they are turned out exactly as for a formal dressage show. They are usually unbraided for the cross-country phase, as the rider may need to grab the mane if the horse should get into trouble at a fence. If time permits, the mane is braided for stadium jumping, but white tape is not used and tail braiding is seldom seen.

In the athletically demanding world of show jumping and eventing, the groom's job is directed primarily toward the aspects of grooming that affect the horse's and rider's safety and ability to perform at their athletic best, and only secondarily concerned with appearance. The groom must be thoroughly familiar with each piece of equipment the horse wears and its correct adjustment. He must check the strength and security of each strap and buckle, the fit of boots and bandages, the adjustment of noseband, martingale and breastplate and the security and balance of the weight cloth. The correct studs must be put into the shoes according to the ground conditions. The groom must also be familiar with the rules and know what could disqualify or penalize a rider—for instance, if an event competitor carries a whip into the dressage arena, he will be eliminated. During an event or between rounds of a class, he may have to help both horse and rider recover as quickly as possible from their exertions and be ready to go on with the next phase or into a jump-off calm, refreshed and ready. In addition, the demands of these events often mean that the groom must contend with a horse that is extremely hot, tired and stressed, and requires more skill and knowledge in cooling out and after-care. This requires more knowledge than can be adequately conveyed in this chapter. Event grooming in particular is best learned through apprenticeship to an experienced event groom, or by going to events and learning on the job by helping as one of the "pit crew" volunteers. An excellent book on the demands of grooming for eventers is *The Event Groom's Handbook* by Jeanne Kane and Lisa Waltman.

Twelve

GROOMING AT HORSE SHOWS

PLANNING AND PREPARATION

Good planning and preparation can make the difference between a well-organized, pleasant and successful show and a nightmare. Rider, trainer and groom should get together to plan, delegate jobs and coordinate their efforts. Equipment and essential items will have to be assembled, checked over and sometimes cleaned, repaired or replenished before they are packed. Using checklists can help ensure that important things are not left undone or left behind when you ship out.

Before the show season, you should start a show calendar and a show information file. This should contain rule books of the American Horse Shows Association and any breed, sport or organization under whose rules you compete, prize lists for shows and the omnibus or season's show listings for your area. You may need to register your horse in order to be eligible for certain awards, and you may be required to produce eligibility documents such as an amateur card, membership card, pony height certificate, etc., when entering, along with your horse's registration papers. Each horse should have an individual folder containing photocopies of his registration papers, Coggins test and any other health or vaccination certificates. These papers should travel with the horse, as you may be required to produce them on arrival at the showgrounds before you will be allowed to unload your horse. A small portable file box is useful to keep all such information organized and safe but easily available, and can be carried along to shows.

You will need to know what kind of conditions to expect at each show, how long you will be staying and the time schedule. This can be obtained from an omnibus (a booklet containing information and prize lists for a series of shows), the prize list or sometimes by calling the show manager or another exhibitor. Get clear, written directions to the showgrounds and know how long it will take to get there.

Checklist 1 DOCUMENTS AND PAPERWORK

_____ AHSA Rule book

_____ Breed or other association rule book

_____ AHSA Membership Card (membership # _____), other membership card

_____ Horse AHSA Number _____

_____ Amateur Card (#_____)

_____ Horse's registration papers (photocopies)

_____ Pony Measurement Card

_____ Current negative Coggins test (photocopies)

_____ Vaccination certificate (if required)

_____ Prize list for show, including show schedule

_____ Clear directions to show (for van driver and others)

_____ Address, telephone and AHSA Membership number of owner, if not present at show

_____ Address, room number and emergency phone number at hotel for rider/trainer (on card to be attached to horse's stall door)

_____ Telephone number of horse's regular veterinarian

Several important chores must be done far enough in advance of the show to allow time for repairs or other services. Certain show procedures should be done in advance to allow the horse to be at his best condition on show day.

Checklist 2 TO BE DONE A WEEK BEFORE THE SHOW

____ Check horse's shoeing; reset or trim if necessary.

____ Check condition of all tack (any needed repairs made)

____ Check supplies and obtain any needed items

____ Have trailer and truck or van serviced and safety checked

____ Have any required documentation on file, plus show information

____ Trim/clip/condition coat and/or mane and tail

____ Rider's clothes clean, fitted and assembled

____ Make any necessary arrangements such as ordering extra feed, coverage of chores at home, transportation arrangements, etc.

In the last day or two before the show you may bathe the horse and do a final show trim to have him looking at his best. Show tack will be cleaned and polished before it is packed and checked off. You will need to plan your schedule for shipping, arrival and setting up at the show and will need to know the time schedule and which classes each horse is entered in. As the trainer may have last-minute schooling in mind, this should be taken into account when planning the shipping and arrival times.

SHOW GEAR AND HOW TO PACK IT

The equipment you will need at a show will depend on the kind of horse you show and the nature of the competition, whether you are stabling overnight or showing from your trailer, and other variables. However, some items will be essential or useful for even the simplest trip. As you show, you will develop some preferences of your own about the essentials and the "nice-to-haves"—these should be incorporated into your own stable's checklist. The main items necessary for a one-day show or a two- or three-day overnight show will be covered here. Packing and managing your show equipment is easier if you have trunks or kits devoted to specific equipment, and if the equipment is always packed in the same place. This saves time when you need a particular item in a hurry. If you show a lot, it is helpful to have certain duplicate items reserved just for show and permanently stored in your show trunk—for instance, "show" brushes, braiding kit, tack care items, etc. This is easier than trying to assemble brushes, seam ripper, scissors and sponges from all over the barn, the house and the tack room and remembering to return them all after you get home! Your tack trunks, tools and other items can be painted in your stable colors to look nice and to easily identify them as yours. Portable kits that can be taken to a stall, wash rack or the warmup ring make it easier for the groom and are easier to assemble, check and transport than a hundred individual items carried willy-nilly. Plastic totes, wooden carrying cases, a many-pocketed grooming apron or even a plastic bucket will suffice. Plastic milk cartons are useful for carrying and storing items and are strong enough to use as a step or stool. A shoe storage bag with many pockets can hang in a tack stall or grooming area and will hold many small items neatly.

As you assemble and pack, be sure that each item is clean, in good repair and ready to go. It will be much easier throughout the season if you clean your show equipment and trunks and repack immediately after each show. Don't check an item off on your list until it is ready to use at the show and packed in its proper trunk.

When you arrive at a show, your first job will be to set up your stalls (or if showing from the trailer, your trailer area) to receive your horses. At times you may arrive after dark to do this, so you need the essential hardware and tools handy and, perhaps, a light to work by. Some stables send an advance crew ahead of the horses when shipping a number of horses to a major show; the crew will set up stalls, tack room, feed stalls, etc. and bed them down ready for the later arrival of the horses.

Checklist 3 TOOL KIT AND SET-UP KIT

These items fit easily in a flight bag or large tool kit, which should be packed where it can be reached easily on arrival.

—— Hammer and assorted size nails

—— Pliers (wire cutting type)

—— Screwdrivers (large, small, regular and Phillips head)

—— Staplegun and staples

___ Hand drill

___ Sharp knife

___ Screw eyes (large and medium—for feed tubs, stall guards, etc.)

___ Double end snaps

___ Plastic electrician's tape, duct tape, baling wire

___ Coil of 1/2-inch rope, baling twine

___ Extension cord (heavy-duty type, 50 feet long), drop light with cord

___ Battery-powered lantern and fresh batteries

If you are using a stall for the day or overnight, you will need equipment for setting up and sometimes improving the stall and for feeding, watering and mucking out. Even if you are showing from the trailer, you must be able to water your horse and feed him hay and should be able to clean up your trailer area before leaving.

Checklist 4 STABLE EQUIPMENT

Showing from trailer:

___ Water bucket with snap for each horse plus extra bucket for washing, etc.

___ Tie rope (*not* a chain end lead shank!)

___ Hay net

___ Rake

___ Shovel

___ Muck basket

___ Trash bags

___ Bug repellent and hornet spray

____ Water container (full)—at least 10 gallons

____ Tack hook

____ Portable saddle rack

____ Waterproof tarp in case of rain

In addition, when using stalls:

____ Stall guards

____ Stall screens (stall doors)

____ Feed tub

____ Manure fork

____ Wheelbarrow or garden cart (space permitting)

____ Broom

____ Bedding for 2 nights (minimum 4 bags shavings)

____ Plywood panels (especially if stabling a stallion)

____ Halter board, blanket rack, tack hook, etc.

____ Cross-ties

____ Immersion bucket/heater for hot water

Another item that should be close at hand when shipping and at the show is a first aid kit. There should be emergency veterinary supplies and a human first aid kit as well. Your personal choice of first aid items and veterinary supplies will be dictated by how much veterinary care and treatment you can handle and perhaps by your own veterinarian's recommendations, but as a minimum you should be prepared to handle cuts, minor illness or injuries. You should also have the basic farrier tools needed to pull a shoe if the horse should twist or spring a shoe, but you must be capable of using them. First aid supplies, medications and liniments or other leg preparations are often kept in a special lockable medicine chest. When shipping, your first-aid supplies should be readily available in case of a shipping accident—not at the bottom of the least accessible tack trunk.

Checklist 5 HORSE FIRST AID KIT

____ Chain end lead shank & twitch for restraint

____ Clean plastic bucket, preferably with snap-on lid (can be used to hold kit)

____ Leg wraps & cottons

____ Vetrap

____ Sterile gauze pads (4 × 4 inches)

____ Bandage scissors (blunt ends)

____ Penlight flashlight with fresh batteries

____ Antibacterial soap

____ Thermometer

____ Clean turkish towel

____ Nitrafurazone salve and/or nitrafurazone powder

____ Rubbing alcohol, leg brace and/or wrapping liniment

____ Elastic adhesive tape

____ Poultice and plastic food wrap

____ Electrolytes

____ Instant ice pack

Any prescription medications, injectables or controlled substances (such as Banamine, tranquilizers, etc.) should be kept in a locked case, as should syringes and needles. These should be prescribed by a veterinarian and should only be used on his orders. Be sure that you are familiar with current regulations regarding forbidden drugs (including seemingly "innocent" drugs such as penicillin), which may contain forbidden substances such as procaine or may be an illegal "masking" drug that blocks drug tests. If you administer a possibly illegal drug for legitimate purposes (such as an attack of colic), you must file a report with the show veterinarian and you may be required to withdraw your horse from competition. Do not administer tranquilizers for clipping or shipping close to the show date—this can result in a positive drug test and severe penalties.

Checklist 6 FARRIER TOOLS

In tool kit:

_____ Hoof knife

_____ Shoe pullers

_____ Farrier's hammer

_____ Clinch cutter or buffer

_____ Farrier's rasp

_____ (optional) Duplicate set of shoes, fitted by your regular farrier

_____ Screw-in studs, assorted types (if used) and cotton for filling screw holes

_____ Wrench for setting studs, sharp nail for cleaning threads of screw holes

Before showing, your horse may need warmup and schooling time. This often entails special schooling equipment such as longe lines or boots, etc. (Add your own essentials!)

Checklist 7 SCHOOLING EQUIPMENT

In tack trunk:

_____ Longe line

_____ Longe whip

_____ Boots or polo wraps

_____ Bell boots

_____ Martingale or other schooling device if used

The horse clothing you take will depend on the weather, the time of year and the kind of horse you are showing. You may need a blanket rack to keep clothing clean, neatly folded and handy.

Checklist 8 HORSE CLOTHING

In tack trunk:

_____ Sheet (for keeping horse clean at night and during shipping)

_____ Blanket (if weather requires), with hood if used

_____ Anti-sweat sheet (for cooling out)

_____ Cooler or walking cover

_____ Scrim fly sheet

_____ Rain cover

_____ Paddock sheet

_____ Stable bandages and cottons

_____ Tail bandage

_____ Polo bandages (if used for warming up)

_____ Blanket rack

_____ Bandage rack or bandage box

Your tack should be cleaned and polished before packing it for the show, but you may need to clean up tack, boots or metal items between classes. You should also have certain spare items to make repairs or to substitute in case of breakage.

Checklist 9 TACK CLEANING AND REPAIRS; SPARE TACK

In cleaning kit/tack trunk:

_____ Tack cleaning bucket (can be container for kit)

_____ Tack cleaning hook

_____ Glycerine saddle soap

_____ Lexol or other leather dressing

_____ One-Step leather cleaner (for quick cleaning jobs)

____ Metal polish

____ Tack sponges, turkish towels, bit scrubber, old toothbrush

____ Leather punch

____ Swiss Army knife

____ Extra small pieces (Chicago screws, martingale rings, rein stops, bit keepers, etc.)

____ Plastic mending tape (black and brown)

____ Speedy Stitcher (sewing awl with thread)

____ Screwdriver

____ Extra stirrup leather

____ Extra halter and lead rope

____ Extra rein

____ Extra girth

____ (optional) Rubber-covered reins for wet days

Grooming items will vary with the groom's individual preference and the type of horse being shown. The grooming kit should be portable, so that it can easily be carried to a stall or to the warmup ring. A separate "last-minute kit" may be taken to the ring for final touches before the horse is shown.

Checklist 10 GROOMING ITEMS

In tack trunk with portable kits for brushes and last-minute kit:

____ Clippers, blades, blade wash

____ Brushes, currycomb, regular grooming tools (in kit)

____ Towels (several per horse)

____ Scraper, sponges, hose for bathing

____ Hoof pick, nail brush, hoof dressing or polish; hoof polish remover

____ Mat or panel to stand horse on while applying hoof polish

____ Coat spray

____ Fly repellent

____ Stain remover

____ Highlighter gel

____ Setting gel for mane and tail

____ Cornstarch, baby powder or French chalk for whitening white markings

____ Shampoo, Ivory liquid, body wash

____ Mane and tail conditioner, brilliantine or un-tangler spray

____ Bot Block or Slick 'n Easy Block (removes bot eggs)

____ Scissors, sharp knife

____ Braiding kit

____ Stool or step to stand on when braiding

____ Tail wrapping necessities (tail bandage, cotton strips, tube sock, tape, etc.)

The last-minute kit, which will be used for final touch-ups to horse, rider and tack just before entering the ring, might include:

____ Towels (2)

____ Sponges (2) 1 for Lexol, 1 dampened with water only

____ Coat spray (containing fly repellent)

____ Lexol or One-Step leather cleaner (to touch up leather)

____ Hoof pick and hoof brush

____ Hoof dressing or polish

____ Cornstarch or French chalk to whiten leg markings

____ Finishing brush (sprayed with coat dressing to collect dust)

____ Brilliantine, baby oil or light oil for mane and tail

____ Bucket for water

You will also want to plan for the comfort and convenience of your human team. You will need a place to sit down, space in which the rider can dress and make his final preparations, cold drinks and other comforts. This may range from the front seat of a pickup truck to a formally appointed tack room with tack room drapes, carpets, personalized director's chairs and a portable bar. It is essential to have a "people place" separated from the groom's working area and the horse's resting spot, for the sake of safety, organization and everyone's sanity!

Checklist 11 TACK ROOM AND "PEOPLE" ITEMS

____ Folding chairs

____ Cooler with cold or warm drinks, depending on the season

____ Human first aid kit

____ Removable hook for clothes hangers

____ Mirror and personal grooming kit

____ Trash can or trash bags

____ Boot jack and boot hooks

____ Combination locks for tack trunks; bicycle combination lock for tack room (*Never* lock a horse in a stall!)

____ Rain gear, including extra poncho and waterproof tarp

____ Blanket for cold weather

____ Umbrella or large parasol for sunny days

____ Notebook, pencils, markers, tape

____ Show schedule, posted with classes entered marked

____ Work schedule (marker board or chalkboard) listing grooms' chores for each horse and any special notes

____ Folding table

_____ Folding cot with blankets and sleeping bag (if staying overnight)

_____ Saddle racks, bridle racks, tack hooks, harness racks, etc.

_____ Privacy drapes for tack room (for changing clothes or if staying overnight)

_____ Battery-operated lamp for tackroom (if staying overnight)

_____ Folding cart (for transporting tack, trunks, etc.)

Finally, you will need to clean, check and pack each horse's tack, being sure to include the correct tack for each class he is entered in. Saddle pads and any washable items should be freshly laundered, and it is wise to have extras so that the horse will not have to appear in a pad that is dirty from several earlier classes. For a two-day or longer show, the horse should have a fresh pad each day. Tack may be shipped in trunks or in saddle and bridle cases or harness bags. Tack should always be covered to protect it from scratches and other damage in shipping.

Checklist 12 TACK ITEMS

For each horse; in tack trunk or in its own case:

_____ Stable or shipping halter

_____ Tie rope

_____ Chain end lead shank

_____ Show halter and lead shank (clean, with silver polished)

_____ Saddle (clean, with metal polished)

_____ Saddle pads (freshly laundered, 1 extra pad)

_____ Breastplate (silver polished)

_____ Martingale

_____ Show bridle (clean, with metal polished)

_____ Extra bits or extra bridle

____ Harness (clean, with metal polished)

____ Show cart (clean, polished, with protective cover)

____ Boots (clean) if worn

____ Show whip or crop

____ Other required appointments (list and check off!)

When showing for only one day, you will probably only take hay and water. It is a good idea to have plenty of hay, as it keeps horses relaxed and contented when they must stand tied to the trailer or in a stall all day. Taking your own water is convenient in case the show's water source is far off or your horse refuses to drink strange-tasting water. You can carry 8-gallon jerrycans or use large plastic buckets with snap-tight lids. Never use anyone else's buckets or feed tubs or let your horse drink from a water trough at a show—this is a way to pick up contagious diseases.

For longer shows, you will need to take hay, grain and sometimes your own bedding. While feed and bedding can usually be ordered on the grounds at large shows, it is better to come prepared with your own if possible, as you may not get the kind or quality of feed you are used to, and it may not be available when you need it.

FEED AND BEDDING CHECKLIST

____ Haynet for each horse

____ Hay (more than normal amount, as horse cannot be turned out during show)

____ Feed, including any vitamins or additives

____ Feed measure (or feeds may be put up in premeasured packages for a single horse that will be away only one night or so)

____ Water (enough to offer horses water en route on a long trip)

____ Electrolytes

____ Bedding (Bagged shavings are most convenient to carry and horses cannot eat their bedding. Allow 2 bags or bales per stall for one night.)

HOW TO BE A GOOD HORSE SHOW GROOM

Anyone who shows horses will quickly appreciate the help of his groom, whether he or she is a professional show groom, a parent, friend or child who can hold a horse for a minute or run back to the trailer for a forgotten number. Nobody can appreciate a groom more than the person who has tried to do his or her own grooming while schooling and showing, too! It is possible to groom for yourself, but it takes extra energy and time and good organization. Ideally, the rider should be able to concentrate on the job of schooling, warming up and showing his horse, and sometimes on following the advice of his coach or trainer. He should not get his clothes messy by kneeling to put on hoof dressing when he is dressed for the show ring, and he cannot dismount in a muddy warmup ring to pick out his horse's tail just before entering the ring. Having a good show groom can take some of the pressure off the rider and trainer (who may be the same person!), and often means better care for the horse.

The rider, trainer and groom are all equally important members of the same team, with the same goal: to get the horse to the show ring ready, on time and fit to do his best and to present the best possible performance. The rider is certainly not the "lord of the manor", nor is the groom a lowly servant. Any rider who forgets this deserves to find out just how hard it is to groom for himself without good help! At the same time, the groom must remember that most show riders are under considerable stress and should not take offense if a rider is a bit tense, flustered or compulsive about double-checking everything. A good groom can help ease the rider's nervousness by having everything well organized and the horse ready in plenty of time, and by being there with quiet, positive support. It is not the groom's job to train the horse, criticize the rider's performance or, in the case of professional stables, to discuss such things with clients or parents of junior riders, and to butt into these areas is to invite trouble and bad feeling. Riders and trainers should remember to show their appreciation for the groom's efforts, and sometimes need to remember to curb their tongues when things are hectic. It is particularly unpleasant to hear a child rudely scolding or preemptorily ordering a parent to get the horse ready, or to fix her clothes, or whatever—especially when said parent probably provided the horse and the clothes, trailered the horse and has made it possible for the child to be showing at all. Show schedules and pressure are no excuse for rudeness and lack of consideration on anyone's part.

A good show groom will keep the horse's performance and needs foremost in mind. This sometimes means that the groom will not get to see as much of the show as he might like to, or have time to socialize or ride for fun. The horse is there to show his best, not for other purposes. Sometimes children want to ride their horses all over the show grounds between classes, or their friends may ask to ride, too. It is really unfair to the horse or pony to permit this, or to sit on him between classes to watch the show. Whenever a horse will not be showing for a while, he should be cooled out and unsaddled and allowed to relax. When the groom has some free time, check to see if there is something that needs doing, such as cleaning tack or rerolling bandages, before going off to watch the show. Grooms work long hours, so they deserve to take a break whenever the work schedule permits, but things should be left neat and organized before going off duty, and the stable area should always have someone there to keep an eye on it.

GROOMING FOR YOURSELF

Grooming for yourself takes good planning and organization and more energy. You will need to do most of your horse-care chores and grooming early, as well as any schooling, so that you have time to clean up the horse and have yourself dressed and correctly turned out in time for your class. This is easier when competing in a dressage show or other show with a fixed time schedule, so you know at what time your horse must be ready. Keep in touch with the announcer and how the show schedule is running; cancellations, scratches or combined classes can alter the schedule, and it is harder to cope without help.

You can save time by wearing a coverall or protective clothing over your show clothes while you groom. Female dressage riders often wear a wrap-around denim skirt over their boots and white breeches between classes; this has handy pockets for grooming tools as well as keeping the breeches clean. Have an area in your tack stall, dressing room or vehicle set up as a dressing area, with a mirror and toilet articles. If you remove and hang up your show coat, hat, gloves and tie as soon as you dismount and clean them up with a clothes brush after your horse is taken care of, they will be ready for your next class. Your grooming tools and routine need to be similarly organized so that your horse is cooled down, cleaned off and ready to go again in plenty of time before your next class. The tack can be touched up with a quick wipe-over using Lexol, One-Step cleaner or saddle soap.

Grooming for yourself is much easier if you have an easy-going horse that will tie safely and does not require extensive schooling before showing. Even if you don't have an experienced groom, it can be very helpful to have someone along who can hold the horse for a minute or run an errand for you if necessary.

SHIPPING YOUR HORSE

Horses should be wrapped and prepared for traveling so that they arrive safely and in show condition. Poor traveling protection can result in rubbed tails, scrapes or even serious injuries, especially when the horse scrambles or does not load or unload quietly.

The legs should be protected with shipping boots or bandages that protect the coronary band in case a horse steps on his own feet while trying to keep his balance. The tendons and other structures of the leg should also be protected against kick injuries or scrapes and cuts that may occur during loading or if the horse scrambles in the trailer. Bell boots offer more protection than shipping bandages alone and are a good idea for horses that are poor travelers. (See Chapter 3 for directions for applying shipping bandages.)

The tail should be protected with a tail wrap (see page 108 for directions) unless the horse will be on the van for an extremely long trip. Tail bandages

FIGURE 1 *Horse prepared for shipping*

should not be used when a horse is shipped by a commercial shipper or for more than eight hours. If the bandage should slip or begin to cut off circulation, it may not be noticed and could cause permanent damage to the tail if not fixed in time. Tail wraps or a tail guard are especially indicated for horses that brace themselves against the butt bar of a trailer, as they may rub their tails raw, but only on trips when they can receive individual attention.

The horse should wear a strong, securely fitted shipping halter. Shipping halters are often covered with fleece to prevent them from rubbing the skin of the face. A shipping halter should be of leather so that it could be cut in the event of an accident.

Horses that are fearful about hitting their heads, especially when unloading, should wear a head protector attached to the halter. Be sure that the halter still fits securely after the head protector is attached—sometimes a protector makes the halter fit loosely so that it can slip over the horse's head.

The horse may need to wear a blanket, sheet, hood or anti-sweat sheet, depending on weather and the vehicle he is being shipped in. Do not underestimate the effect of a draft in a moving vehicle, especially on a clipped horse. On the other hand, a closed trailer can develop extremely high temperatures when parked in the sun—enough to cause serious dehydration and even collapse from heat exhaustion in some horses during very hot weather. It is important to monitor the horse's condition, especially on long trips and in extremely hot or cold weather. The appropriate clothing should be on hand to put on the horse if he needs it.

Horses that are to be shipped should be fed lightly for a day or two prior to shipping. Their grain should be cut by half, and they should not be grained just before shipping; in fact, it may be better for some horses to withhold grain entirely. They should have a haynet available in the van or trailer, which will keep them busy and contented. If a horse becomes upset by travel, a full grain feed before leaving could contribute to an attack of colic. If the horse is to be shipped for twelve hours or longer, grain is usually withheld for two days before shipping and the veterinarian may give the horse mineral oil by tube to prevent digestive upsets caused by change, stress and standing idle for a long period.

Loading should be accomplished quietly, calmly and with a positive attitude. If the horse is inexperienced at loading, he should have a practice trip before show day—don't try to train a horse to load when you are in a hurry. Start early and leave extra time for loading; just knowing that you are not behind schedule will make your job easier and your attitude more relaxed and confident. Most loading problems are caused by people who are in a hurry, disorganized and unsure of themselves or irritable. If you must load or unload near a road or in the open, attach a longe line to the horse's halter. Should he pull back for any reason while loading or unloading, he is much less likely to get away from you than if you were using only a lead shank.

SETTING UP AT A SHOW (STALLS)

Your first job on arrival is to get the stall ready so that your horse has a safe place to be. Inspect the stall carefully before bedding it down or bringing the horse in. It may have been used as a tack room and have nails, staples or trash left in it. Remove any feed tubs or buckets—they could infect your horse with contagious diseases. If there are electrical outlets nearby, be sure that the horse cannot reach a cord and chew it. Sweep down the walls, and if the floor is clay, dampen it before bedding down.

Temporary stalls are often made of boards with open spaces between them. These can allow horses to get their legs caught between the boards when they roll (as they usually do in a new stall.) Some horses, especially stallions, may sniff at their neighbors and squeal and fight through the gaps. You may need to reinforce such stalls with 4 × 8-foot panels of plywood, or a heavy tarpaulin fastened at the top and bottom of the stall panel. It is a good precaution to keep horses' legs wrapped in temporary stalls, even if they are not usually wrapped at home.

The stall may have a regular stall door, a sliding board gate or no door at all. In the latter case, you will need to set in screw eyes and hang a stall screen as a door, or you may use a fabric or vinyl stall guard. Some horses need two stall guards so that they do not duck underneath, but be sure that they cannot get a foot through the lower stall guard. A stall screen is hung on the inside of the doorpost, and the hangers are slipped down into the screw eyes. Be sure to secure each hanger to the screw eye with a piece of heavy wire, so that the horse cannot lift the door up and pull it off the hinges. Stall screens open inward, so they can only be used in a roomy stall. A stall screen should be placed high enough to prevent the horse from reaching out and nipping passing horses, but not high enough that he can injure his knees by pawing underneath the door. Stall screens permit good ventilation and allow you to see the horse without going into the stall.

Set in the screw-eyes for the feed tub, water bucket and hay net. Keep buckets high enough so that the horse cannot paw them. The hay net must be hung high enough so that the horse cannot get a foot into it, and should

Setting up a temporary stall

    A. *Temporary stalls often have dangerous gaps between the boards which can trap a horse's leg.*

    B. *Plywood nailed over boards on inside of stall.*

    C. *Tarpaulin used to create a solid wall to prevent fighting with adjacent horse.*

    D. *Feed tub with screw eyes and snaps.*

    E. *Water bucket.*

    F. *Stall screen hung on inside of doorway. Hangers wired to screw eyes so horse cannot lift door up off hangers.*

    G. *Hay net hung safely so that horse cannot catch a foot in it when empty.*

    H. *Bedding banked high against walls to prevent horse from getting cast.*

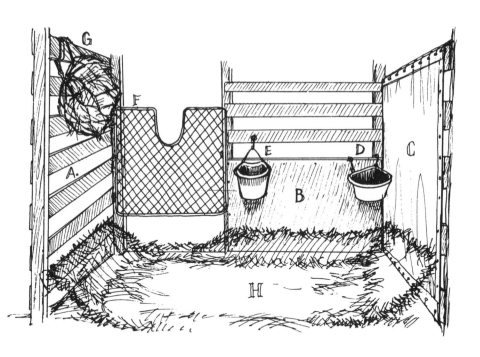

FIGURE 2 *Temporary stall set up safely*

FIGURE 3 *How to tie a hay net safely*

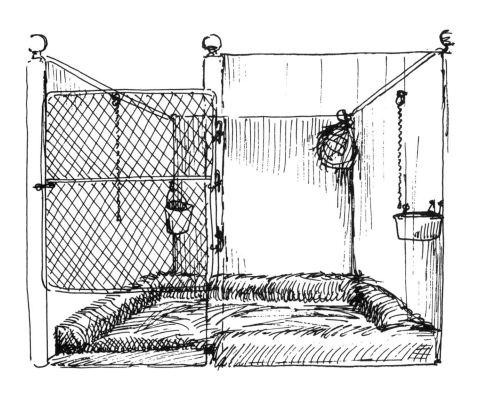

FIGURE 4 *Making banks and rolling straw at entrance*

be double-tied so that it will not hang low enough for the horse to paw it when it is empty. (To double-tie a hay net, run the ties through a high ring or over the top board of the stall and then tie to the ring at the bottom of the hay-net with a slip knot, or fasten it to the bottom ring with a double-end snap.) Set in cross-tie rings or a tie ring so that you can tie the horse in the stall.

Finally, bed down and bank the stall. Use plenty of bedding at a show; it keeps the horses cleaner and encourages them to lie down and rest. The bedding should be banked well up against the walls and corners of the stall to prevent the horse from becoming cast (or stuck) if he rolls. Straw or shavings can be simply piled high against the walls and patted down firmly with a fork, or if you use straw, you can make fancy English square banks. For square banks, the straw is piled higher along the walls and patted down hard on top; the fork is then used to tuck and shape the sides into a square bank. The banks are a source of clean bedding when you clean the stall and rebed it. The entrance to the stall should be swept clean so that the horse will not drag bedding out into the aisleway when leaving the stall. For a straw stall you may roll the edges by setting a broom handle down over the edge and kneeling on it. You then twist and tuck the straw edged under until a neat, folded edge is achieved. When you have filled the water bucket and tied up a full hay net, your horse can be left to investigate his new quarters.

If you are showing several horses, you may rent a tack stall. If your stable is not large enough to rate a tack stall for your exclusive use, you may be able to share a tack stall with another exhibitor. The tack stall is your base of operations throughout the show, so it takes some planning and preparation to devise an efficient, workmanlike but attractive setup. Professional show stables have elaborately appointed tack stalls with drapes, saddle racks, chairs and accessories in their stable colors, with ribbons won and photographs of their current champions on display. Remember that neatness and efficiency should take precedence over decoration, however.

To set up a simple tack stall, sweep down the walls and floor and put up nails or hooks for bridles, tools and clothes. Your saddle rack and tack trunk should be set up in a convenient place, and you will need to hang a drape or curtain for privacy when changing clothes. Have folding chairs and a cooler full of cold or hot beverages for the convenience of your human helpers. It is best to keep people activities away from the horse preparation area; remember that the main purpose of the stable area is to take care of the *horses*, not for socializing, playing, eating or entertaining. A place should be designated for horse grooming and care, for the rider to dress and fix his clothes, for tack to be hung up and cleaned, and for needed items to be stored. Put any items

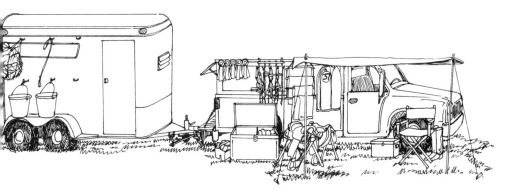

FIGURE 5 *Safe set up for showing from trailer*

you have used back in their trunk or kit as soon as you have finished with them; this keeps the area neater and more organized and makes it less likely that you will lose, spill or spoil things. Post a copy of the show schedule prominently and underline the classes your horse is entered in; list tack changes or times when a horse may have to hurry from one ring to show in another. A battery-operated lamp or lantern or a drop light on a long extension cord makes it easier to work in the tack room and is essential after dark. You may also want an electric bucket immersion heater, but this must be used with care to avoid a fire hazard. Finally, have a lock and chain to close the tackroom securely (a bicycle lock with a combination is handy) when you must be away from it for a while.

SHOWING FROM THE TRAILER OR VAN

When no stabling is available, you will have to tie your horse to your van or trailer, keep him in his van stall or have someone hold him when he is not showing. If you tie to a trailer, it should be hitched to the tow vehicle and the wheels should be blocked—you might be surprised to learn how far a frightened horse can drag an unhitched trailer. Never tie your horse to a fence board, a car door handle or anything else he could break off or move.

Try to park your van or trailer so that you have convenient access to the show ring, schooling area and entry office, but not so close you will be bothered by dust or your horse will be disturbed by the action. Park in the shade if possible, and leave plenty of space between your rig and the next one. Be sure that you are close enough to hear class announcements.

Take a good look at your trailer's exterior before you tie your horse to it. Remember, if a horse can find a way to get hurt, he will! The trailer should have tie rings set far enough apart for your horses to be safely separated, and the horses should not be tied so that they could swing around and catch a leg, head or tie rope on a door latch, ramp or springs. Never tie a water bucket or hay net to the same ring you tie your tie rope to; if the horse should pull back and pull the tie ring loose, the water bucket would be attached to his head by the tie rope and could panic him. Be sure that he cannot paw against a sharp-edged fender and cut himself.

When you tie a horse, tie fairly short and always use a quick-release knot that can be jerked loose in an emergency. If the rope is too long, the horse may put his head down and get a leg over it or catch the rope across his poll and scare himself. Even though your horse may tie perfectly well at home, there is more excitement and more chance of his pulling back at a show. Use a strong tie rope with a sound snap, and *never* tie a horse with a chain lead shank. A chain shank will break if a tied horse pulls back on it, and if it is over the horse's nose or under his chin, it could cause serious injuries or even a fracture. The same goes for tying a horse by the bridle reins.

Hay nets should be tied high, with the long ties run back through the center ring and then tied in a slip knot or fastened with a double end snap. If the full hay net is simply tied with the ties at the top, it will hang lower and lower as the hay is consumed, until the horse can get a foot caught if he paws it.

If your horse doesn't tie safely, you will need someone to help out by holding him whenever he is not showing. This can be tedious, but it is far safer than leaving an excited horse tied insecurely to a trailer, or having to recapture him after he has gotten loose. If you are holding a horse, it may be necessary to use a chain lead shank with the chain over the horse's nose or under his chin for control. Be careful not to let him step on the shank and scare himself when he grazes, and keep horses away from hazards such as lawn chairs, wire fences, electric cables and crowded areas like food stands and entry booths.

If your horse loads easily and your van or trailer is roomy, you may let the horse stand in his trailer or van stall between classes. Be sure that your trailer is parked in the shade and that ventilation windows and doors are open, as the temperature inside a trailer parked in the sun can easily reach over 100 degrees. Always untack the horse before putting him on the van or trailer; loading or unloading with a saddle or bridle on exposes your horse and your tack to the risk of catching some piece of equipment on the trailer stall and scaring the horse as well as damaging your tack.

Keep a full hay net in front of your horse when he must remain tied during a show. This gives him something to do and keeps him quiet and contented. Use fly repellent and scrim fly sheets if the bugs are bad, and never leave a tied horse by himself while you go to watch the show.

In rainy weather, good organization can minimize the mess and inconvenience. Have a waterproof rain cover to put over your horse; you can tack and unsaddle underneath it. Other waterproof tarps can cover your tack rack and show trunk, and you may be able to set up a canopy or shelter on one side of your car or truck. If the ground becomes terribly muddy, a bag or two of shavings spread underfoot will make the area cleaner, if not dry. Have plenty of towels to dry off wet horses, people and tack, and have extra coolers so that a dry one can be substituted for a wet one. Your horse may need an anti-sweat sheet, especially if his rain cover keeps him warm and sweaty. Finally, don't forget hot beverages for your wet, cold human helpers!

DUTIES AT THE SHOW

On arrival at the show, once your stable area is set up, you will need to let your horse relax and settle in. He can be taken for a walk around the show grounds to see the sights, but he may be flighty and excited, so handle him with care and stay alert. He may need the chain shank run over his nose for control. If possible, walk a green horse with a quiet, calm stablemate. Stay away from other horses and watch out for hazards like guy wires, tent ropes, electrical cables and holes where your horse could be injured.

Before it gets too close to show time, your horse should be schooled and get accustomed to the warmup area and, if permitted, the show ring. He may be longed first or schooled under saddle. Sometimes schooling over obstacles is permitted before the show, but do not rush a horse off the trailer and into a hasty, desperate schooling session; this can hurt rather than help the confidence of both horse and rider. Instead, plan to arrive early enough for an unhurried schooling session, with time for the horse to rest and be cleaned up before he warms up for his first class.

If your horse has been bathed, groomed, braided and trimmed at home, you will not have much preparation to do at the show except for removing travel stains and final touches to the coat, feet, mane and tail. If you are braiding at the show, try to get it done very early in the morning before there is too much activity around the stable area. Some horses will happily eat their grain or pick from a hay net while you braid.

Your grooming schedule will depend on how many horses you are responsible for, the kind of grooming they need and the class schedule. The work schedule for the day should be posted prominently, showing who is responsible for what chores for each horse and for the stable area. You should have a copy of the class schedule in your pocket, marked with your horse's classes and approximate times. Stay alert for class announcements and be aware of how quickly classes are running; remember that class changes, scratched entries or cancellations can alter the time schedule you have planned on. Keep in touch with how the classes are running and know which ring your horse will be showing in.

A typical schedule for a groom at a weekend show might go something like this:

FRIDAY AFTERNOON

Arrive ahead of horse van; set up stable area, bed stalls, hay and water. When horses arrive, unload, remove shipping wraps, walk them around grounds. Feed, settle them in stalls. Post work/show schedules for next day. If horses are schooled, cool out afterwards. Brace and bandage legs. Clean off tack. Check horses late at night. Leave area clean and secure.

SATURDAY MORNING
(Horses showing at 8 A.M.)

4 A.M.: Feed. Pick out stall while horse is eating. Remove wraps and check legs. Braid while horse finishes hay. Groom and remove any stains.

6 A.M.: Tack horse for longeing or schooling and school for 45 minutes. Cool out horse and clean him up, removing stains. Clean up tack. Do final grooming, including picking tail, coat spray, quarter marks, highlighter, etc., just before horse goes to warmup ring. Take last-minute kit to warmup ring to touch horse up after warmup.

After Horse Shows: Cover with cooler or sheet and cool him out. If he has more classes later, put him back into stall with hay and water; plan for enough time to have tack cleaned and horse tacked up with final grooming done for the next class.

After Last Class: Braids are removed and the horse's legs braced and wrapped. If he is sweaty or the ring is muddy, he may need a bath. Horse should have been cool and dry for an hour after work before feeding grain. If ground is hard or horse has worked hard, legs may be poulticed or feet packed. Pick out stall, leave tack clean and area neat, and leave horse with hay, water and last feed. Check on horse late at night.

SUNDAY SCHEDULE

Chores will be similar to Saturday's schedule, but times may vary.

Midafternoon or as Last Classes Approach: Begin repacking any equipment that will not be used again during the show. Take down and repack tack room items.

After Last Class: Horses must be cool and dry for at least 1 hour before shipping. Take out braids; wrap legs for shipping. Pack equipment in van or trailer. Load horses and ship out, with stalls stripped and stable area left clean.

AT HOME AFTER A SHOW

Unload horses; unwrap and settle in stalls. Check for injuries. Poultice legs. Unload show equipment and replace tack and tools in proper places. Clean trailer or van. Clean tack. Launder saddle pads, bandages, etc. Check equipment for needed repairs, replacements. Make list of any supplies needed. Repack show equipment, clean and ready for next show. Horses should be jogged out in hand to check for injuries or stiffness; usually they will have a day off with turnout time after a show.

When you go to the ring with your horse, take along a bucket or kit with the items you will need for any last-minute touches after he has schooled or warmed up. In cold weather, you may need a cooler or paddock sheet; a light cover might be necessary during warm weather to keep dust off his coat as he waits at ringside. If it is muddy, take along a bucket of water, sponge, scraper and towels; the horse's tail should be tied up in a mud knot or bandaged to keep it clean while he warms up. You may need to touch up hoof polish or apply hoof oil, and the tail and mane may need to be picked out and the coat brushed and put straight. Take along Lexol, a damp sponge and a rag to wipe over the tack and the rider's boots. Before leaving the stable area, be sure your rider is wearing the correct number and that his tack and appointments are correct.

In the warmup ring, don't annoy the horse and rider by unduly fussing over them, but you can quickly sponge, scrape and wipe off sweat marks, pick the mane and tail and wipe over the tack and the rider's boots. If enough time has been allowed for a proper warmup, these touches can be done efficiently without rushing.

After the horse has performed, he may be wanted again for further work-offs or for an award. The rider may need to return to ringside to watch his competition or listen to the judge's instructions for a ride-off. The groom should cover the horse according to the weather, scrape him down if he is sweaty and walk him nearby, out of the way of other entries warming up but ready to go back in as soon as he is needed. Loosen the girth and noseband, but remember to readjust them when the horse is mounted again. Remember that a hunter must return to jog for a ribbon in the same complete bridle he wore when showing over the course or he could be disqualified. Tie up the martingale strap if the saddle is removed, so that the horse cannot step on it, and loosen the noseband but do not unbuckle it, as the horse can shake his head and hit his eye with the buckle end if it is undone. Stay clear of other horses; strange horses may be kickers.

After his class is over, the horse should go back to the stall or trailer to relax until he is needed to show again. He can be cleaned up if he has classes later, but he should be allowed to relax and not fussed over unnecessarily. He should be left with hay and water when he is cooled out; in the meantime, the groom (or the rider, if he is available!) can clean tack for the next class.

After the last class, the horse should be cooled out thoroughly and prepared for the night or for shipping. If he is shipping home, he does not need to be fed grain. If remaining overnight, he may need his legs poulticed, braced or massaged and protective stable wraps will probably be used as a precautionary measure. He should be grained only after he has been cool, dry and relaxed for an hour, and a late-night check should be made to be sure that he is well and happy for the night.

GROOMS IN, PLEASE!

You may be called into the ring to assist in grooming in certain stake classes where the horses are stripped and judged for conformation after they perform, to act as a header for harness classes, or to lead a horse in to receive a ribbon when a rider has placed with more than one horse in a jumping class. Since you will be in the public view, you should be neat, clean and correctly attired for the class. Even if you don't expect to be called into the ring, the way you appear around the warmup ring reflects on yourself and your stable, so you should look professional. Clean slacks or jeans worn with a clean shirt (tucked in) and possibly a jacket with your stable's logo are appropriate for most occasions when you may have to groom in public. If you are acting as a header in a harness class or assisting in a Saddle Horse Stake class, you will look more correct if you wear jodhpurs, jodhpur boots and a shirt and vest. Grooms who ride on a carriage in driving classes must wear the correct livery for their equipage and for the requirements of the class, as their appointments will be counted in the judging.

You should have a kit with a rub rag, sweat scraper, damp sponge and soft brush to carry into the ring. Wait until the horses are lined up and you hear the call "Grooms in!"; you are not permitted in the ring until it is given. Run briskly to your horse and assist the rider in unsaddling; set the saddle neatly on end with the stirrups run up and the girth out of the dirt. Quickly scrape your horse and wipe over him with the rub rag. Use the sponge to clean the foam from his mouth and the bits; help the rider to get him properly posed or parked out before the judge comes by. It is permissible to shake your rag at your horse or speak to him to get his ears up, but do not engage in antics that attract the judge's attention to you instead! When permission is given, quickly resaddle, taking care as you do that all saddle and bridle parts are correctly adjusted. Give your rider a leg up and wipe off his boots after he is mounted; you may also have time to wipe the lather off the reins and saddle.

You may be called upon to assist in a combination class (in which the horse is both ridden and driven) or a versatility class. In these classes, the changes from harness to saddle or from one type of saddle to another are made in the ring; watching the quick transformation is part of the fun for the spectators. When unharnessing in the ring, remember that a horse must *never* be unbridled, even for a second, while it is hitched to a vehicle. When changing bridles, be sure that you have a halter secured around the horse's neck—you do not want to provide comic relief by having to recapture your escaped horse! If this is a combination class, you will now put the harness in the vehicle and pull it out of the ring. Whenever assisting in the ring, try to be as quick, efficient and unobtrusive as possible; this way the entry gives a more professional impression.

If you lead a horse in to receive a ribbon, have him as clean and well turned out as you did when he competed. His saddle may have been removed and he should be scraped and have any saddle marks rubbed out, or he may be covered with a cooler. Remember that hunters must return to jog for the judge in the same complete bridle in which they competed, including the martingale—substituting a halter is a violation of the rules. If the saddle is removed, the martingale strap should be knotted up so that it does not hang down where the horse could step on it as he jogs.

If you are asked to assist in a model or in-hand class, you will need to know how to set the horse up in the correct pose and how to run him out in hand. This takes practice beforehand and probably some advice from the trainer. Keep your horse safely separated from other horses so that he can be seen by the judge and cannot get kicked by another entry.

STABLE SECURITY

The stable area should never be left unwatched, as there are many hazards at a horse show that would not be present at home. Most horse show spectators are horse lovers of some kind, but they may know little or nothing about horses and about safe and appropriate behavior around horses. Well-meaning strangers can spook or irritate horses by approaching too closely with balloons, baby strollers and boisterous children or dogs, and they are apt to poke fingers, handfuls of hay and even hot dogs into the stall for horses to nibble. You must protect the public from the horses as well as the horses from the public. Stall screens help to keep stray fingers out of stalls, and stall curtains allow the horses some measure of quiet and privacy. Another way is to set up a barrier of rope attached to standards that keeps spectators several feet from stall fronts, but be careful not to create a hazard for people who must get horses in and out.

Dogs are a mixed blessing at best at a horse show and can create a nuisance or even a real danger. A protective dog, kept tied in your tack room, can discourage uninvited visitors or thieves, but don't bring a biting dog to a horse show—it can end in a lawsuit. No dog, however cute or well behaved, should be allowed to run loose on the show grounds—*leash your dog or leave him at home!*

You should be especially vigilant about smoking and fire hazards at a horse show (and at home also!), as some temporary stabling arrangements could be real firetraps. Absolutely forbid smoking in your stable area; post No Smoking signs and call attention to them and complain to the management if fire regulations are not enforced. Be very careful in your use of electrical appliances and extension cords; don't overload outlets or use indoor extension cords for outdoor conditions. If you do not leave a halter on your horse when he is in the stall, a halter and lead shank should be hung on his stall. Keep aisles and doorways clear for fire exists, and again, *never lock a horse in a stall.*

A neat, organized and well-supervised stable area is less susceptible to accidents and to petty thievery. Put equipment away and close up trunks when you are through using it; this not only looks neater, but it does not leave your equipment displayed so anyone can walk off with it. Do not leave small, valuable items like cameras or wallets casually out in the open or leave tack at the wash rack or the warmup ring; this invites theft, and the chances of recovery are very poor. Your saddles and good leather items should be marked with your driver's license number on the underside; do not rely on brass nameplates, which are easily removed. Any time you leave the tackroom, it should be locked with a chain and combination lock. Trunks that stand outside the stalls should have padlocks, also.

Night security is usually handled either by having one or more of the grooms sleep in the tackroom, or by hiring a horse-watching service. The commercial services will check in on your horses several times during the night and will call you at your hotel or call a veterinarian if indicated. Any time you leave a horse stabled away from home, you should post a stall card on his door giving an emergency number where you can be reached. If someone else is checking on him or feeding him for you, essential information on the horse and his habits should also be included.

PUBLIC RELATIONS

Horse shows are the shop window of the horse world, whether you are a trainer, instructor, breeder or dealer in show horses—or even just a horse owner, proud of your horses and the impression you make on the public. When you are at a show, everything you do will be scrutinized, in the ring and out of it. Those who watch you may be experienced horse people who know what they are looking at when they watch a horse or a handler, or they may be ignorant but interested in horses and what goes on around them. The manner in which you present yourself, your horses and your stable can make a lasting impression for or against your stable, yourself and your breed or type of horse.

Your stable area should be as attractive as possible, without being inefficient or needlessly ornate. Neatness makes the greatest difference. Stalls should be kept well bedded and picked out, aisles swept, trash picked up and equipment neatly hung up when not in use. Clean, shiny tack hung up neatly looks nicer and is ready for the next class; blankets and bandages should be freshly laundered and neatly folded or rolled up and hung on their racks. Naturally, your horses should be properly trimmed and well groomed.

The dress and attitude of the stable's personnel are important, too. It is incongruous to see a beautifully appointed stable area and tack room, immaculate horses, and the stable help looking like bums in grubby tee shirts and filthy jeans. Naturally, you don't wear your best clothes to muck out stalls, but you should take pride in the impression *you* make, and you can look neat, clean and professional. Many stables supply shirts, jackets or caps with the stable's logo and colors; this looks much more professional, especially when you are out in the public eye. Your language and behavior also reflect on your stable as well as yourself; foul language and rude behavior create a very bad impression and will turn people off.

A horse show is not the place to train horses or to settle a serious behavior problem with a horse. Discipline is necessary at times, but a violent altercation with whip or shank is seldom worth the adverse reaction it will cause from spectators, other horsemen and even show officials. People are put off by anything that smacks of cruelty, callousness or rough handling. By preparing your horses properly at home and avoiding public problem sessions or questionable methods, you will avoid distressing incidents and give a better impression of your stable, your horses and your horsemanship.

Be helpful and friendly to spectators whenever possible. It might be easier to close off your aisles and warn off all strangers with an unfriendly glare, but you will not commend yourself, your stable or even your sport to people that way! You sometimes hear comments like "Those snobbish hunter people!" or "That saddle horse clique . . ."; some people have the impression that all horse people, or at least all horse show people, are snobs. An unfriendly attitude is what starts and perpetuates such petty divisions and feuds and can even create enemies for all horse people. Remember that the person you are short with today could be tomorrow's client, or may someday vote on whether or not horses will be zoned out of your neighborhood. If you are too busy to answer questions at the moment or if your horse has had about all the petting he can stand, you can say so in a polite manner and suggest that the person stop back later, or tell him when he can watch one of your horses in a class. Spectators love to have someone special to root for; they are interested in the people and horses behind the scenes, and it is no more trouble to be civil than to be unpleasant. You'll make a lot of friends this way also.

Lastly, leave your stable area cleaner than you found it. If you have parked your trailer on the host stable's grounds all day, clear away the manure your horse has left around it and pick up all your trash, bottles and cans. Make a last check of the area before you leave—you never know what you'll find that would have been forgotten.

Appendix 1 TRIMMING STYLES BY TYPE AND EVENT

TYPE OR EVENT	MANE	TAIL	OTHER NOTES
Combined Driving	Trimmed according to breed or type of horse used. Often pulled as for sport horses. May be braided in sewn-in button braids (yarn matches mane color).	According to breed or type of horse, but very seldom braided. Upper hair of dock may be pulled.	Trim bridle path and head as usual, but do not boot up legs on marathon horses. May be body clipped, even in summer, for more efficient cooling.
Combined Training (Eventing)	Pulled to 3 1/2"–5". Braided and taped for dressage. Unbraided for cross-country. Braiding (no tape) optional for stadium jumping.	Upper hair of dock pulled (optional). Banged tail optional. Braided tail optional but unusual for stadium jumping.	Head and legs trimmed. Often body clipped for 3-day events to aid cooling, even in summer. Bridle path no more than 1". Quarter marks optional.
Dressage	Pulled to 3 1/2"–5"; usually braided with knobs and taped. Scalloped braids optional. Sewn-in button braids optional. Long-maned horses: French braid or Continental braid optional. Forelock may be braided or not. Ribbons, bangles, etc., prohibited.	Usually pulled short at top of dock. Banged tail optional. Braided tail optional but inadvisable; may cause stiff movement.	Head and legs trimmed. Do not wipe foam from mouth. Ears trimmed outside but often not trimmed inside. Bridle path no more than 1"–2". Quarter marks optional.

TYPE OR EVENT	MANE	TAIL	OTHER NOTES
English Pleasure, Saddle Seat	Long, full and natural. Bridle path 6"–8". Some breeds use braided forelock and 1st lock, but some prohibit braiding.	Long, full and natural. Most breeds prohibit tail setting and addition of tail wigs, etc.	Head and legs trimmed closely. May be booted up. Ears clipped clean, with points.
Equitation, Hunter Seat	Pulled to 3 1/2"–4 1/2" and hunter braided with matching yarn. Forelock braided. Mane always braided on right side.	Hunter braided tail optional. Natural or pulled tails are acceptable.	Head and legs trimmed. Booted up if necessary. Bridle path no more than 1". Quarter marks optional for formal turnout.
Equitation, Saddle Seat	*3-Gaited Saddle Horse:* mane and forelock roached off. *All others:* Long mane, natural or forelock and 1st lock braided with ribbon (according to breed.)	*3-Gaited:* set tail, with dock trimmed or feathered. Wigs and tail braces permitted. *Others:* Tail long, full and natural, according to breed.	Head and legs trimmed, often booted up. Ears clipped clean, with points.
Equitation, Stock Seat	Pulled to 3 1/2"–4 1/2", with 5"–6" bridle path. Should fall on left side. Banding optional. Forelock sometimes braided. Roached mane seldom seen today.	Long, full and natural.	Head and legs closely trimmed; ears clipped clean. Often booted up.
Fine Harness	Long and full; 6"–8" bridle path. Forelock and 1st lock braided with ribbon.	Set or may use spoon crupper or tail brace (some breeds require natural tail.) Long hair at top of dock. May use tail switch or wig.	Head and legs closely trimmed; ears clipped clean. Often booted up.

TYPE OR EVENT	MANE	TAIL	OTHER NOTES
Gymkhana	Long and natural, with 5" to 6" bridle path, or Pulled to 3 1/2"–4 1/2" with 5"–6" bridle path, or Roached, with wither lock and forelock left.	Long, full and natural. Shortened tail permissible but out of style.	Head and legs trimmed closely. May be booted up.
Hunter and Pony Hunter	Pulled to 3 1/2"–4 1/2". Hunter braided with yarn in color to match mane or conservative contrasting color. Scalloped braids or sewn-in button braids optional. Forelock braided. Mane always braided on right.	Long and full. Braiding tail is optional. Tail is never braided unless mane and forelock are also braided. Mud knot or braided stick optional on wet days. Banged tail or switch tail optional.	Head and legs trimmed closely. Show hunters may be booted up, but not field hunters. Bridle path no longer than 1". Quarter marks optional when formally turned out.
Jumper	Pulled to 3 1/2"–4 1/2". Hunter braids optional. Forelock may be braided or not.	Long and full. Pulled top of dock optional. Braiding tail optional, but never done unless mane is braided. Mud tail or braided stick optional on wet days.	Head and legs trimmed closely. Bridle path no more than 1". Quarter marks optional when braided and formally turned out.
Parade Horse	Long, full and natural. Bridle path 6"–8". Forelock and 1st lock braided with ribbon; may be metallic or have added bows.	Long, free and full. Some breeds permit set tails, tail braces and tail wigs or switches. Ribbon braids sometimes attached to top of dock to fall with tail hair.	Head and legs trimmed closely; legs booted up. Ears trimmed clean, with points. Glitter on hooves and dusted over croup.

272

TYPE OR EVENT	MANE	TAIL	OTHER NOTES
Park Horse	Long, free and full. Bridle path 6"–8". No braiding.	Long, free and natural. No braiding or pulling. Most breeds prohibit tail setting, ginger or any artificial appliances.	Head, legs and ears trimmed closely. Ears clipped clean, with points. *Legs* booted up.
Pleasure Driving	Long, free and full. Bridle path 6"–8". Some breeds require natural, unbraided mane; some permit braiding forelock & 1st lock with ribbon.	Long, full and natural. Most breeds prohibit tail setting, ginger, tail braces or tail wigs or other artificial appliances.	Head, legs and ears trimmed closely. Ears trimmed clean with points. *Legs* usually booted up.
Reining and Western Performance	Long, full and natural; bridle path 6"–8". May be pulled to 3 1/2"–4 1/2" and left free or banded. Forelock usually free; may be braided. Roached mane with forelock and wither lock permissible but out of style.	Long, full and natural. Shortened tail out of style.	Head, legs and ears trimmed closely; legs may be booted up.
Roadster	Long, free and full. Bridle path 6"–8" inches. Forelock & 1st lock braided with ribbon in stable colors.	Long, free and full. Some breeds permit tail braces and tail wigs; others require tail free and natural.	Head, ears and legs trimmed closely; legs booted up. Ears trimmed clean with points.
Saddle Horse (3-gaited)	Roached mane and forelock.	Set tail with top of dock trimmed or feathered. Tail usually tied. Tail braces, wigs and switches are permitted.	Head, ears and legs trimmed closely. *Legs* booted up. Ears clipped clean, with points.

273

TYPE OR EVENT	MANE	TAIL	OTHER NOTES
Saddle Horse (5-gaited)	Long, full mane; bridle path 6"–8". 1st lock & forelock braided with ribbon.	Tail set and may be tied or use brace. Long and full, including hair of upper dock. Tail wigs or switches permitted.	Same as above.
Walking Horse	Same as 5-gaited Saddle Horse.	Same as 5-Gaited Saddle Horse, except that set tails are prohibited in Plantation Pleasure divisions.	Same as above.
Western (Pleasure and Performance, also Halter)	Pulled to 3 1/2 to 4 1/2 inches. 6–8 inch bridle path. Mane usually falls on left. Long, natural mane optional. Forelock sometimes braided. Pulled mane may be banded. Roached manes now out of fashion.	Long, full and natural. Never shown braided. Shortened tails now out of fashion.	Head, ears and legs trimmed closely. Legs may be booted up. Ears clipped clean, with points.

274

BREED	MANE	TAIL	OTHER NOTES
American Saddle Horse			
1. *3-Gaited*	Roached completely, including forelock.	Set, top of dock trimmed, clipped or feathered but not long hair. Tail braces, wigs or switches are permitted.	Legs, head and ears trimmed closely. Ears trimmed inside and out, with points left on.
2. *5-Gaited and Fine Harness*	Long, with 6"–8" bridle path. 1st lock and forelock braided with satin ribbon.	Set, with long hair at top of dock. Tail braces, wigs and switches are permitted.	As above.
3. *Pleasure*	Long mane, braided as above.	Long natural tail, unset, without brace or artificial appliances.	As above.
Andalusian	Long, full and natural mane and forelock. Bridle path no more than 1". French braid with traditional bullfighting ribbon puffs may be used for special occasions, but not for dressage competition. French braid or Continental braid for dressage classes.	Long, full and natural tail, unset and unbraided.	As above.

BREED	MANE	TAIL	OTHER NOTES
Appaloosa 1. *Western*	Pulled to 3 1/2"–4 1/2"; should fall evenly to left side. 6"–8" bridle path. Mane may be banded for show. Roached mane is permissible but less common. Forelock sometimes braided.	As long and full as possible.	Sparse mane and tail hair are a breed characteristic. Clear hoof polish should be used as striped feet are a breed characteristic & should be visible. Legs, head and ears trimmed closely.
2. *English/Hunter style*	Pulled to 3 1/2"–4 1/2". Bridle path 1 inch (longer for horses also showing western.) Hunter braids with conservative colored yarn, braided on right. Forelock braided if mane is done.	As long and full as possible. Tail may be hunter braided if mane is braided. Mud knot or braided stick may look better if tail is short.	As above.
Arabian (Part-Arabs)	Long, full and unbraided. 6"–8" bridle path. Braiding prohibited except in Hunter or Dressage classes.	Long, full and free. Tail set, ginger or any artificial appliances prohibited.	Head, ears and legs trimmed closely. Ears trimmed inside and out, with points left on.
Buckskin (usually shown western)	Pulled to 3 1/2"–4 1/2", falls to left; 6"–8" bridle path. Pulled mane may be banded. Long natural mane acceptable. Roached mane permissible but out of style.	Long and natural; no artificial appliances. Shortened tail permissible but out of style.	As above.

BREED	MANE	TAIL	OTHER NOTES
Connemara	Pulled to 3 1/2"–4" as for hunter; 1" bridle path. Hunter braids with yarn or sewn-in button braids with thread. Forelock braided.	Long and natural. May be hunter braided if mane is braided. May be pulled as for dressage horses.	As above. Ears need not be trimmed on inside.
Hackney (horses and ponies)	Pulled to 3"–3 1/2". 1"–2" bridle path. For formal classes, sewn-in button braids with yarn of conservative color to match livery.	Docked and set. End of tail hair banged off square.	As above. White legs are booted up. Ears trimmed inside and out, with points left on.
Miniature Horses	Long, natural mane. Bridle path 1"–2".	Long, full and natural.	As above.
Morgan	Long, full and natural, unbraided. 6"–8" bridle path. Braiding prohibited except in Hunter, Dressage or ADS Carriage classes.	Long, full and natural. Tail set, ginger or artificial appliances prohibited. No hair may be added to tail or mane.	As above.
National Show Horse	Long, full and natural mane. Bridle path 6"–8". Adding hair to mane prohibited.	Long, full and natural tail. Tail set, ginger, adding hair to tail prohibited.	As above.
Palomino 1. Stock type	Pulled to 3 1/2"–4 1/2", falling to left. May be banded. Long, natural mane acceptable. Bridle path 6"–8".	Long, full and natural. Artificially changing the color of the mane or tail is prohibited.	As above.

BREED	MANE	TAIL	OTHER NOTES
2. Pleasure type	Long, natural mane with 6"–8" bridle path.	As above.	As above.
Paso Fino	Long, full and natural mane with no more than 4" bridle path. No braiding or artificial hair coloring.	Long, full and natural. Look of hair cascading down from tail bone is desired. Tail hair is parted down center of dock. No artificial color or appliances.	Face, ears and legs trimmed, but natural look is desired. Clipping should not be obvious.
Peruvian Paso	Long, full and natural. Under PPHRNA rules, bridle path may be up to 2". Under OBPPH rules, no bridle path permitted. Geldings may have forelock roached and mane cut to 1/2 inch, standing up, for 3/4 length of neck. The last 1/4 neck is left long.	Full, long and natural. Narrow at dock and wide at skirt, with skirt banged.	Natural appearance is desired, obvious close trimming may be penalized. Trim well in advance of show so hair will be back to natural color. Obvious use of cosmetics, including coat sprays, may be penalized. Natural texture of coat considered in judging. Feet are cleaned but not polished.
Pinto			
1. Stock type	Pulled to 3 1/2"–4 1/2", with 6"–8" bridle path. May be banded, on left side. Forelock may be braided. Long, natural mane acceptable.	Long, full and natural.	Face, ears and legs trimmed. Legs usually booted up. Ears trimmed inside and out, with points left on.

BREED	MANE	TAIL	OTHER NOTES
2. Pleasure type	Long, full & natural with 6"–8" inch bridle path. Forelock and 1st lock braided with ribbon for gaited and fine harness.	Long, full and natural.	As above.
3. Hunter type	Pulled to 3 1/2"–4 1/2" inches, with 1 inch bridle path. Hunter braided with matching yarn, on right side. Forelock braided.	Long, full and natural. May be hunter braided if mane and forelock are braided.	As above.
Paint	Pulled to 3 1/2"–4 1/2", with 6"–8" bridle path. May be banded for western classes. May be hunter braided for hunter seat classes. Forelock is sometimes braided for western classes.	Long, full and natural. May be hunter braided when mane is braided.	As above.
Pony of the Americas	Pulled to 3"–3 1/2", falls to left. Bridle path 4"–6". May be banded when shown western. May be hunter braided when shown English (on right). Roached mane with forelock and wither lock left is acceptable but less common.	Long and natural. Hunter braided when mane and forelock are braided. Mud knot or braided stick may be better when tail hair is sparse.	Face, ears, head and legs trimmed closely. Sparse mane and tail hair are a breed characteristic. Clear hoof polish should be used as striped feet are a breed characteristic and should be visible.

279

BREED	MANE	TAIL	OTHER NOTES
Quarter Horse			
1. *Western*	Pulled to 3 1/2"–4 1/2", falls to left. Bridle path 6"–8" inches. May be banded for western, but no braiding permitted in western classes. Longer mane preferred on reining & performance horses. Roached mane with forelock and wither lock left is permissible but out of style.	Long, full and natural. Shortened tail permitted but out of style.	Head, ears and legs trimmed closely. Legs may be booted up. Ears clipped clean inside.
2. *Hunter*	Hunter braided, on right, with yarn in matching or conservative color. Forelock braided. Shorter bridlepath (1"–2") preferred for hunters.		As above.
Shetland Pony	Long, full mane with 4"–6" bridle path. Forelock and 1st lock of mane braided with satin ribbon.	Long, full tail; may be set but tail braces and all artificial hair (wigs or switches) prohibited. Tail may be tied.	As above.

BREED	MANE	TAIL	OTHER NOTES
Tennessee Walking Horse	Long, full mane with 6"–8" bridle path. Forelock and 1st lock of mane braided with ribbon. Bows may be added to braids.	Long and full. Set tail, with or without tail brace and tail wigs permitted in Show Walking Horse classes. Natural, unset tail in Pleasure Walking Horse classes.	As above, but leave extra hair on front of pasterns to protect them. Permitted lubricants (Vaseline, glycerine or mineral oil) may be applied to pasterns to prevent rubbing by action devices. Any horse showing evidence of previous soring of pasterns (scar, callous or granulation tissue) will be barred from showing.
Thoroughbred	Pulled to 3 1/2"–4 1/2", falls to right. Bridle path 1". Hunter braided on right, with matching or conservative-colored yarn. Forelock braided (may be left unbraided on jumpers or dressage horses.) Scalloped braids or sewn-in button braids permissible.	Long and full; may be banged or switch tail. Hunter braided tail optional when mane is braided. Mud knot or braided stick optional, especially on wet days.	Head, ears, and legs trimmed closely. Legs may not need to be booted up if hair is fine. Quarter marks sometimes used on solid colored horses when turned out formally.
Warmbloods (Hanoverian, Trakehner, Holsteiner, Dutch Warmblood, Swedish Warmblood, etc.)	Pulled to 3 1/2"–5", may fall to either side. Bridle path 1"–2". Braided as for dressage, using knob style braids; may be taped. Sewn-in button braids or scalloped braids permissible. Forelock may be braided or not.	Pulled or trimmed at top of dock to "turnover" point. May be banged or switch tail. Braiding is permitted when mane is braided but is seldom seen.	Head and legs trimmed neatly. Legs may be booted up. Europeans seldom trim ears or whiskers; edges of ears may be trimmed & hair left inside. Quarter marks sometimes used on solid colored horses when formally turned out.

BREED	MANE	TAIL	OTHER NOTES
Welsh Pony *1. Section A*	Full, natural mane with 3"–5" bridle path. Long, full forelock. Braiding of forelock and 1st lock of mane with ribbon allowed only in Roadster and Formal Driving classes. Hunter braiding permitted on hunter ponies.	Long, full and natural. Set tail, ginger, spoon cruppers and artificial stimulants or appliances prohibited. Hunter braiding permitted when mane is braided hunter style.	Head, ears and legs trimmed closely; legs may be booted up. Artificial coloring of mane or tail prohibited.
2. Section B	Usually mane is pulled to 3"–3 1/2"; bridle path 1". Hunter braided with matching or conservative-colored yarn. Sewn-in button braids or scalloped braids acceptable. Always braided on right; forelock is braided when mane is braided.	Hunter braided tail optional. Mud knot or braided stick may flatter some ponies.	As above.

282

Appendix III SAMPLE WORK SCHEDULE FOR SHOW GROOMS*

HORSE	STALL	GROOM	CLASSES & TIMES	BRAID MANE	BRAID TAIL	EXERCISE	MEDICATION	WRAP FRONT	WRAP BACK	NOTES
Red	26	Sue	33, 34, 36, 42	brown yarn	no	hand walk 30 min.	none	yes	yes	wash socks and tail for model class
Sky	27	Sue	28, 29, 30, 42	black yarn	yes	longe 20 min.	electrolytes	yes	yes	
Beau	28	Bob	15, 16, 18, 20	black yarn	mud tail	Jim will school at 6:30 A.M.	poultice front legs	yes	yes	Change to Jim's saddle for class 20
Silver	29	Bob	20, 21, 22, 23	gray yarn	no	longe 20 min.	blue lotion left hock	yes	yes	

*Can be made up on a marker board or chalkboard.

Appendix IV HORSE PREPARATION CHECKLIST*

HORSE	GROOM	TACK CLEAN/CHECKED	BATH/ PREP	TRIM/ CLIP	SHOEING CHECKED	BLANKETS/ CLOTHING	TRUNK PACKED	SHIPPING/ LEG WRAPS	HEALTH PAPERS	HAY NET/ BUCKETS	OTHER NOTES

*At home, before shipping to show.

284

Index